PUBLIC POLICY
DECISION MAKING
AND REGULATION

Douglas G. Hartle
Department of Political Economy
University of Toronto

Institute for Research on Public Policy/Institut de recherches politiques

Distributed by
Butterworth & Co. (Canada) Ltd.
Toronto

ISBN 0 920380 20 4

Legal Deposit First Quarter
Bibliothèque nationale du Québec

Institute for Research on Public Policy/Institut de recherches politiques
3535, chemin Queen Mary, bureau 514
Montréal, Québec H3V 1H8

Foreword

How much regulation is enough? Does anyone know for certain? I think not; but it is a question which must be exhaustively explored because regulations pervade all aspects of our daily lives.

As a result, regulation—or deregulation—is a subject which generates vociferous public controversy and debate. This book is no exception, particularly as it puts forward the view that demands for massive deregulation are ill considered to the point of being mindless.

The virtue of this study rests on the fact that it attempts to provide a conceptual framework that will assist the reader in understanding the factors that determine how governments make decisions to adopt particular regulations. Remembering Barnum's dictum that you can please only some of the people, and at that, only some of the time, this study provides a host of informative and useful insights, together with an interesting public policy decision model.

Anyone interested in understanding the complex and often contradictory process involved in creating regulations should profit from reading this book.

Dr. Hartle's study was commissioned for and financed by the Economic Council of Canada in connection with its ongoing study of regulation in Canada. The Institute and the Council are cooperating in the dissemination of research in this important field. The findings of this study are the personal responsibility of the author and, as such, have not been endorsed by Members of the Economic Council of Canada.

Michael J.L. Kirby
President
March 1979

Avant-propos

Quelle est la juste dose de réglementation? En avons-nous une idée exacte? Je ne crois pas; toutefois, il convient d'analyser cette question en profondeur puisque la réglementation intervient dans tous les aspects de notre vie quotidienne.

C'est d'ailleurs pourquoi la réglementation—ou sa suppression—est un sujet controversé et âprement discuté par le public. Ce livre ne fait pas exception, l'auteur déclarant, entre autres choses, que les demandes d'abrogation massive sont peu fondées, voire parfaitement hors de propos.

Cette étude a pour caractéristique principale de proposer un cadre conceptuel susceptible d'aider le lecteur à comprendre les facteurs qui déterminent le processus décisionnel des gouvernements, en ce qui a trait à l'adoption de réglementations particulières. Comme le disait Barnum, on ne peut plaire qu'à certains, et encore en certaines occasions seulement; ainsi cette étude présente-t-elle une variété de perspectives valables et utiles, et même qu'un modèle de décision politique intéressant.

Quiconque cherche à saisir le processus complexe et souvent discordant de l'élaboration de la réglementation tirera avantage de cette lecture.

L'étude de M. Hartle a été réalisée à la demande et aux frais du Conseil économique du Canada, parallèlement à l'étude sur la réglementation canadienne qu'il poursuit actuellement. L'Institut et le Conseil collaborent à la diffusion des recherches dans ce domaine d'importance. Les conclusions de cette étude sont la responsabilité personnelle de l'auteur et, par conséquent, n'engagent en rien les membres du Conseil économique du Canada.

Michael J.L. Kirby
Président
Mars 1979

Acknowledgements

I wish to acknowledge with gratitude the advice (not always accepted) of Professors Richard Bird, John Dales, Donald Dewees, Rodney Dobell, Stefan Dupré, Scott Gordon, Hudson Janisch, Leonard Waverman, Thomas Wilson and some bureaucratic friends who must remain nameless. The assistance of Jack Miller, Lok Ho, Barbara Lane, and Lorelle Triolo was important too. And most especially the forebearance of Lexia.

As someone once wrote over four hundred years ago: ''When in disgrace in fortune and men's eyes . . . .Happily I think on thee . . .''

Preface

Without wishing to deny their importance, this study does not consider: federal-provincial relations; international relations; or economic stabilization policy.

The Canadian parliamentary system is assumed throughout.

The study is designed to be comprehensible to the informed general reader. Although many basic economic concepts are used, technical terms have been avoided or defined.

Table of Contents

Executive Summary

Some of the moves made recently in the United States towards deregulation, particularly with respect to transportation, seem to have produced dramatically successful results. It would be folly for Canada not to explore carefully similar opportunities. And there are, no doubt, regulations now in effect in Canada that apply in other fields that should be reformed (including abolished). Nevertheless, some of the vociferous demands for massive deregulation seem ill-considered—ill-considered to the point of being mindless.

The domain of Canadian regulations is extraordinarily vast if one defines the term, as the study does, to include all government rules. Some of these regulations protect the shared rights of individuals. These rules afford a kind of protection that is extraordinarily valuable yet cannot be provided by the private sector any more than that sector can provide defence protection. Moreover, some regulations have bestowed enormous financial benefits on some special interest groups at the expense of the many. One wonders, for example, how most farmers would react if agricultural marketing boards lost their regulatory powers to restrict output and set floor prices in order to raise farm incomes. Would organized labour readily acquiesce if regulations that enhance its bargaining power were dismantled? How would the holders of broadcast and cable licences respond if entry to these industries were unregulated? And what about the professions that control entry through their licensing regulations? Would they welcome deregulation? In short, many of those who demand deregulation appear to have a highly selective list in mind: regulations that bestow particular advantages on themselves should be retained. Regulations that bestow benefits on others and costs on themselves should be abolished.

In more general terms, it is not difficult to understand the demand for deregulation as a manifestation of the hostility in many quarters towards government intervention in all its forms. This hostility has arisen from the inevitable disillusionment that follows when voter expectations about the miraculous powers of government have been proven unrealistic by the persistence of a seemingly intractable economic malaise, despite repeated government efforts—including, of course, regulatory efforts—to find a "cure." It is not so obvious, however, aside from the pursuit of narrow self interest, just what those who call for massive government deregulation really want. Moreover, it is even less obvious why governments in the past chose to intervene by means of regulations where, in many instances, tax changes (including tax concessions) or subsidies or grants (or some combination of the three) frequently would have produced the same effects. Furthermore, the effects of many regulations, both direct and indirect, on the allocation of productive resources and on the distribution of income and wealth are almost certainly at variance with voter perceptions. Consequently, the impact of the withdrawal of particular regulations would likely result in some allocative and distributional changes for good or for ill that are not now widely anticipated.

The study attempts to provide a conceptual framework that will assist the reader in understanding the factors that primarily determine a government's decision to adopt a particular regulation. The competition among parties for electoral support, the circumstances under which special interest groups can be formed and exert pressure on ministers and officials, the perceptual limitations of the electorate, and the use of rules and procedures to bias the outcome of regulatory bodies are considered. Some hypothetical illustrations are also offered as a means of conveying how the framework can be applied to the analysis of several distinct types of regulations. A summary of the basic conclusion and recommendations follows.

(1) THE ROLE OF GOVERNMENT

If one defines the term regulation to mean rules of all kinds as we do, regulation is, we are convinced, the most general policy instrument of government. Taxation and expenditures, rather than being the main policy instruments, are essentially special cases that attract much more attention because their *direct* effects are so manifest because they leave dollar tracks on the books for all to see. It is precisely because regulations do not leave these obvious tracks that they are often introduced, rather than taxes or subsidies.

The times are evocative of those that prevailed at the time of Adam Smith when in 1776 he published his panegyric treatise to market competition and his vehement protest towards suffocating government intervention.

If one were to make a prediction it would seem plausible that the demand for minimal government has not yet run its course, and in some instances justifiably so. Nevertheless, surely it would be a grievous error to forget the dreadful faults of the minimal government system in its heyday and the unique circumstances of that time, both in Britain and in the rest of the world.

The fact that these too are troubled times calls for an Adam Smith for our unique times but not a return to Adam Smith's prescription for his unique times. His insights about the pursuit of self-interest and incentives are as valid today as they ever were. But the size and strength of institutions, the state of knowledge and technology, the world balance of power are all so utterly changed that it is idle to pretend that what was "good enough for Smith is good enough for us." A new conceptual framework is required. It would take into account, among a host of others, the following factors:

- The ever receding range and significance of competitive open market decisions. That is to say, more and more crucial decisions are now made *within* and *among* organizations of increasing size on a negotiated basis rather than on a free market basis.

- It is impossible to conceive of the corporate-labour giants and the regulated professions becoming small competitive microcosms, particularly when so many of the former are international in scope.

- It is also inconceivable that the distribution of income/wealth that would emerge from a minimal government approach would, in the longer run, gain adequate voter support in a nation with a semblance of democratic government.

- Minimal government, in the sense of minimal government intervention in markets where workable competition can prevail, coupled with some form of guaranteed annual income—tax reform scheme, might be devised. However, such a combination would remove one of the most important rationales for government intervention that *purport* to assist the disadvantaged but, in fact, provide much more assistance to the advantaged. Would those strong interest groups that have been able to parade under the false colours of government intervention for an ostensibly laudible purpose, in order to achieve inordinate benefits for themselves, readily acquiesce in such a scheme? To ask the question is to answer it.

- It is imperative to avoid some kind of shadow government with all the major pressure groups represented that relied for its effectiveness on the exercise of prerogative powers of a ministry under a bundle of statutes that, by their vague wording, were essentially enabling statutes. Such a decision-making system would make a mockery of Parliament and any notion of accountability to the electorate would be completely lost.

(2) COLLECTIVE RIGHTS REGULATIONS

The regulations that seek to protect our collective rights (rather than some vital civil rights) have had the shortest history and, unless they are defended with vigour, will be the first to be attacked by the deregulation enthusiasts. Without wishing to appear to be defending their present form, or the manner of their enforcement, these *kinds* of regulations are part and parcel of the *minimal* role of government. Just as defence and police services protect our tangible collective and exclusive rights, enforced collective rights regulations stand guard for the intangible but vital rights we cannot protect individually.

(3) REGULATORY AGENCIES

It is proposed that the authority of ministers and the ministry as a whole to dispose of the decisions of so-called "independent" regulatory agencies almost at will, under the euphemistic term "right of appeal to the Minister or Governor in Council," be withdrawn. Instead, we would strongly suggest that a minister or a ministry be empowered to declare, in advance of a decision by a statutory regulatory body, that it deemed the matter of such general concern or importance that it would consider the agency's recommendation but would take ministerial responsibility for the decision. If a ministry wished to declare that one or more particular regulatory agencies henceforth would play an advisory role only, so much the better.

The provision of a continuing open forum, through open regulatory agency hearings in specialized subjects of continuing and general concern, is most valuable. However, some means must be found to finance adequately what we have called "collective rights" groups. The ideal financing method would be by public subscription. This route should be pursued more systematically and aggressively. In the meantime, pressure should be put on governments to fund such groups out of general revenues. To reduce such funding as an "economy measure" would be outrageous, given some of the other expenditures that remain untouched.

Ultimately what is required, over and above the foregoing, is to increase the authority of Parliament *vis-à-vis* the executive branch. As the extent and depth of government intervention have increased, the dangers of excessive executive prerogative powers in Canada have grown commensurately.

(4) SUNSET PROVISIONS

It has been proposed by some that beyond a stipulated date (fixed?, appropriate?) every regulation would no longer have force or effect unless formally reaffirmed by the authority under which it was issued.

There are some immediate and obvious mechanical difficulties that hardly need to be mentioned. First, given the enormous ambiguity of the term "regulation" and the multitude of available synonyms, and the mind-boggling range of governmental rules (instruments?), it would be virtually impossible to draft an omnibus bill that would neither catch everything nor would not have loopholes so large that it would catch nothing. Furthermore, even if the gauge of the net were "just right," in some sense, how would the various decision-making bodies find the time to rethrash old straw when they can barely cope with the current crop?

Both of these difficulties could be readily avoided if, instead of an omnibus "sunset" bill, such a provision were added *on a highly selective basis* to some existing statutes, like those now contained in the *Bank Act*. Public pressure may induce a ministry to consider such provisions in draft bills more seriously in the future—an excellent idea. But these courses of action are not panaceas whereby, with the passage of but another rule, all "bad" and "superfluous" rules come to an end after a few years.

(5) GENERAL RESEARCH PROPOSALS

Many regulations have highly significant effects on the allocation of resources. These need to be examined and the results made available to the public. What we would emphasize, however, is that the income/wealth distributional effects have, in the past, tended to be downplayed relative to the allocative effects. This imbalance should be corrected in so far as possible. We are not suggesting that analyses of regulations contain any judgments about the fairness or unfairness of their distributional effects. Rather, we would urge that such analyses simply set forth these effects as clearly and precisely as the available data and analytic techniques permit. Let such results speak for themselves, in so far as the normative assessment of them is concerned.

Regulations often fly under colours that bear little if any relationship to their actual effects on the distribution of income and wealth or on the allocation of resources. Thus, statements of intended purposes or stated objectives, formal or informal, should not be taken at face value for analytic purposes. All that needs to be done is to place in juxtaposition these kinds of statements and the estimated actual distributional/allocative effects.

The principal analytic questions to ask in assessing particular regulations are:

(a) What would be the impact on the income and/or of a particular change in a particular regulation on individuals with certain attributes relative to the alternatives—including the abolition of the particular regulation, of course? The impact of such a change on other individuals and on the system as a whole would also have to be considered if the analysis were to have much meaning.

(b) Each analysis should also include estimates of the effects of the particular regulation on the allocation of resources, compared with the alternatives.

The volume of regulations extant is overwhelmingly large—so large, in fact, that if all the competent analysts in the world were to work diligently for a decade they could not seriously consider them all. Indeed, unless the flood is stemmed such a group might well lose ground in terms of the work to be done relative to that accomplished with the passage of time. A highly selective research approach is therefore imperative. In some instances, the research work should be directed towards areas where it seems possible to devise acceptable alternatives. In others, perhaps, what is called for are debunking analyses—analyses designed to show that ostensible purposes are being subverted by seemingly laudable regulations. In still others, there is a desperate need for more information on which to make more informed judgments about where to proceed, either with respect to further investigations or in devising alternatives.

While not wishing to suggest that we are proposing any overall research plan, the issues listed below seem to us to warrant special attention. The order is of no importance and the list does not purport to be exhaustive.

- The Canadian pulp and paper industry seems to be in fundamental difficulty. What has been and is likely to be the relative importance of environmental protection measures as a contributing factor? Are there alternative ways of "cleaning up" the environment that would leave the firms able to compete in international markets without bestowing windfall gains on the shareholders? What are the trade-offs?

- Regulatory compliance would appear to be particularly onerous for small businesses relative to larger enterprises. Is this true? To what extent? What could be done to ameliorate the situation if there is, indeed, a problem?

- Have regulations that conferred significant bargaining power on some labour and professional groups, or have been instrumental in raising some factor and product prices, been a significant factor in making it increasingly difficult to attain reasonably full employment without increases in the general level of prices (over and above those accounted for by international forces)?

- Federal-provincial jurisdictional questions in the regulatory realm are incredibly complex. The water quality regulations of the two jurisdictions exemplify many of the difficulties. An in-depth multidisciplinary case study could prove most illuminating.

- Many statutes confer regulatory powers on ministers who in turn delegate, in most instances, the responsibilities to their officials. It is important to investigate, again in depth, how these powers are exercised and their effects. Are the officials involved inordinate risk averters, as one would expect? Does the system now in effect forestall innovation? The problems are particularly acute where a high science-technology component is involved in regulation. The realities of the application of the *Food and Drugs Act* would provide some needed insights into an aspect of the regulatory world that seems largely a "black box" except to those immediately affected. In particular, what are the rights of appeal against the "opinions" (that are, in effect, decisions) of scientific and technical bureaucratic "experts" who have every personal incentive to be cautious and no incentive to count the social cost of inordinate timidity?

- Is there any reason why broadcast frequencies, cable territories, and satellite channels could not be sold or leased on an auction basis with the contractual conditions applicable to the successful bidder clearly set forth?

- In the field of transportation, have we fully explored the possibility of establishing only maximum rates and opening all routes to competition, with the stipulation that a corporation, having once begun a particular service, could neither drop the service nor raise the rate for a significant period of time?

Abrégé

Les mouvements récemment apparus aux Etats-Unis, en faveur de l'abrogation de divers règlements—particulièrement en matière de transport—ont, au moins en apparence, rencontré un inquiétant succès. Au Canada, il serait à coup sûr judicieux d'envisager sérieusement de telles mesures et d'identifier les domaines dont il convient certainement de modifier, sinon de supprimer, la réglementation. Toutefois, les requêtes bruyamment exprimées et visant à une suppression pure et simple de certains règlements semblent peu fondées, au point d'être parfaitement hors de propos.

La réglementation au Canada recouvre un champ particulièrement vaste si l'on englobe sous ce terme, comme le fait la présente étude, toutes les lois gouvernementales. Les règlements qui assurent la protection des droits collectifs se révèlent ainsi infiniment précieux et d'une efficacité beaucoup plus grande que ne pourrait l'être celle du secteur privé dans ce domaine. Par ailleurs, certains règlements ont accordé d'énormes avantages financiers à quelques groupes d'intérêt, aux dépens de la collectivité. En conséquence, on peut se demander comment réagiraient la plupart des cultivateurs si les offices de commercialisation étaient dessaisis de leurs pouvoirs de limiter la production et de fixer les prix minimums en vue d'accroître les revenus agricoles. Les syndicats accepteraient-ils facilement de voir abroger les réglementations qui accroissent leur pouvoir de négociation? Quelle serait l'attitude des détenteurs de licences de radio-télédiffusion et de câblodistribution si l'entrée sur ce marché n'était plus réglementée? Comment les associations professionnelles dont l'accès est limité par l'octroi de licences accueilleraient-elles la suppression des règlements? Bref, un grand nombre de ceux qui exigent l'abrogation des règlements semblent avoir en tête une liste très sélective: sans toucher aux règlements qui les avantagent, l'abrogation doit s'appliquer à ceux dont ils font les frais au profit d'autres catégories.

Plus généralement, ce mouvement apparaît clairement comme un signe de l'hostilité manifestée dans divers milieux à l'égard de toute forme d'intervention gouvernementale. Cette hostilité est née de l'amertume inévitablement ressentie par les électeurs lorsque la vanité de leurs illusions quant aux pouvoirs miraculeux du gouvernement s'est trouvée démontrée par la persistance d'un malaise économique apparemment insoluble, en dépit des efforts constamment déployés—notamment, bien sûr, en matière de réglementation—afin de ''remédier'' à la situation. Cependant, les objectifs réels de ceux qui sollicitent l'abrogation massive des dispositions réglementaires sont moins évidents que leur volonté de défendre leurs intérêts propres. De plus, les raisons de l'attitude adoptée dans le passé par les gouvernements ne se révèlent guère plus compréhensibles: en effet, pourquoi ont-ils choisi d'intervenir au moyen de la réglementation, alors que très souvent il aurait suffi de simples subventions, de primes ou de changements de régime fiscal (l'octroi d'avantages fiscaux) pour aboutir aux mêmes résultats? Enfin, les électeurs perçoivent et apprécient, à coup sûr, différemment les conséquences directes et indirectes des nombreuses dispositions réglementaires sur l'utilisation des ressources productives et sur la répartition des revenus et des richesses; l'abrogation de certaines de ces dispositions entraînerait probablement des changements, pour le meilleur ou pour le pire, dont on ne prévoit pas pour l'instant la réalisation.

Cette étude a pour objet de définir un cadre théorique permettant au lecteur de mieux comprendre pourquoi un gouvernement choisit d'adopter une réglementation déterminée; par ailleurs, plusieurs questions sont tour à tour examinées: les luttes entre partis briguant le soutien des électeurs, les modalités selon lesquelles certains groupes d'intérêt peuvent prendre corps, puis exercer des pressions sur les ministres et les fonctionnaires, le caractère limité des informations dont disposent les électeurs et le recours aux lois et aux procédures pour faire obstacle aux organismes de réglementation. Quelques exemples hypothétiques permettent de déterminer comment procéder à l'analyse de différents règlements, dans le cadre théorique proposé. Cette étude s'achève par l'exposé des principales recommandations et conclusions qu'elle suggère.

(1) LE RÔLE DU GOUVERNEMENT

La réglementation, si l'on s'entend pour inclure sous ce terme l'ensemble de toutes les règles adoptées, sans distinction, constitue très certainement l'instrument politique le plus couramment utilisé par le gouvernement, tandis que la taxation et les dépenses ne sont que des instruments particuliers, certes plus spectaculaires, en raison de leurs effets *directs* et des traces qu'ils laissent dans les comptes, au vu et au su de tous. Aussi le gouvernement recourt-il souvent, de préférence à l'instauration de nouvelles taxes ou de nouvelles subventions, à l'adoption, plus discrète, de règlements.

Les controverses actuelles évoquent la polémique ouverte par Adam Smith, lors de la publication en 1777 de son vibrant éloge à la libre concurrence, s'opposant farouchement à l'intervention étouffante de l'Etat.

S'il fallait émettre un pronostic, il semblerait plausible d'affirmer que le mouvement en faveur d'une réduction de l'intervention gouvernementale n'a pas fini de se manifester et ce, dans certains cas, à juste titre. Cependant, il serait à coup sûr profondément erroné d'ignorer, d'une part, les énormes erreurs commises lors des beaux jours des systèmes de gouvernement pratiquant le non-interventionnisme et, d'autre part, d'oublier le contexte dans lequel était appliquée cette doctrine, en Grande-Bretagne comme dans le reste du monde.

Les difficultés de notre époque requièrent la présence d'un Adam Smith contemporain, mais non des solutions qu'il préconisait au XVIIIᵉ siècle. Ses conceptions en matière de défense des intérêts particuliers sont toujours aussi justes; par contre, l'importance des institutions, l'état du savoir et de la technologie, l'équilibre mondial des pouvoirs ont subi de tels changements, qu'il serait vain de prétendre appliquer aujourd'hui le système proposé par Adam Smith. Le nouveau cadre théorique qu'il importe de définir doit prendre en considération une multitude de facteurs, parmi lesquels:

- La portée et le nombre de plus en plus restreints de décisions prises dans un contexte de concurrence libre et ouverte; maintenant, en effet, les choix décisifs sont davantage négociés *à l'intérieur* même de divers organismes d'une importance sans cesse croissante, et *entre* eux.

- L'impossibilité de concevoir la transformation en petits organismes rivaux de groupements professionnels régis par des statuts et de syndicats tout puissants, souvent d'envergure internationale.

- A plus long terme, et dans un pays se voulant démocratique, les électeurs ne peuvent soutenir la nouvelle répartition des revenus et des richesses résultant d'une politique de non-intervention des pouvoirs publics.

- Dans l'hypothèse de la mise en place d'un nouveau système de taxation supposant un revenu annuel garanti, associée à une intervention restreinte sur les marchés où une saine concurrence peut s'exercer, une telle politique irait à l'encontre de l'un des principaux fondements de l'intervention gouvernementale: sous *prétexte* de secourir les personnes démunies, elle assurerait, en fait, davantage la protection des intérêts des nantis. De plus, de puissants groupements ont manifesté bruyamment et hypocritement leur soutien à une politique dirigiste, menée apparement dans un but louable, mais leur permettant concrètement d'obtenir d'énormes avantages. Il semble hors de question qu'ils acceptent l'instauration d'un tel système.

- Il faut à tout prix éviter la présence d'une forme quelconque de "gouvernement fantôme" où les principaux groupes de pression sont représentés et dont l'efficacité repose sur l'exercice des prérogatives d'un ministre par le biais d'un ensemble de règlements réduits, par leur formulation ambiguë, à l'état de dispositions habilitantes. Un tel processus de décision ne laisserait au Parlement qu'un rôle entièrement factice, toute notion de responsabilité devant le corps électoral ayant disparu.

(2) RÉGLEMENTATION DES DROITS COLLECTIFS

Les règlements visant à la défense de nos droits collectifs (autres que les droits fondamentaux de la personne), les plus récents, seront les premiers à subir les attaques des tenants de l'abrogation et requièrent donc une défense vigoureuse. Sans vouloir justifier leur forme actuelle et leurs conditions d'application, ce *type* de règlements incombe aux pouvoirs publics, et en constitue l'une des fonctions *essentielles*. Tous comme la défense nationale et les services de police protègent concrètement nos droits collectifs et individuels, l'application de cette réglementation garantit l'inviolabilité des droits fondamentaux dont nous ne pouvons nous-mêmes assurer la protection.

(3) ORGANISMES DE RÉGLEMENTATION

Il conviendrait de retirer aux ministres et au Cabinet le pouvoir quasi absolu de s'opposer aux décisions d'organismes de réglementation prétendument "indépendants", en vertu d'une disposition nommée par euphémisme "droit d'appel au Ministre ou au gouverneur en conseil". Par contre, nous suggérons vivement de leur offrir la possibilité, préalablement à la décision de l'organisme officiel responsable, de déclarer la question suffisamment importante ou d'une portée assez générale pour devoir être tranchée sous l'autorité du ministre, en tenant compte néanmoins des recommandations formulées par l'agence impliquée; ainsi, plusieurs agences pourraient se voir attribuer un rôle strictement consultatif.

Consacrées à diverses questions spécialisées, mais présentant un intérêt soutenu pour l'ensemble de la communauté, les audiences publiques des organismes de réglementation jouent le rôle d'une tribune ouverte et permanente, dont l'existence est particulièrement appréciable. Il importe par ailleurs de mettre au point un mode de financement approprié pour les associations dites de "défense des droits collectifs"; tout en continuant de recourir, sans doute plus systématiquement et plus énergiquement, aux souscriptions publiques, il faudrait exercer des pressions sur les gouvernements afin qu'ils subventionnent ces associations. Il serait scandaleux de ne pas donner suite à de telles demandes, sous prétexte de "mesures d'économie", compte tenu du maintien de certaines autres dépenses.

Enfin il est de toute première importance d'accroître les pouvoirs du Parlement, car l'ampleur et la portée croissantes de l'intervention gouvernementale ont introduit un déséquilibre des pouvoirs au profit de l'exécutif.

(4) CLAUSES DE DISSOLUTION

Certains suggèrent de définir une date fixe ou variable, au-delà de laquelle une réglementation ne serait plus en vigueur, à moins d'avoir été formellement reconduite par l'autorité qui l'a édictée.

Faut-il mentionner les évidents obstacles qui s'opposent à une telle suggestion? Tout d'abord, la très grande ambiguïté du concept de réglementation, l'extrême diversité des notions qu'il recouvre et, enfin, l'ensemble inextricable des procédures gouvernementales (s'agit-il de moyens d'action?): il s'avérerait pratiquement impossible de rédiger une loi d'ensemble, précise sans excès. A supposer qu'un tel "juste milieu" puisse être défini, comment les divers organismes responsables de ce genre de décisions trouveraient-ils le temps de ressasser de vieilles arguties, alors qu'ils ont à peine celui de régler les questions en cours?

Ces difficultés pourraient être levées si les clauses de ''dissolution'' n'étaient définies *qu'en ce qui concerne certains règlements bien particuliers*, comme actuellement certaines dispositions de la *Loi sur les banques* et non aux termes d'une loi d'ensemble. Grâce à la pression de l'opinion, un ministère pourrait avoir la bonne idée d'envisager plus sérieusement l'introduction de telles clauses dans les projets de loi déposés. Cependant, l'adoption d'une simple loi ne pourrait constituer une panacée, permettant d'abroger au bout de quelques années toutes les législations inappropriées et inutiles.

(5) THÈMES DE RECHERCHE PROPOSÉS

La réglementation a souvent une incidence très importante sur la répartition des ressources: il importe d'étudier ce phénomène et de présenter au public le résultat de ces travaux. Cependant, nous tenons à souligner que les règlements ont eu dans le passé une portée plus faible sur la distribution des revenus et des richesses que sur la répartition des ressources; il convient donc de faire disparaître ce déséquilibre dans toute la mesure du possible. Il ne s'agit pas d'analyser les réglementations en jugeant de l'équité de la distribution des revenus qu'elles entraînent. Nous suggérons simplement d'énoncer clairement et précisément leurs effets, ce qui suffira à en constituer une évaluation.

La finalité apparente des textes réglementaires n'a souvent que très peu de rapport avec leur incidence réelle en matière de distribution des revenus et des richesses ou d'utilisation des ressources. Par conséquent, l'énoncé, explicite ou non, de leurs buts et de leurs objectifs ne doit pas être pris pour argent comptant, mais plutôt confronté à leurs effets prévisibles.

Afin d'évaluer une réglementation particulière, il convient de l'examiner en posant les deux questions suivantes:

(a) Quel serait l'impact de chacune des alternatives envisagées d'amendement à une réglementation déterminée, sur les individus d'une catégorie particulière et sur les revenus (y compris l'impact d'une abrogation de cette réglementation)? Pour être significative, une telle analyse doit également prendre en considération l'incidence d'un amendement sur les individus des autres catégories et sur l'ensemble du système.

(b) Quelles seraient les répercussions d'une réglementation donnée sur l'utilisation des ressources, par rapport à celles entraînées par d'autres solutions?

L'ensemble des textes en vigueur constitue une masse de documents d'un volume écrasant, à tel point que tous les spécialistes du monde réunis ne pourraient en venir à bout, au terme d'une décennie de travail assidu; en fait, les seuls règlements édictés au cours de cette période suffiraient à les déborder. Par conséquent, une approche très sélective s'impose, se limitant, dans certains cas, à l'étude des seuls domaines où la définition de solutions de rechange acceptables semble possible, ou à un travail nécessaire de démystification, afin de démontrer la dénaturation de la finalité initiale—apparemment louable—de certaines réglementations. Dans d'autres cas, la priorité évidente consiste à recueillir suffisamment d'informations supplémentaires pour formuler un avis judicieux quant à la marche à suivre: c'est-à-dire la poursuite des recherches entreprises ou la définition de solutions de rechange.

Nous ne prétendons pas proposer un programme complet de recherches; cependant, les points suivants nous semblent mériter une attention particulière. L'ordre de présentation de cette liste, non exhaustive, n'a pas d'importance.

- L'industrie canadienne des pâtes et papier semble traverser de graves difficultés: en quoi les mesures de protection de l'environnement ont-elles constitué et constituent-elles encore l'un des facteurs de cette situation? Existe-t-il d'autres moyens de garantir l'intégrité de l'environnement, sans limiter le potentiel de concurrence des entreprises sur les marchés internationaux et sans réduire à néant les dividendes de leurs actionnaires? Quelles sont les options en présence?

- Est-il exact d'affirmer que l'observation des règlements coûte davantage aux petites entreprises qu'aux grosses sociétés? Comment résoudre ce problème, si toutefois il existe?

- Certains règlements ont conféré un réel pouvoir de négociation aux syndicats et aux groupements professionnels ou ont contribué à susciter la hausse du prix de certains produits et facteurs. Ont-ils réellement contribué à rendre plus difficile l'obtention d'un taux d'emploi acceptable, sans accroissement du niveau général des prix (abstraction faite de l'incidence des mécanismes internationaux)?

- L'interaction des juridictions fédérale et provinciale crée des problèmes d'une incroyable complexité, dont la réglementation de la qualité de l'eau constitue une illustration significative. Une étude de cas, approfondie et effectuée dans un cadre multidisciplinaire, s'avérerait sans doute particulièrement révélatrice.

- Les statuts défèrent souvent le pouvoir réglementaire aux ministres; ceux-ci, dans la plupart des cas, le délèguent à leur tour à leurs fonctionnaires. Une étude sérieuse des conditions d'exercice de ces pouvoirs et de leur portée réelle s'impose. Ne peut-on s'attendre à ce que les fonctionnaires impliqués ne manifestent une prudence excessive? Les procédures et l'administration actuelles étouffent-elles toute innovation? L'acuité des problèmes posés est évidente lorsque le domaine régi par la réglementation en question relève d'une technologie avancée. L'application de la *Loi des aliments et drogues* a révélé utilement un aspect des difficultés liées à la réglementation, souvent considéré comme totalement ''hermétique'', sauf par les initiés. Quels sont, plus précisément, les droits d'appel contre les "avis" (ou plutôt les décisions) techniques et scientifiques des "experts" bureaucratiques, davantage enclins à la prudence qu'à la prise en compte du coût social d'un conservatisme excessif?

- Pourquoi les fréquences d'émission, les zones de distribution par câble et les canaux de transmission par satellite ne pourraient-ils être vendus ou loués au terme d'une procédure d'adjudication permettant un exposé clair de toutes les obligations contractuelles du futur acquéreur?

- Dans le domaine des transports, avons-nous pleinement envisagé la possibilité de ne définir que des tarifs maximums et d'autoriser le libre jeu de la concurrence, limité simplement par l'interdiction—pendant une période de temps déterminée—de supprimer un service particulier instauré ou d'en élever le tarif?

Introduction

Most analyses of public policies take for granted the institutional framework from which policies emerge. The roles of Parliament, the courts, political parties, the bureaucracy, special interest groups (or in some instances their notable weakness, if not absence!) are taken as given. Moreover, those who function within these institutions are treated as automatons: people going about their tasks devoid of personal interests. It is ignored that those involved in the decision-making process are faced with reward-punishment (incentive) systems that are often unique to the function they perform that greatly encourages some kinds of behaviour on their part and conversely.[1] The voters are perceived—if they are taken into account at all—as some kind of massed choir singing in perfect harmony, without direction, a stirring hymn entitled "The Public Interest" with music and lyrics by God.

When the policy issue under consideration is relatively narrow, and, hence, highly technical almost by definition, the detailed consideration of all of the surrounding circumstances, including those just mentioned, is out of the question. Each analysis would have a preface as lengthy as this book! However, when the subject for consideration is a policy instrumentality as broad, flexible and amorphous as *government regulation,* to assume away the host of factors cited above would be to assume away the problem itself. For regulation, in the broadest sense, is *the* essential function of government. Indeed, taxation and expenditures, the other two principal instrumentalities, can be thought of as special cases of regulation. Enforcement, after all, involves expenditures and the benefits bestowed on some by regulation are as real as a cash subsidy. Similarly, the penalties for regulatory infractions can raise money, and compliance with regulations often impose, directly or indirectly, costs that are as real as a conventional tax.

From this perspective, to examine government regulation is to examine the role and function of government itself—no small task! Just as the forces impinging on and interacting within the structure and processes of government are multitudinous, so too are the perspectives that can be taken in viewing the overall phenomena. When approaching a discussion of government regulation one feels like a photographer trying to take a picture of a many-faceted diamond (or is it quartz!). There is an almost infinite number of backgrounds, lighting arrangements, film types, camera angles, ranges, lens openings and shutter speeds from which to select—each with its own

---

[1] For example, ministers who embarrass the ministry are "punished" by demotion or expulsion from the Cabinet. Deputy ministers who are "helpful" to a minister or ministry are assigned to more prestigious departments. There is a host of examples discussed in Chapter 3.

1

advantages and disadvantages. Needless to say, ten photographers could, and almost certainly would, produce ten quite different pictures of the same "thing." In a contest to "pick the fake diamond from among these ten pictures" there is little doubt that each one of the pictures would be selected by someone. With this general caveat having been stated, the next few paragraphs seek to briefly describe what we try to capture in this book.

Assumptions

Our fundamental assumption is that the effects of alternative regulations and rulings, or any other government policy decision for that matter, should be assessed in terms of their ultimate impact on the interests of individuals. Those interests are multidimensional and include much more than the income and wealth of the individual in the conventional accounting sense. In addition to the obvious items just mentioned, individuals hold rights and bear liabilities that are exclusive to them but cannot be bought and sold and, in some instances, cannot even be assigned a meaningful monetary value. Oscar Wilde's "one-liner" to the contrary, economists do *not* know the prices of everything and the value of nothing. There are some things that are extraordinarily valuable to the individual that cannot be priced. Pride of country is an example. When we speak of the interests of individuals these unpriced but valuable rights (assets) are included.

Individuals have still another set of interests. These are their shared interests—their non-exclusive rights to collectively provided government services (e.g., roads, defence and police-fire protection). They also encompass the quality of the physical environment, extant legal, political, social and economic systems, and the prevailing conditions (favourable or unfavourable) in each of those systems (e.g., unemployment-inflation in the economic system). We will term them "collective rights."

The Supermarket Analogy

Changes in government policies and decisions, regulatory or otherwise, can and do affect, directly or indirectly, materially or trivially, each and all of these many individual interests. It is of the utmost importance to recognize, however, that each individual does not hold the same portfolio or bundle of interests although some of the kinds of interests can be found in all portfolios. To illustrate, imagine an enormous and certainly peculiar supermarket carrying all types of goods (rights) on its shelves. These shelves stock everything of any importance to individuals. There are sections devoted to jobs, others arraying shares and bonds, bank balances, real property rights, pension rights, personal health, social status, the state of the economy . . .

Everything that each individual "owns" (but not necessarily exclusively) is contained in his[2] shopping cart. Each cart thus contains all of that individual's interests, at that point in time. Some carts are overflowing, others are nearly empty. Some contain an unusually high proportion of some items and unusually small proportions (including none) of others.

Stretching our imaginations a little further, conceive of a control booth located high above the floor of the supermarket. The booth contains a staggering array of magic levers. A few levers, that are particularly difficult to find, when activated can add something valued by all of the customers to each of their shopping carts. The amounts of the thing added may differ from cart (individual) to cart (individual), but no one is worse off in an absolute sense. The vast majority of levers have quite different effects. By activating them, items can be shifted automatically from cart to cart. Other levers, when activated, will increase a particular kind of item in all carts while *simultaneously* and *necessarily* reducing another kind of item in all carts. Consequently, the customers' attitude towards its activation will depend almost entirely on whether or not the affected items are in their carts at all, and how large a proportion they are of their carts' total contents.

But these are the simple levers. There are others that are much more complicated in their effects. Some will affect certain combinations of items in the carts; others will only affect carts with total contents of certain sizes. There are an infinite range of permutations and combinations of levers and effects but, with the rare exceptions mentioned at the outset, activating levers necessarily involve gains *and* losses. Whether a particular individual is a winner or a loser on *balance* as these diverse levers are constantly activated depends, of course, on what he started out with when he entered the store and what levers have been pulled in the meantime. His attitude will depend in part on whether the contents of his cart are more or less than what he expected them to be, whether he expects future changes to make things better or worse for him, *and* how he views his cart's contents in comparison with the contents of the carts of those he sees around him in the crowded aisles.

As goes without saying, the customers are vitally concerned about *who,* individually or collectively, has access to the controlling levers *and* what they are actually doing with the levers. They can riot; they can organize into groups to influence the decisions; they can set up selection rules and procedures; they can set up rules for arbitrators to settle disputes—all the machinery of government. The point of the far-fetched analogy is to drive home that although individual interests broadly conceived are the focal point of our approach, it is also imperative to recognize that many of those interests

---

[2] Throughout this paper, the term "individual" occurs endlessly for essentially philosophic reasons. But "he" and "his" are also used in referring to individuals of either gender. The constant use of "he and/or she" and "his and/or hers" yields such a laboured style that we have decided to opt for the epithet "sexist" rather than that of "clumsy."

are in conflict. The "public interest"—the interest that is unanimously shared with no reluctant losers—is so rare as to be irrelevant to a serious discussion of public policy. If it had any serious meaning, the "control of the levers" problem in our analogy could be readily resolved. *One* individual, serving his own interests, could be *elected by acclamation,* for each of his decisions would be precisely the same as would those of each of the store's other customers. This is pushing imagination too far!

We have pushed the supermarket analogy to the limit (if not beyond it!). It is not apt and, indeed, perhaps misleading, in several vital respects.[3] However, the point is as easily made as it is constantly overlooked or forgotten: the essence of public policy making is the resolution of the almost invariably conflicting interests of *individuals.* It is an exercise predicated on dissonance, not harmony.

Significance of Organizational Forms

The interests of the individual and not the interests of abstract entities such as corporations, unions, associations, bureaucracies, ministries, and so on, are at stake. These organizational *forms* are of great importance, for they permit individuals to work together collectively and, therefore, often immensely more effectively than they could acting separately. Nevertheless, they are forms, not substances, although frequently substantial in their impact. Ultimately, such organizational *forms* can only be assessed in terms of their impact, for good or for ill, on the interests of individuals. And those interests may be, and often are, complex. Consider a large corporation that produces, let us suppose, steel in the usual manner. The individual interests in that corporation encompass, among others, those of:

— *shareholders and bondholders,* including, among others, insurance companies for which these corporate stocks and bonds are assets and form the "backing" of their policies and annuity obligations that are held by hundreds of thousands of individuals;
— *managers* whose remuneration, job security, prestige and pride are dependent upon the corporation's success;
— *workers* with rights (more or less) to their jobs and the remuneration attached to their performance of those jobs (more or less);
— *customers* who have an interest in getting the most for the least in order to supply *their* customers—individuals who also want more for less;
— *"neighbours"* of the corporation whose interests are hurt by the smoke, fumes, and noise arising from the production process;

---

[3] A vitally important dimension of policy that is *not* readily conveyed by the supermarket analogy is that, over time, the policy decisions made now affect the growth of the inventory of items on the shelves in the future.

— *the lawyers, accountants, and public relations specialists* in whose interest it is to increase the corporation's profits in a host of ways including minimizing taxes, writing briefs in support of protective tariffs, and "softening up" the community towards the environmental impact.

And one could go on and on. Corporations as such do not pay taxes; ultimately individuals do—through the diverse routes, and many others, just mentioned. Similarly, regulations do not hurt or help corporations as such, they ultimately hurt or help individuals.

What has just been said about the corporate *form* is equally true of the other organizational forms. One of the more significant points we make later is that some individuals, *by virtue of the offices and employments they hold* (an exclusive non-transferable right), have, as one of their responsibilities, the pursuit of the interest(s) of others. Not the interests of all others, with a few notable exceptions, but the interests of those who pay them (in one way or another) to act on their behalf. In other words, there are offices and employments where it is in the self-interest of the incumbents to serve the interests of *some* others. These are the corporate executives, union leaders, trade-industry association executive officers and, *the exception,* those who head consumer, environmental, safety and civil rights type organizations that *come close* to serving everyone's interest, but whose success in serving the shared interest of the generality must invariably hurt the particular interests of some most substantively (e.g., those individuals whose interests would be hurt by "cleaning up the environment," and clearer labelling, and so on). As we have just said, we will designate them as collective rights leaders.

Rights and Actions

If the bundle of broadly defined rights held by an individual at a particular point in time can be thought of as his wealth, as broadly defined in Chapter 2, there are a number of alternative courses of action open to him. Ignoring how he obtained his wealth, generally speaking it will generate (usually when coupled with work!) a flow of money and a flow of time (to ignore a number of other more subtle items) that have to be devoted to the *maintenance* of himself and his dependents. The remainder (if any) can be allocated in essentially three ways: spent on goods and services that give immediate satisfaction and in leisure; saved (e.g., purchase of a bond or just kept in the bank); invested. The term "invest" is given a special meaning in this paper and is precisely defined in Chapter 2. However, the basic idea is that individuals can and do invest their time and money in education, job search, tax liability minimization, and a host of other ways. But of particular importance for our purpose is the individual's possible investment in obtaining favourable changes in government policies including, of course, regulatory policies and rulings thereunder. Such investments cover a wide spectrum—from investing in information in order to be able to vote intelligently, to holding office in a political party, to membership in an association that pushes an interest the individual wishes to push.

This raises the "free-rider" problem in its starkest form. Why should the individual invest his time and/or money in trying to secure a favourable policy change if the benefits, if successful, will be widely shared? To illustrate, suppose that, by the investment of 10 thousand dollars, a policy change could be obtained that would confer a benefit of 100 million dollars. (We will ignore who will bear the cost!!!) That is to say, each dollar invested would yield a return of 10 thousand dollars. Rather attractive, one might conjecture. However, if there were only ten men willing to contribute a thousand dollars each, and the benefit would be divided equally among a population of 20 million, each of the investors would gain five dollars at a cost of one thousand dollars! A somewhat different picture. Conversely, if the 20 million potential beneficiaries each contributed a dollar they would each have a net gain of four dollars. But, why invest one dollar if you will obtain five dollars solely by dint of the investment costs borne by others?

Much is made of the virtues of a pluralistic society in which those individuals with some common interests can organize themselves and press those interests through the media, representations to government, and by many other routes. One of the major flies in this sticky ointment is that because of the "free-rider" problem, the greater the stakes in a policy change and the smaller the group that will share in them, the simpler it is for an organization to protect itself against "free riders." Thus, the investment in policy change will be commensurate with the large potential gain *per investor*. For this reason, the much vaunted countervailing power rationalization is equivalent to the assertion that the teeter-totter, despite all appearances to the contrary, *must* be balanced because the bags of feathers perched precariously at one end are equal in number, and sitting the same distance from the fulcrum, as the bags of scrap iron so securely ensconced at the other.

Just as there are individuals in whose self-interest it is to pursue the interests of some others, so too are there individuals in whose self-interest it is (where "interest" includes prestige and personal pride) to reconcile the conflicting interests of others. These are the politicians in general and ministers in particular. And there are others, senior public servants, or bureaucrats if you will, in whose self-interest it is primarily, but not exclusively, to serve the interests of ministers. We try to explain the enormity of the task faced by a ministry—any ministry, regardless of political party—in filling this conflict resolution role. In large part that difficulty is obviously greatly intensified by the competition among political parties. That very competition is the font of our individual liberties, as limited as they sometimes seem to be. Not only do we not wish to denigrate this competition, we strongly believe that it needs to be greatly enhanced. Any ministry in Canada has an enormous set of advantages in the competition, and this statement is also made without regard to party affiliation or personalities. Some of those advantages are discussed in this paper and some ameliorative changes are proposed that would help to right the gross imbalance in interparty competition between the "ins" and the "outs."

There are, however, some unfortunate aspects of this interparty competition that are immutable. Firstly, voters cannot be fully informed on all issues all of the time. They cannot devote all of their available time and money to invest in casting just the "right" ballot. (What a dreary world it would be!) And further, journalists, even if there were no undue constraints on the information available to them, proceed, of necessity, on a highly selective basis while they competed for audiences. Secondly, it seems an inherent human quality to simplify reality in order to distinquish between good and evil—between that which is in one's interest and that which is not—by adopting rules of thumb, usually associated with certain symbols, as an aid in identifying the former from the latter without having to consider the evidence in detail to arrive at some balanced judgment on ethical and other issues. As a consequence, the competition among political parties for voter support involves, not only changing reality or promising such real changes, but also in taking advantage of the voter's lack of information[4] *and* by the use (manipulation ?) of symbols.[5]

The greater political competition in the opportunistic sense, the less informed the voters, and the more readily voters accept symbolic change for substantive change, the greater the likelihood that the emergent policies, again regulatory or otherwise, will serve the interests of the informed, the realists, and those who have the largest personal stakes in the outcome (for all the reasons alluded to above) at the expense of the many.

If one casts one's eye backwards to earlier times—back fifty years— back a hundred years—back five hundred years . . . the informed, the realists and the powerful (and hence wealthy) have always gained at the expense of the many—revolutions and wars notwithstanding. No doubt this is an inescapable dimension of the "human condition." But it is also true that this same time perspective also reveals reason to hope. For, by fits and starts, and sometimes even for all the wrong reasons, enormous improvements have been made. This book is offered in that spirit. There seems no reason to believe that further improvements are either unnecessary or beyond attainment. However, there also seems no reason to believe that they will readily be achieved.

---

[4] This lack of information results in part from an individual's incapacity to learn or the absence of opportunity. But of greater importance are the rules of thumb that individuals adopt in order to be able to reject at a glance the flood of information with which they are bombarded that has proven in the past to be of inadequate significance, given their interests, to warrant the time and effort required to obtain it.

[5] See Edelman (1967).

Conceptual Framework

The essence of what we have to say begins with the conceptual framework presented in Chapter 2. This framework is then applied in and elaborated upon in the following chapters. Those who are in basic agreement with the point of view expressed in this Introduction can readily bypass Chapter 1. It is devoted primarily to explaining why some of the things they expected to find in this paper are not in it or have been relegated to appendices. It also attempts, as a secondary purpose, to put the framework adopted into a wider and broader context.

As a guide to the reader who is in doubt whether or not to proceed directly to Chapter 2 the section headings and their first few paragraphs should prove of some help. It will be appreciated that because we seek to address the widest possible group of readers we have had to recognize that what is obvious to some is news to others. And what is inconsequential to some is of considerable interest to others with different backgrounds or purposes.

In order that the basis for some of the judgments made in this paper, and that an understanding of the conceptual framework provided in Chapter 2 may be gained, our basic assumptions are explicitly stated. Assumptions (9) and (10) are particularly important in the latter regard.

Basic Assumptions

(1) The means to the satisfaction of individual wants are inherently scarce both because of the niggardliness of nature (including a limited lifespan!) and the inherent zero-sum game nature of prestige, influence and power that are direct sources of satisfaction to individuals.

(2) Individuals seek to maximize their current satisfaction *and* the present value of their expected lifetime flow of satisfaction derived *from all sources,* net of the costs, in terms of satisfaction forgone, incurred to obtain them.

(3) An individual's welfare may be affected, positively or negatively, by his perception of the welfare of others. It follows that some voluntary sacrifices made in aid of others are possible and not inconsistent with the pursuit of self-interest in its broadest sense. By the same token, so are actions based on jealousy and vindictiveness.

(4) It follows from these propositions that both personal and inter-personal conflict is inevitable. That is to say, hard choices have to be made and opportunity costs—that which is forgone—are ubiquitous.

(5) Moreover, choices have to be made in the face of uncertainty, and a lack of information arises either because the latter does not or cannot exist or the costs of acquiring it are too high relative to the anticipated gains.

(6) Conflicts are resolved by the imposition of rules that both constrain and permit choices. Three categories of rules can be differentiated:

(a) internalized (largely unconscious) rules enforced by the individual's conscience (where conformity is rewarded with feelings of personal pride and non-conformity with feelings of guilt);
(b) social customs and practices enforced by social pressures and rewards (e.g., prestige); and
(c) formal rules enforced by governments and all formal organizations.

(7) Four types of formal rules can be differentiated:
(a) rules concerning the scope of the government's authority (dubbed "constitutional rules");
(b) rules concerning the authority to change the constitutional rules (which might be called "constitutional amendment rules");
(c) rules made under a given set of constitutional rules (termed "derivative rules") that thereby have authority *de jure;* and
(d) further derivative rules may, in turn, be derived from derivative rules, *ad infinitum.*

(8) One set of derivative rules gives rise to collective decision-making processes and procedures. Among the more important:
(a) constitutional change processes and procedures;
(b) legislative processes and procedures;
(c) executive (administrative) processes and procedures;
(d) judicial processes and procedures.

These "processes and procedures" rules usually answer, among other things, the following questions.
— How are decision makers to be selected?
— What are their powers (jurisdiction)?
— What procedures are they to follow?
— To whom and on what grounds can their decisions be appealed?
— What are the penalties for non-compliance?

The three preceding assumptions concerning rules are brief to the point of being enigmatic.

(9) If one defines, as we do, all of the sources of individual satisfaction as property rights, then the ultimate sources of the sources of satisfaction are, when they are enforced, the rules and procedures just discussed. It follows that changes in the rules, and the decisions made under existing rules, can and do create, increase, decrease, destroy and reallocate property rights and, hence, change the level and allocation of individual satisfaction.

(10) Some property rights are exclusive and transferable. When such rights are voluntarily exchanged, one can assume that this makes at least one of the parties better off. However, when one of the parties (including a group of individuals with similar interests) is able to secure a decision or a change in the rules that confers a benefit on it without an adequate *quid pro quo* (i.e., compensation that would be acceptable to those who would lose under the change), coercion takes place.

(11) Needless coercion is an absolute evil. But coercion is not always needless. Unfortunately, the human condition sometimes requires the acceptance of more of one evil in order to achieve less of another. It is our belief that there is no universal ethical rule that provides the "correct" answer to all questions that involve the trade-off among alternative evils. To say that "it all depends" hardly constitutes an intellectually stimulating or emotionally satisfying "answer." Nevertheless, at least, it shows a significant degree of self-control in resisting the ever present temptation to pontificate with certainty on the inherently unknowable.

(12) Without denying its normative importance, the concept of coercion as just defined can be looked upon from a positivistic point of view: how does the existence or prospect of coercion affect individual and collective behaviour, considering both the behaviour of those being coerced and those doing the coercing? How do the coercers proceed? Under what conditions do they succeed? How do the victims react? How do they escape? What are the political, social and economic consequences of the struggle? It is from this positivistic perspective, for good or for ill, that we intend to proceed.

REFERENCES

Edelman, Murray (1967) *The Symbolic Uses of Politics* (Champaign-Urbana: University of Illinois Press).

Chapter One

Some General Perspectives

One of the problems we face in writing this book is that the wider the audience one wishes to reach, the more difficult it is to decide upon the selection of the perspective to be taken. As we have tried to explain in the Introduction, what is obscure to one is boringly obvious to another and what is of serious concern to one is picayune to another. This chapter represents our resolution (not solution) of the dilemma and presents a number of different perspectives. The reader is advised to glance at the section headings and their opening paragraphs and simply skip those that consider matters in which he has little interest.

The sections are:

1.1 Canada's Current Economic Malaise and the "Deregulation" Prescription
    1.1.1 Tax and Expenditure Growth in the Past and the Current Dilemma
    1.1.2 Consumer and Environmental Protection
1.2 The Contending Ideologies of Economists and the Role of Government
1.3 The Contending Approaches of Economists and Political Scientists Towards Public Policy Decision Making
1.4 The Adversarial Nature of Public Policy Decision Making and the Scope for Leadership

1.1 CANADA'S CURRENT ECONOMIC MALAISE AND THE "DEREGULATION" PRESCRIPTION

Canada has now suffered through several years with serious economic problems of near crisis proportions. There is still no light at the end of the tunnel. Voters are frightened, disappointed, disillusioned, and angry with government. It has demonstrably not been able to solve the economic problems that beset the nation and, what is more, it is now perceived to stand in the way of those who could. It is widely *believed* that:

(1) taxes are too high;

(2) expenditures are wasteful and that the indolent are being carried on the backs of the industrious and the provident;

(3) regulations are both costly and hopelessly constraining;

(4) that together these factors mean that initiative is stifled and the economy is, therefore, incapable of staggering to its feet, much less breaking into a run; and

(5) it therefore follows that by reducing taxes, cutting expenditures, and by "deregulation," their evil consequences as described in (4) can be eliminated.

There is, of course, an element of truth in the first three propositions. The conclusion of the fourth ignores some other, probably much more significant, factors. The deduction contained in (5) is almost certainly invalid unless dramatically qualified. Finally, some of the regulations now in place that may be having a significantly deleterious effect on the economy were created in response to the demands of those who are now calling for deregulation, or put in place because of what was perceived to be their irresponsible behaviour in the past.

What is desperately needed is some perspective on why we are where we are rather than a mindless demand for panacea. This section seeks to sketch some aspects of such a perspective in order to cool the ardour for simplistic answers to complex questions. To begin, we will ignore regulation altogether and consider some other factors.

1.1.1. Tax and Expenditure Growth in the Past and the Current Dilemma

Of enormous significance in explaining the growth in government expenditures[1] and other involvements in the economy was the crucial fact that it was not only politically costless, but almost politically desirable to raise tax levels to unprecedented heights during World War II. And, of special importance, was the massive increase in personal income tax rates that occurred. As the country's defence spending needs dropped like a stone, tax rates, generally, did not fall either as rapidly or as deeply. And the personal income tax remained, after the war, an extraordinarily important part of the tax structure.

However, it was not simply the fact that the level of personal income tax rates remained relatively high and largely withheld at source, thereby dulling taxpayer perceptions of rising tax burdens, that was important. Of greater significance was the fact that because of the progressive rate structure of the personal income tax, the government's revenues grew substantially *more rapidly* than national income grew, even when the latter was measured in inflated dollars. Not only did the funds flow in at an increasing rate, they arrived on the doorstep of government *without political cost*. The extra funds were at hand without raising tax rates. This was unprecedented. From a political point of view: "Why not spend the funds and buy voter support

---

[1] Bird (1970) and *The National Finances, 1977-78*.

because we are not having to bear the blame for raising the taxes to finance them?'' To make matters worse, government did not anticipate the current slump and lightly entered into spending commitments based on the comforting assumption that the goose that laid the golden tax revenue eggs would not only continue to produce them, but produce them at a rate that increased more rapidly than a rapidly growing economy. The faltering of the economy and the decision to partially index the personal income tax to reduce the effects of inflation[2] together greatly weakened the goose and the flow of eggs ''ain't what it use to be.'' Some of the ''fat,'' indeed flatulence, of government spending can be traced easily and directly to this pre-slump revenue bonanza. It explains, to some degree, the rate of inflation that it fed on. It also explains the current deficit, for the revenues have faltered while the expenditure commitments have lingered on. And the deficit has made it more difficult to take decisive stimulatory fiscal action because of the fear that this would set off another round of inflationary expectations. And thus gross government extravagance *in the past* has created a situation in which the economy cannot be (or at least has not been) given the needed medicine. The response from the private sector has been and is still for the steps outlined at the outset, including deregulation.

All of this is painfully reminiscent of the Herbert Hoover – R.B. Bennett days when the shibboleth of the balanced budget incapacitated governments in the face of a horrendous employment crisis—depths to which we have not yet fallen. In a peculiar way, the ''don't increase the already frightening deficit'' maxim is playing the same role today as the balanced budget maxim played then. And one can see, given the inflationary experiences of recent years, why the inflationary fears are held by so many and so strongly. The balanced budget pre-1930 was a disciplinary device that kept government honest. Keynesian economics plus World War II ended the unemployment problem for decades, but the discipline of the balanced budget was not replaced in the post-war period by a more rational and appropriate yardstick, unfortunately. What was needed, and what was said at the time, were some whopping surpluses in sustained periods marked by full employment and, by current standards, gently rising prices. An indexed personal income tax, introduced years earlier, also would have been most salutary. In fact, the only surpluses that arose were accidental—the productivity of the golden egg-laying goose had been underestimated and the government machinery was too clumsy to spend in the appropriate fiscal year the windfall tax revenues. Similar comments could be made about the increases in the money supply designed to hold down interest rates.

Some kinds of regulation are contributing to, if not creating, escalating prices despite unemployed labour and capital. These regulations certainly are

---

[2] Why this was done is a fascinating story, but not one to be told here.

not helping in the resolution of the simultaneous inflation-unemployment problem we face. It goes without saying that those who benefit from such regulations, in ways we explain later, are hardly in favour of deregulation as it applies to their interests.

1.1.2 Consumer and Environmental Protection[3]

Government regulations, as that term is commonly understood, did not arise on the scene yesterday. Public concern with both "take what the traffic will bear" rail rates and industrial combines in restraint of trade led to legislation in the early part of the century. Other less laudible pressures were also at work even (but not especially!) in those days. In the United States, for example, in the 1850-1870 period there were some rail routes where strong intercompany competition prevailed. This was, needless to say, thought of by the companies as "ruinous." Government rate regulation eliminated that problem to the benefit of the shareholders of both earlier competitors.

Mackenzie King's concern for maintaining competition was probably greatly tempered by the fear that the tough anti-trust legislation enacted in the United States just before the turn of the century should not be transplanted unpruned to Canadian soil.[4] Like so much Canadian legislation then and now, Canadian opinion was "infected" by American opinion. But the Canadian "solution" was to enact legislation that had the appearance of "wrestling it to the ground" without seriously disturbing the substance of what was happening for those in the know. The first *Combines Investigation Act* in 1910 was a typically Canadian response and a typical Mackenzie King response at that: a symbolic response to a real problem. The American response was not dramatically successful either but it did turn out to have wider and sharper teeth than the Canadian legislation.

The scope and intensity of government involvement in the affairs of men and women have increased at an unprecedented and, at least until very recently, at an exponential rate since World War II. The unprecedented intrusions of government during the war into matters and in ways that would have been thought to be outrageous in peace-time were readily accepted under the circumstances and individuals became accustomed to them, at least to a degree. The very success of the Allied war effort, and the Canadian part in it, also created a feeling that governments could solve any problem—for even the seemingly implacable were defeated. Moreover, the return of the much feared post-war depression was averted and unprecedented prosperity followed, for which governments claimed the credit. This reinforced the view that governments were omnipotent.

---

[3] These are defined later as elements of "collective rights."
[4] See Canada (1910) House of Commons Debates, pp. 6832-34.

Hand in hand with the perception of government omnipotence, that was of course reinforced by political parties claiming that they could, if elected, wipe out anything from poverty to discrimination, went the public perception of government benevolence. Our forbears, particularly immigrants from Europe, had a basic fear of government. It was, in their eyes, a potential tyrant. Certainly it was thought of as a blatant liar and both a grand and petty larcenist. This was forgotten. But governments with those nasty attributes had been destroyed forever in the war had they not? ("Well there were still the Communists, but . . . .") Under some circumstances the price of liberty may be eternal vigilance, to coin a phrase, but why pay the price when there is nothing about which to be vigilant?

As it turned out, some discovered that there was, indeed, something about which to be vigilant. It was not the government, however, except its lack of decisive intervention. Rather it was the large corporation and especially the large multinational corporation. These organizations were believed by many to be "ripping off" the public and, even worse, gobbling up irreplaceable resources, despoiling the environment, sometimes irreversibly, and creating health hazards that threatened life in general and the human species in particular. To make matters worse, all of these dire events were thought to be completely unnecessary and done for the most selfish and narrow of motives—the conscious pursuit of corporate profits. The government must "do something" and the competition for votes led inexorably to escalating promises and at least symbolic government intervention.

Affluence also played a part in the drama. Painfully conscious of the ostentatious waste and vulgarity that unaccustomed affluence so frequently brings, those who firmly believed (some still do) in the worst of the dire consequences just sketched were appalled that these were the fruits that some said could not be "sacrificed" to reduce either the likelihood or the severity of the coming disaster. Ironically, it was the progeny of the affluent who had the opportunity to gain the education that created their awareness of the problem and the financial security to be able to pursue their battles against it. They were willing to accept personal deprivation to "fight the good fight" because they were revolted by many aspects of conventional success.

This dedicated, educated, articulate, confident and secure group of individuals introduced a new element into the political scene. They were groups of virtual martyrs who pursued "the public interest," as they saw it, with religious fervour. We use the term "public interest" here in a non-derogatory sense for about the last time. Usually it is a euphemistic blanket under the cover of which many a special interest has been served. But these collective rights supporters were quite unique in their dedication to their cause.[5] Needless to say, the observations of economists about the costs

---

[5] Just how unique they were, and to some extent still are, is shown by the fact that a large proportion of the same cohort essentially withdrew from reality in some self-destructive ways that are tragic in their irreversibility.

(and we mean that word in its widest sense) involved in pursuing many of the courses of action these groups espoused were, and still are, dismissed by them as materialistic, short-sighted, and based on totally unacceptable ideological premises.

It should be noted that the emergence and effectiveness of the collective interest groups was (and still is) but one manifestation of the gradual shift in power, first from those possessing rights to land to those possessing commercial-industrial property rights, and now to those possessing intellectual property. This property is embodied in their heads and is exercised by these individuals through their holdings of rights to offices, employment or professional licences (see Chapter 2).

These groups not only pressed the government directly, but more importantly were able to convince some other voters who were feeling slightly guilty about their affluence. The latter were also alarmed at the dreadful potential consequences that were so readily dramatized by the media and confused by the vague warnings of economists. Moreover, they resented and feared corporate giantism too.

Opposition came, of course, from those voters who perceived the predicted dire consequences as leading to government policies that would lessen their hope of attaining affluence, and from those who were already affluent and dreaded the thought that they might become less so if the government acted effectively to "correct" the problem. The first did not believe that distant and uncertain dangers warranted government decisions that would visit them with immediate and certain disappointments. The second claimed (whether they really believed it only the administration of truth serum would reveal) that there would be no dire consequences now or later that could possibly warrant government intervention. This group espoused the view that any dire consequences would be as a result of the intervention and not of the "mythical" problems themselves.

The unanticipated growth in affluence partly explained, we believe, the demand for government intervention through regulations to stop the perceived depletion, pollution and consumer rip-offs we cited before. By the same token, the unanticipated decline in the growth of affluence, and, for some individuals, its absolute fall, coupled with the widespread feeling that the best is over and the worst has yet to come, have led to a new attitude towards government and a new set of demands.

It goes without saying that the martyrs find a much less responsive audience for their dire warnings. Furthermore, those who were hurt, or more accurately, were fearful of some day being hurt, by the government's resulting regulatory interventions have been quick to point the finger of blame for "stagflation" at this kind of government intervention. That it is in their interest to do so is undeniable. Do these assertions have a basis in fact?

This is a question we have not attempted to address. However, in order to assist the reader in putting the argument in perspective, we would suggest that these points/queries be borne in mind.

(a) Canada now has environmental, occupational safety, product health/safety, advertising, and competition maintenance regulations *on the books*. It would be most illuminating to test the hypothesis that, with a few possible exceptions (e.g., environmental protection regulation in pulp and paper and mining), the consequences have been *immaterial* except for the legal and other expenses incurred in avoiding them and the minor expenses incurred in appearing to enforce them. To be crude, have most industries been gummed rather than bitten by these regulations? Secondly, do those actually bitten constitute such a significant part of the industrial scene to attribute the general malaise to this source?

It can be argued by those who represent industrial interests that their current agony is derived from the anticipation of future pain that, if nothing else, increases the level of uncertainty under which their investment plans must be formulated. This is valid argument. However, in the myriad uncertainties that are swirling around the business community at the present time, one would have thought that the weight attached to regulatory uncertainty must be as a meadow brook is to Niagara Falls. Moreover, given the proven capacity of the business community to emasculate, again with a few exceptions, tax structure reform and competition policy reform (Stanbury, 1977), one would have thought they would be full of confidence when approaching the regulatory hurdle. Parenthetically, it might be added that in recent years the Government of Canada has had an uncanny knack of first stirring up business concern (and hence increasing uncertainty) and then backing off without achieving much other than the diversion of managerial time and effort and, of course, higher expenses in preparing briefs, submissions and lobbying.

(b) The two most successful economies (in growth terms) in the Western world are those of West Germany and Japan. How do their environmental, occupational safety, product safety and industrial competition regulations *as actually applied* compare with Canadian regulations? This is, of course, another factual-analytic question that needs to be addressed. If such differences are found, how important are they relative to other factors such as the apparently different attitudes on the part of organized labour and business towards each other and the *structure* of industry?

In particular, the differences in the approach actually applied to industrial competition in both Western Germany and Japan, *vis-à-vis* the approach taken in the United States and, to a much lesser extent, Canada, deserve careful analysis. To put the matter in a different way, in neither West Germany nor Japan are the ostensible benefits to the *domestic* consumers of industrial competition given much, if any, weight, nor are the political dangers of the close interconnection between government and industrial power given much, if any, weight. These nations rely primarily on the competition of foreigners to keep their industries efficient. And as for the political dangers . . . .

(c) There are some overwhelming *economic* forces at play in the world that are having, and are likely to continue to have, an enormous and largely painful impact on the Western world. As the Economic Council's (1975) recent report on international trade entitled *Looking Outward, A New Trade Strategy for Canada* discussed, there are enormous imbalances in the current national endowments of natural resources, human capital, industrial capital, and the consequent disparities in living standards. The "oil crisis" of a few years ago rocked Western economies and created shocks that have not been entirely absorbed. Other shocks are likely to follow, and then more. Canada relies heavily on international trade. International shocks hit the Canadian economy both directly and also through their impact on our international markets. From this perspective, Canadian government regulation hardly looms as the most menacing spectre with which we have to contend.

To descend from these Olympian heights (or to ascend from these abysmal depths, depending upon one's perspective), we wish to point out that the critics of government regulation have, no doubt inadvertently, opened a Pandora's Box. That box contains not only regulations that have been ostensibly detrimental to Canadian business. There are also regulations that have been extraordinarily, yet unobstrusively, helpful to some business and labour interests while being detrimental to the interests of many other Canadians. As the regulations tumble in profusion out of the box one can anticipate with absolute certainty cries of anguish: "But we didn't object to *that* one . . . or *that* one . . . or *that* one . . . ."

The sad fact is that, under the guise of regulations, and rulings promulgated "in the public interest," fortunes have been made. And as the chill, efficiency-generating winds of competition have been converted into gentle, relaxing breezes, the least fortunate have been made more unfortunate to add to the advantages of the advantaged. Moreover, the regulatory process itself has made it possible for the well-to-do, the well-connected and the well-informed to glide quickly and silently through seemingly impenetrable barriers, like pike through a weedbed, with their eyes fastened on their prey. The unnumbered minnows have disappeared without a ripple on the surface.

1.2 THE CONTENDING IDEOLOGIES OF ECONOMISTS AND THE ROLE OF GOVERNMENT

Most economists conceive of government regulations as but one of the potential means or instruments at the disposal of governments to achieve their purposes. But what are those purposes? Does it matter how they are determined? How are we to identify the "real" purposes? By and large, those who adhere to this "means-ends" approach to government regulations and other government policies assume both that these "purpose" questions lie beyond the purview of their disciplines and that stated goals can be taken at face value or inferred from previous policy choices. This group would, by and large, assess specific regulations in terms of their effectiveness in realizing goals, relative to alternative policy instruments, in order to minimize costs, broadly defined. This approach is discussed in great detail in Appendix B. Analyses based on the "rational actor" approach have something to contribute to the conflict resolution process. However, unless seen in the context of an adversarial decision-making process but rather viewed as, in some sense, "answers" to policy questions they are at best misleading. The reason is that they almost always ignore income/wealth distributional considerations and these are at the heart of virtually all policy decisions—and certainly those of a regulatory nature.

There are a few economists, known as "public choice theorists," who, particularly in recent years, have focused their attention on the rules that determine government decision-making processes. In particular, they have emphasized the coercion involved when a majority voting rule rather than a unanimity rule is adopted. The "Virginia School"[6] approaches the government rule-process question from an explicitly normative (ideological) point of view, while those on the periphery of that school are more inclined to analyse the conditions under which individuals and groups try to change rules and processes in the pursuit of their self-interest. They have also been concerned with the behavioural effects of particular rules and processes on individuals and groups. These economists are concerned with the analysis of bureaucracies, pressure groups, political parties and voters, using the most basic concepts of economics to derive theories about what have traditionally been thought of as institutional-political behaviour.[7]

In many ways the "Chicago School" is similar to the public choice (Virginia) school.[8] Some of those attached to it[9] take a strong normative stance in favour of market decisions and an equally strong opposition to almost all government intervention including, of course, regulations. The emphasis is on individual freedom and economic efficiency. Although they do not use the term frequently, most government interference in individual market choices is thought of as coercive. Here too there are many "members" of this school who use the economic tools and framework of market analysis to critically examine, from a positivistic standpoint, the allocative consequences of government intervention.[10] Needless to say, given their philosophic presupposition, they find them most unfortunate!

---

[6] In particular, see Buchanan and Tullock (1962).

[7] See Downs (1957); Olson (1965); Niskanen (1971); Breton (1974), among others.

[8] See Samuels (1976).

[9] Notably Milton Freidman.

[10] Too numerically large to cite all the names but some examples are George Stigler, Gary Becker and Steven Cheung.

Scott Gordon (1977), in a paper prepared for the Economic Council of Canada,[11] discusses three "ideals": welfare, justice and freedom that he terms, following Rawls (1971), "primary social goods." Welfare, justice, and freedom are usually treated as overarching goals or ideals. And Gordon, too, considers them in that light. The particularly interesting point that he makes, and he makes it most persuasively, is rather surprising, however. In his view, justice and freedom, in particular, are terms that cannot be precisely and simply defined so as to derive rules of universal applicability. Moreover, he believes that those who claim to have simple, universal rules are worse than foolish—they are positively dangerous. He argues that when such rules are consistently applied, they invariably have disasterous consequences in the sense that the logical extensions are so extreme as to be unacceptable to sensible men. He makes the valid point that it is usually much easier to obtain agreement as to the existence and nature of a problem than it is to obtain inadequate realization of some goal(s) that is the source of the problem. In other words, men seem to be able to agree when they perceive that welfare, justice and freedom do not prevail in particular situations, but can rarely agree on what those concepts mean in abstract, universal terms.

In our view, this perhaps reflects neither more nor less than that both denote the *absence* of that which we believe to be bad. Thus, justice is the *absence* of capricious arbitrariness and "unfairness" and freedom is the *absence* of needless constraints imposed by others. But what is judged as unacceptably and unnecessarily capricious, arbitrary and constraining depends upon one's upbringing and experience. This, in turn, suggests that the underlying rules upon which individual judgments are made about justice and freedom are so deeply ingrained in the individual's subconscious that they become, to all intents and purposes, absolute imperatives for that *individual*. Because these imperatives are learned at a very early age, that which is learned is not critically examined. And, because that which is learned comes from a few sources (e.g., mother, family, neighbourhood, etc.) upon which the child is physically and emotionally dependent, he can exercise little if any choice with respect to what he learns. Because contiguous families tend to become similar with respect to what their children are taught by word and by deed, and/or because those that think and behave similarly tend to congregate, the sense of what constitutes injustice and what constitutes tyranny is widely shared within the group.

To the concepts of justice and freedom (as we have just defined them) has to be added another—the concept of "welfare." This concept is defined precisely later in the paper, but for our immediate purpose it might be thought

---

[11] This paper is recommended reading for anyone seriously interested in government economic policy from a wider perspective than that taken by most economists.

of as the *sense* of well-being of the individual, where the word "sense" means "feeling of satisfaction" or "utility."

Policy decisions, including, of course, regulatory decisions, involve a trade-off among these three "primary social goods" unless *and only unless* there are inefficiencies, where the term inefficiency means precisely that: the availability of costless gains. As we will seek to explain later, almost by definition it would be unanimously agreed that all costless gains should be realized *and* immediately. The rub comes in the fact that *obtaining* these "costless gains" is hardly ever, if ever, costless. Furthermore, the conflict concerning who is to enjoy them may preclude their realization.

Another gross simplification, that ignores many of the qualifications expressed by the authors themselves, is to say that the public choice theorists and the Chicago school adherents believe that, with free markets and no government interference other than the provision of the "necessities" (in particular, the maintenance of property rights) and meticulously adhering to the unanimity decision rule, freedom would be maximized *and* welfare would flourish *at least in aggregate*. They tend to ignore the justice dimension of welfare—the fairness of the distribution of income and wealth that provides access to the collective pot of available goods and services that yield individual satisfaction.[12] By this we mean to suggest that, *relative to most other economists*, at least until recently, the Chicago and Virginia schools have been thought to have taken a most conservative stance toward government intervention. However, with the disillusionment about government previously discussed, more and more so-called "liberal-minded" economists are *perforce* finding the Chicago and Virginia schools increasingly acceptable ideologically. Two of the "logical" alternatives—Marxism and Fascism (corporatism)—involve a rejection of humanistic values that most find unacceptable. The third alternative, and it is more a matter of degree than of kind, is so-called welfare economics. To a discussion of that subject we now turn.

Welfare Economics

In our opinion, welfare economics has extraordinarily little to contribute to the analysis of public policy other than a classification scheme of market imperfections. This is not to denigrate some of the insights such as the "free-rider" problem, the externalities problem,[13] and the transactions costs problem to which we allude later and on which much of our argument depends. These are vital concepts from a positivistic point of view.

Just as the border between, say, Manitoba and North Dakota is clear enough on the map, and the writs of the Government of Canada and the

---

[12] But are by no means the only source of individual satisfaction as discussed in Chapter 2.

[13] "Externalities" can be looked upon as non-exclusive rights and obligations. See Chapter 2.

Province of Manitoba on the one side, and those of the United States and the State of North Dakota on the other, run to this border, so does the concept of Pareto optimality divide two philosophic-ideological perspectives. The Pareto optimality concept essentially differentiates between an economic efficiency question and a distribution of income and wealth question. An economic efficiency question, as defined by the Pareto optimality concept, is one that encompasses deviations from a condition(s) under which no individual can be made better off without making someone else worse off. A distributional question, on the other hand, is one that encompasses changes in which the gain of one or more individuals is necessarily at the expense of one or more others. The significance of this distinction lies essentially in the assumption that an improvement in economic efficiency—a change that would make one or more individuals better off without hurting others is, by definition, an improvement that would command unanimous consent and, therefore, raises no normative (subjective value judgment) issues. Conversely, distributional changes necessarily entail subjective value judgments—who *should* gain and who *should* lose—that would not command unanimous consent for the losers would, in essence, be coerced. The important, and in a sense practical, implication that stems from the distinction between efficiency and distributional questions is that where instances of economic inefficiency are found the economist can, *under extraordinarily stringent conditions,* [14] state as a matter of logic rather than of personal belief that such and such a change would constitute an unequivocal improvement. The inference can then be drawn that government intervention in the market, over and above the provision of "pure public goods,"[15] (e.g., defence, and the maintenance of the rule of law) is warranted—indeed, a "good thing" *by definition.* However, the Chicago school adherents[16] argue that these kinds of market imperfections are extraordinarily rare. Moreover, they argue that, generally speaking, interventions to correct market imperfections often (invariably?) do more harm than good and are (almost always?) a cloak under which self-interest is pursued at the expense of individual freedom and the economic well-being of the collectivity.

The social democratic "liberal" position would be something as follows: "We *believe* that 'pure' capitalism would result in a distribution of income and wealth among individuals that would be ethically unacceptable. Government intervention to alter that distribution is, therefore, warranted even if this does create some inefficiencies in the Pareto optimality sense. Moreover, the market system is riddled with imperfections. Thus it will not, without government intervention, give Pareto optimal (pure efficiency)

---

[14] See Appendix A for a statement of these conditions.

[15] Pure public goods are those from which the benefits cannot be denied to those who do not pay for them and are available to all without diminution.

[16] For references to the work of this group, see Samuels (1976).

results." Therefore, there are two grounds for government intervention—the first admittedly normative, the other based on "logic."

The explicit discussion among economists on these issues over the past fifty years or so has become increasingly complex, refined and inward looking. Following the debate, which has often been turgid, conjures up, in the mind of the non-economist at least, the seemingly endless often pointless controversies that characterized medieval scholasticism. Yet to dismiss it as irrelevant would also be facile—inordinately facile.

There are several types of market imperfections that have engendered government regulatory intervention. The word "engender" conveys the impression, perhaps, that the intervention took place because of the ideas and arguments of professional economists. That is highly unlikely. Populism (anti-"big business"), consumerism and environmentalism have been pushed by large social-political groups at one time or another, with more or less vigour and more or less success. Some economists certainly have provided the theoretical rationale, if you will, for these movements. But it is doubtful that the ideas of economists were responsible for them except, possibly, in a most roundabout manner.

In a recent and extremely helpful paper by Trebilcock, Waverman and Prichard (1978), a brief review of the market imperfection arguments of economists is presented. At the end of that review their views, and the findings of others are summarized.

> Plausible rationalizations for regulatory interventions in private markets in order to eliminate market failures were presented in the previous section. However, in this section, an analysis of a limited number of actual forms of intervention indicate that eliminating market failures does not appear to be the sole or even primary motivation. Studies of the total effect on economic efficiency of various regulatory regimes indicate that social welfare is reduced not increased in many cases.[17] If regulation is intended to eliminate market failures and increase economic efficiency, how can this be allowed to happen? We now turn to an analysis of the distribution of gains and losses from regulation and a discussion of redistributive rationales (Trebilcock *et al.*, 1978, p. 28).

We agree with this assessment, and our paper seeks to explore the same fundamental issues, from a more explicit conceptual framework, as that set forth in the last sentence in the quotation from their paper. However, as they noted elsewhere in their paper and as we also agree, there are some aspects of the market imperfections argument that *are* germane to the question of government regulatory intervention. As a matter of expository convenience, that should not be construed as an attempt at denigration, Appendix A provides a summary and assessment of the principal ideological-theoretical

---

[17] Trebilcock *et al.* (1978), cite the following: Peltzman (1973; 1975); Posner (1975); MacAvoy and Pindyck (1975); Stigler and Friedland (1962); Wilson (1964).

aspects of the market imperfections discussion in the literature of welfare economics.[18]

1.3 THE CONTENDING APPROACHES OF ECONOMISTS AND POLITICAL SCIENTISTS TOWARDS PUBLIC POLICY DECISION MAKING

For many decades now, academic economists and political scientists have been speaking at cross-purposes about public policy—when they could bear to be in the same room with one another when the subject was broached. The economist insisted that each and every public policy question had to be formulated as an optimization problem. The typical dialogue went something like this, with the economist responding to a question raised by the political scientist concerning how the government of the day could (should?) formulate its economic policies.

"The answer is straightforward. First the government must specify *all* its objectives and constraints. Then it must define the set of policy instruments to be used. It is then a simple matter to express in precise mathematical terms the marginal conditions to be met in order to realize the objectives within the constraints at the lowest possible cost.

"Moreover," continued the economist, "if they have all the data needed they can determine whether the objectives can be simultaneously attained. If they cannot be, the government will have to back off on some of the objectives and/or constraints and/or introduce more policy instruments. If that seems too static an approach, then they could go to control theory . . . ."

"But," interrupted the political scientist, "that is all very well. But that is *not* the problem at all, as I see it. Governments don't think that way either. Their objective is simple enough. They want to stay in office. Actually that is *too* simple. Most of them want to keep the country together and improve it as they see it. But they certainly first have to get into office or stay in office. But they do that by making decisions everyday. It depends upon the situation in the House of Commons and the feedback they get from their constituents, from the polls and so on. They are always trading off this policy to please this group and another policy to please that. Why, didn't you read in the paper this morning . . . ."

"Oh, get off it," interrupts the economist, impatiently. "That's just a *description* of what happens, not a *theory*! That's the trouble with you political scientists . . . ."

Although put facetiously, the lack of communication has had some consequences that have been anything but amusing. And, as is so often the case, there has been virtue on both sides. The economist has had an analytic method of proven efficacy *in some uses* and was insisting that the problem be formulated in such a way that his method could provide the ''answer.'' The political scientist was unwilling to push the problem with which he was

---

[18] Gilles Paquet (1978), in a recent paper, begins with the same basic postulate as we do (and thus as do Trebilcock *et al*.)—the unsatisfactory nature of much of the traditional economic analysis of regulation. Although the conceptual framework presented by Paquet is quite different in many respects from that presented in our paper, the spirit of his approach (if one can use such a word when dealing with government!) is much the same as ours, although it addresses the political issues involved less explicitly.

struggling into the economists' procrustean analytic bed, believing, and rightly so, that the resulting "answer" would be an answer to a different problem.

In essence, the political scientist was discussing an extraordinarily complex gaming problem that is not "solvable" analytically, particularly because of the multiplicity of probabilistic relationships concerning both information flows and competitive reactions. Had the political scientist asked the question in the following terms, the discussion might have been more fruitful.

> Suppose there are four corporations, each seeking to maximize the market value of its shares. Suppose that they compete with one another in an oligopolistic market in which each firm sells similar but brand-name products to poorly informed consumers. Assuming price leadership does not prevail, what is the optimal strategy for any one of the firms?

In all likelihood, the economist's "answer" would be similar to the political scientist's *description* that the economist so quickly dismissed in the earlier hypothetical dialogue. The outcome is indeterminate. Perhaps, by dint of much imagination, effort, *and* computer time, it would be feasible, using some highly simplified *assumed* behavioural responses and by limiting the range of many of the probabilistic variables, to come close on a trial and error basis to simulating what usually occurs in such situations. Hardly a theory!

With this by way of explanation, the next section presents a *description* of the adversarial process of collective decision making. But we cannot forbear a comment. If economists would concern themselves more with the analysis of the actual distributive impact of alternative public policies and spend less time attempting to arrive at statements that are logically valid only under impossibly stringent conditions, their unique knowledge and expertise could make an invaluable contribution. If economists, as economists, are content with the self-denying ordinance of analysing distributional effects without offering normative comment so much the better. But collective decisions about policies that have enormous distributional consequences are made. And, in a democracy, they are made through an adversarial process, for the reasons discussed in the next section. One would have thought that the process might work more effectively if the economists provided the voters and the decision makers with more information on the actual distributional and allocative effects of the alternative decisions. They could do this rather than pontificate *after the event* about the adverse allocative effects (effects that may be real and significant) of policy decisions, but effects which are not at issue in the debate unless economists raise them!

1.4 THE ADVERSARIAL NATURE OF PUBLIC POLICY DECISION MAKING AND THE SCOPE FOR LEADERSHIP

Words like "goals," "objectives," and "purposes" imply a normative imperative. It is impossible, of course, to determine non-subjectively whether a particular goal is good or bad. Either it must be assumed to be good or it must be assumed that the goal was arrived at by some kind of process or by some kind of group or person that *ipso facto* makes it good. From this standpoint, and it is one to be qualified greatly later, it follows that the pursuit of these "good" goals is therefore good: the more effectively they are pursued, the better.

One constantly hears plaintive pleas from all quarters, including the members of political parties, members of Parliament, bureaucrats and journalists that the government of the day is somehow remiss in failing to specify its goals except in a highly vague, rhetorical fashion. It all seems too obvious to practical men—men of affairs—that in order to be able to move expeditiously towards where we want to go we first have to decide upon the destination that we seek! "How can we plan when we don't know where we are going?" "We are all going in different directions and offsetting one another's efforts." "Let's all pull together."

These kinds of comments are as ubiquitous as they are innocent, if not misguided. They reflect a painful lack of awareness of the full richness of the political problem. Take, for example, the constant use of the word "we." "We" in this context suggests a high degree of consensus, if not complete unanimity, among Canadians about what they want the government to do for them (or to them) as a collectivity. It is implied, if not stated, that at least a clear majority of Canadians want full employment, a stable price level, better quality of goods and services, greater security of persons and property from internal and external threats, a cleaner physical environment, greater access to better social and cultural amenities, greater equality of opportunity, less poverty . . . . There is little doubt that the vast majority of Canadians would accept all of these goals (and many more too).[19] The rub comes not in compiling lists of quasi-motherhood statements—that is easy enough—but in contending with two painful facts: these goals are not independent of each other nor of other goals; voters are not indifferent about who will obtain the benefits and who will bear the costs, to put the charged reality as mildly as possible.

Most goals cannot be considered independently from one or more other goals because the greater realization of one has effects, sometimes positive and sometimes negative, on the realization of others. There are often important trade-offs or complementaries. The most obvious instance of a trade-off is that between a reduced unemployment rate and a reduced rate of

---

[19] This point is elaborated in painful detail in Appendix B.

inflation. It is widely believed that, at least without fundamental structural changes, the greater realization of one of these goals necessarily entails that the other will be less fully realized. The adverse effects of the pursuit of one goal on the realization of the other means that the goals are, in essence, simultaneously both goals and constraints: the pursuit of full employment is constrained by the undesired impact on inflation and conversely. Now, if policies are inefficient so that one goal can be further realized without any adverse effects on one or more of the others, one would expect that there would be almost universal support for a policy change. But, as soon as the trade-off becomes operative, consensus tends to evaporate because there are, then, potential net losers as well as net gainers. This arises not only because individuals have different tastes and preferences, but also because they are not equally wealthy (or poor) and because the composition of their portfolios of rights (assets) differs widely, as explained in Chapter 2. An individual who is unemployed may well feel quite differently towards the ''right'' trade-off between inflation and unemployment than a retired individual on a fixed pension. When, as is usually the case, there are trade-offs between the goals there are bound to be conflicts among individuals because their personal interests differ—sometimes substantially. Under these circumstances potential losers will seek to avoid these losses and potential winners will attempt to obtain the gains by influencing government policy in a whole variety of ways—the more important of which are discussed in subsequent chapters. The point is, however, that whatever government decides to do, it is, under these conditions, helping some individuals at the expense of others and this involves an explicit value judgment about whose interests should be served.

Modern welfare economics has sought to avoid making these normative judgments (that, if nothing else, are seldom widely accepted) by postulating a so-called ''social welfare function.'' This is neither more nor less than the assumptions that a government has a long list of objectives that have been defined and that the government has assigned relative weights to each of them which, in effect, constitute the (shadow) prices it is willing to pay to achieve a unit increase in a particular goal in terms of the less adequate realization of competing goals. It implies the existence of a complete, stable consensus or a complete, stable conformity within the Cabinet both with respect to what is of concern and with respect to the relative importance of these concerns. By adopting this postulate, economists have neatly side-stepped the inherent politics of the decision-making process. Therefore, they can specify, assuming a knowledge of the precise trade-offs involved and of the effects of all policy instruments, what *should* be done to most fully realize simultaneously the government's goals, taking into account the relative importance assigned to them.

All of this is very elegant, and the precise conditions for optimization can be specified in precise mathematical terms that are familiar to those who are aware of the conditions that must be met to solve a complex, but static optimization problem by the use of the calculus, or the conditions that must be met to solve a dynamic optimization problem by the use of control theory, difference equations, or dynamic programming. The difficulty is that elegance has been gained by sacrificing relevance. The logic is impeccable but the implications are empty because there is not now, and almost certainly never will be, a government that can, even if it wished to do so, specify such a social welfare function. Moreover, much if not most of the other information required is not available, at least on an "all objectives—all policy instruments" scale. The data does not exist. The analytic problems are horrendous. But it is the postulation of a social welfare function that is particularly unfortunate because it tends to steer economists interested in policy matters towards a course that leads nowhere. To postulate the existence of a stable and known social welfare function is like assuming that Shakespeare could have written Hamlet without introducing the Prince of Denmark. It might be a play, but it would not be Hamlet. To analyse government policy without taking into account the conflicts among politicians (especially Cabinet ministers who advocate different interest groups), without taking into account the pressures brought to bear by competing factions, and without taking into account the constant shifts in the alliances and coalitions among them all, is to simplify the problem to the point where it is at least a different problem and more likely a non-problem.

A quite different framework commends itself to us: a framework that explicitly confronts the problems of interpersonal and intergroup conflict, the ubiquitous nature of transactions' costs (and, in particular, information costs, full-line forcing, log-rolling) and the symbolic character of many of the government's actions and statements.[20]

This conflict resolution approach to government is, of course, not novel. It is the basic concept of pluralism that has been of great importance in political science, particularly in the United States, for decades.[21] Economists have come to the concept much more recently.[22]

Without going into a detailed description of the formal political system that exists in Canada it can be roughly characterized by a few points. Those familiar with the basic structure of the Canadian political system should ignore the following fourteen points. Others might find it a useful reminder.

1. We have a federal system of government with a division of powers between the Government of Canada and the Provinces specified in the *British North America Act*, as amended, together with some court decisions.

---

[20] Probably the most comprehensive discussion (with references) of these terms is to be found in Breton (1974).

[21] See MacIver (1926); Dahl (1956); Bentley (1967); Truman (1951) and others.

[22] See Downs (1957); Solo (1974); Breton (1974); Buchanan and Tullock (1962); Wilson (1963); Niskanen (1971).

2. We have a parliamentary system under which the party with the largest number of seats forms the government of the day and the leader of that party is also simultaneously a member of the House of Commons and the head of the executive branch of government.

3. The maximum length of a government's term is fixed (five years) but an earlier election is mandatory if the party in power cannot sustain a majority (perhaps through the support of another party) on a matter of substance, or the prime minister can persuade the Governor General, the titular head of state, that effective government requires a new mandate.

4. All citizens have a vote in federal elections but the weight attached to each vote differs markedly from riding to riding because of the wide disparity in the number of eligible voters among the ridings.

5. Cabinet ministers and the most senior bureaucrats are appointed by the prime minister and hold office at his pleasure during his term of office although most senior bureaucrats have not, in the past, been dismissed or demoted following changes in government.

6. Most other bureaucrats are appointed by the Public Service Commission on the basis of merit and cannot be dismissed without just cause—a rare occurrence.

7. Each department and agency reports to a minister. Some ''independent'' regulatory agencies and Crown corporations report to the House of Commons *through* a minister, an important distinction that is discussed at length in Chapter 3.

8. Cabinet solidarity requires that all ministers support *in public* all Cabinet decisions unreservedly or resign—whatever their personal views or feelings.

9. Although there is usually an attempt to develop a consensus among the members of Cabinet on each policy issue, this is a matter of prime ministerial style. He can make unilateral decisions if he is willing to risk defections.

10. The methods used to select candidates vary from party to party, from constituency to constituency. Because each eligible voter does not have to declare his or her party affiliation, and because many party supporters do not join a party formally, it is often unclear whether or not the selection of the candidate truly reflects the prevailing opinion in the riding as distinct from prevailing opinion in the riding *association*, because memberships in the association can be packed by one of the contenders if he or she has sufficient funds to advertise and solicit support.

11. Members of Parliament rarely desert one party for another. This is explained in part by the feeling that this is somehow reprehensible behaviour unless the switch is closely tied to a major issue of principle. (Almost by definition, in political contexts these are very rare.)

12. Short of interparty switches, members of Parliament are kept in line by party leaders through threats to withhold party financial support in

subsequent campaigns and/or to force the withdrawal of the recalcitrant M.P. from House committees and other perquisites (e.g., parliamentary assistantships).

13. The Cabinet is chosen by the prime minister to reflect both political realities—those members of Parliament who are in his party and have political clout (e.g., have a personal following or can manipulate those who can bring in the vote)—and the diverse interests of the electorate. These are regional, linguistic, religious, occupational, industrial, rural/urban, worker/management, old/young, male/female, right wing/left wing, and many more.

14. There are essentially five kinds of government departments and agencies:

— *central agencies* that are concerned with matters that transcend the interests of any one department or agency and are essentially extensions of the prime minister's concern for the executive branch as a collectivity. These include the Privy Council Office, the Department of Finance, the Treasury Board Secretariat, and the Public Service Commission;

— *common service departments* that carry out such activities as purchasing and construction on behalf of other departments and agencies, including the Department of Public Works, and the Department of Supply and Services;

— *operating agencies*, including among many others, the Department of Transport, and the Department of Agriculture;

— *regulatory agencies*, with a greater or lesser degree of autonomy (as discussed later) including among many others: the Canadian Radio-television and Telecommunications Commission, the Canadian Transport Commission, and the Tariff Board;

— *Crown corporations* that are given a great deal of independence by statute and where government control is usually indirect (e.g., through control over access to funds or through rate setting by regulatory agencies) e.g., Air Canada, Petro Canada, etc.[23]

This brief discussion of a large and highly complex organizational structure and its many interrelated procedures and processes cannot do justice to the reality we seek to describe. But perhaps one point emerges with reasonable clarity. Like our courts of law that have gradually developed rules and procedures that allow adversaries to contend within recognized constraints with one another when the facts or the meaning of the law are in doubt, so too the decision-making process in a country like Canada legitimizes inherently arbitrary decisions (who should win and who should lose?) by proceeding within a legitimate framework. In short, in neither instance is it possible to know, except subjectively, whether the decisions are

---

[23] For the gory details of the number, powers, and organizations of federal government departments and agencies, see the mammoth *Organization of the Government of Canada* (1976).

right or wrong. Rather, general acceptance is gained because the decisions are only reached after "due process"; through appeal procedures, in the case of the courts, to ministers and the courts in the case of quasi-judicial agencies, and free elections, Supreme Court rulings and defections of M.P.'s from the party in the case of government policy decisions.

These procedures and processes provide *some* protection against continued arbitrariness and perversity by the executive branch of government. By allowing dissidents to air their queries in public, by making a particular minister responsible for each policy area, the disaffected are inclined to acquiesce in their disappointments at least to the extent of refraining from the use of illegitimate means to achieve their ends. They have, generally speaking, a modicum of hope that they will overcome the obstacles before them by acting within the existing system so that recourse does not have to be had to violence, treason and subversion.

It cannot be emphasized too strongly, however, that *it should not be inferred that the word "legitimate" connotes either non-coercive or just.*[24] Sometimes, under some conditions, some procedures and processes reduce the likelihood of gross coercion and gross injustice. "Legitimate" in our lexicon, at least in this context, has a much more pragmatic meaning: generally acceptable and, hence, a means of coercion where the losers are expected to acquiesce in their losses relatively gracefully or, less facetiously, the losers would find it more difficult to rally public support for their cause on the basis of the "injustice" ("illegitimacy") of the decision.

Let us now briefly examine the interrelated questions of coalitions, log-rolling and full-line forcing, and the timing of elections. The *sine qua non* of a stable coalition is the perception of the members of the component groups that their separate group interests and their shared interests (if any) will be furthered more by acting as a collectivity of groups than by acting alone, and that the particular coalition has more to offer than the alternative coalitions available.

Without going into the complexities, coalitions usually involve some kind of log-rolling: "we will support your group's position on X if your group will support our stand on Y." Obviously, log-rolling is not without its costs because the members of a group may find it difficult to swallow the stands taken by their leaders in order to buy the support of other groups whose members will be equally disconcerted when their turn comes to repay the favour. Clearly, there are limits beyond which interest group leaders cannot go in log-rolling without alienating their supporters. But the limits are probably quite wide on many issues as long as the group leaders can convey the view, without admitting it publicly, that some embarrassment on issue X is the price of success on issue Y. It is important to note that, at least for the

---

[24] On this question we depart from Novick (1974) and Buchanan (1975) who, to all intents and purposes, define as absolute justice the decisions emerging from just processes.

initiated, these kinds of coalitions may arise without any explicit agreement, verbal or written. Professional interest group leaders and politicians are well aware that a favour received is an obligation incurred. Those who ignore this basic rule find themselves rejected by all sides and unable to fulfill their functions.

The power of pressure groups derives from several factors which are considered extensively in Chapter 3. Perhaps the most important source of their strength is the fact that many proposed policy changes would bestow substantial benefits on a relatively small group while the costs would be spread thinly and widely. This means that the potential gainers can afford substantial expenses (in terms of money or time) to push for the adoption of the policy proposal, while the opponents are too numerous to organize and the stakes on *an individual basis* too small to warrant an expensive battle. For example, removing an industrial tax concession (e.g., depletion) would have a major effect on a relatively few firms: the extra revenues, if used to reduce personal income taxes, would mean only pennies for the average taxpayer. The former cannot afford not to mount a major defensive action; the latter, if they pursue their narrow self-interest, will hardly bother to read the story in the newspaper!

Because interest group members often believe that the stakes are high they are willing to invest heavily in exerting pressure and influence and they may find it expeditious to make contributions to campaign funds—a matter of great concern to politicians, of course. These "contributions" are usually not as vulgar as old-fashioned bribes. However, it is difficult to believe that simple charity rather than some kind of anticipated return on the investment (albeit often indirect, such as a favourable regulatory interpretation or as subtle as gaining access to "the right person") is the motive.

An important factor in log-rolling is what has come to be known as full-line forcing (a term taken from theories of industrial organization). When an uncommitted voter is trying to decide which candidate/party to support the choice is between alternative *packages* of policies (actual or promised). In order to try to obtain policy A, a policy the voter desires intensely that is offered by a particular party, he has to support a candidate/party that is also likely to implement or retain a large number of other policies, some of which are less attractive, some of which are a matter of indifference, some are slightly unattractive, and some indeed may be considered by the voter as most unattractive. The trick for the political party is to put together a package of policies that, by achieving a careful balance relative to the packages offered by the other parties, will commend itself as a whole to swing voters in swing ridings. (There is no point in worrying about firmly committed voters of any stripe!) Because parties are selling packages rather than individual items they can contain a host of mildly unpleasant items that are of little significance to the vast majority of voters but of great significance to a small pressure group. This means that the log-rolling among pressure groups need not jeopardize the party's general support if there are enough policy items of some value to the voters whose support is required.

Barring calamities, most majority governments are in office for about four years after their election. This means that the package of actual policies is gradually assembled over this period in a dynamic series of compromises because there is time to alter the package in response to feedback from the voters whose support is necessary. Because, by and large, the government of the day can select the date for an election within an upper boundary, the flow of compromises can be stopped almost at will when a snapshot (political poll) gives the most favourable picture to it.

In contrasting the relative advantages of the "ins" and the "outs" it should not be forgotten that other factors are also in play. The government of the day has not only the advantage of being able to call the election at a time most favourable to itself, it also has demonstrated that it at least once had wide public support and could put together a team of ministers with a modicum of competence. But, and it is a major qualification, the government of the day has to live with its record. Promises to make change if re-elected are a little hollow. "If these changes are so desirable why were they not made in the past four years?"

Opposition parties are much less burdened by the record, of course, particularly if they have not held office for a substantial period (if ever). Promises can flow like water: inconsistent promises, vague promises, uncosted promises, promises that are hopelessly unfulfillable. The trick for them is to appear to be all things to the uncommitted voter *and* a credible alternative with growing public support. This puts a limit on the rashness of the promises. Credibility consists of more than plausible promises, however. It also requires that the opposition party persuade the public that it can field a reasonably strong ministerial team and that other voters now see it as a credible alternative to the point where just a little more support will produce a winner. Apparently there is a considerable attraction to voters that is self-reinforcing, to think of themselves as being "in on the ground floor."

Although the advantages are not entirely one-sided, it would appear that the balance is usually tipped in favour of the party in power. Success breeds success: the government of the day finds it easier to attract attractive candidates; the government of the day also has control over the pork barrel and, in a sense, can buy support in advance of an election rather than promise benefits when and if elected.

There is an old adage to the effect that opposition parties are not elected to office: rather the party in office is voted out of office. The factors we have sketched give support to this proposition—as does the track record of Canadian political parties!

It should be made explicit, perhaps, that the bureaucracy itself constitutes an extremely powerful interest group that can have, on occasion, a decisive influence on the rolling series of compromises that the government of the day must achieve. It has several sources of strength: (i) many bureaucrats have a virtual monopoly over the flow of technical information and political advice on which ministers must base their decisions with the result that ministers may be unaware of attractive alternatives or the dangers implicit in others; (ii) even good policy decisions can be thwarted by clumsy implementation and it is usually difficult, and often impossible, to prove that implementation problems arose because of conscious obstructionism; (iii) senior bureaucrats are extremely conscious of the fact that if the prerogatives and/or authority of one is whittled away, then all are vulnerable with the result that senior officials who usually compete strongly against one another can coalesce against a ministry and make it appear much less competent than it would appear to be with full bureaucratic support. A ministry must, therefore, tread the tightrope between being captured by a bureaucracy that is often insensitive to political realities and overly sensitive to administrative convenience and precedents, on the one hand, and alienating those who can make it or break it, on the other.

Where then does this leave us? What *is* the role of government? Is it nothing more than a highly complex means of resolving, through an endless series of compromises, the conflicting interests of those subject to its authority in such a way as to avoid the open use of force: "the war of all against all," to use Hobbes' phrase? The answer is usually yes, but occasionally no. There is a role for government leadership by which we mean the adoption of policies that are unpopular in prospect but come to be accepted perhaps even with enthusiasm and pride, after they have proven themselves.

If one were to try and capture *the* single most important and persistent objective pursued by a ministry it would undoubtedly be to "remain in power." For the opposition parties it is, of course, to gain power. A politician without elected office is like a fish out of water gasping for the air of immediacy, involvement, risk taking, public attention, personal power, income and perquisites. But politicians, like everyone else (excluding psychopaths!) have feelings of altruism, a concern for their country, and the well-being of other individuals. Moreover, from their vantage point they may see some emerging problems more clearly than the average citizen. Politicians, like everyone else (again, with the notable exception mentioned parenthetically above!), have personal moral standards that they break only at the cost of a loss of self-esteem. No one doubts that the statements of politicians often are laced with rhetoric, self-congratulation and implausible rationalizations. It is true, nevertheless, that some politicians some of the time are willing to risk their careers by pushing for the adoption of policies in which they believe, but that have little public acceptance. If most politicians behaved like martyrs most of the time the political system would be hopelessly unstable. Resignations would be an everyday occurrence: compromise would be impossible because every issue would be "a matter of principle.'' But, on the other hand, it is also true that without the efforts of some politicians to nudge the system toward a slightly different and unpopular course, from time to time, the ability of a nation to adapt to changing circumstances would undoubtedly be less than it is.

Political leadership does not usually entail that the outstanding politician personally discover a new theory or a new concept or a new policy or a new constraint, or foresee emerging trends hidden to others. Rather, it means that the rare politician is able to discern in the discoveries of a few others an insight "just slightly ahead of its time," and through a mixture of persuasion and demonstration bring it to bear on policy decisions before it has been widely recognized by voters.

But let us return to the question posed earlier. As stated above, the daily bread of political compromise is leavened by the yeast of leadership. Another major factor is the existence of widely shared voter preferences on some issues. When all voters want the same thing compromise is, of course, unnecessary. It is only when a faction or coalition of factions is sufficiently large and/or strategically placed so as to preclude electoral success, if not placated, that compromise becomes the order of the day.

Most of us seem to ignore or denigrate the politician's role as a consensus builder. No politician would prefer a painful compromise over a decision supported unanimously. And, to some degree at least, the choices of individuals can be altered by providing them with information and by persuasion (the provision of biased information) as advertisers well know. Many of the rituals that attend the political/legal process can be thought of as serving the function of helping to legitimize the outcome—an outcome which may be distasteful to the losers. Many political speeches also have a symbolic significance: they seek to reaffirm that the speaker shares the same values as his audience. Many government decisions too are primarily symbolic: they are designed to show that the government cares about the well-being of a segment of the population even if it is not able (or perhaps willing) to do much to further those interests in a material way.

Ideologies also serve an important function. Obtaining, sorting, discarding, storing and retrieving information is costly in time, effort and money. Voters can reduce those costs by choosing a political party on the basis of its ideology and supporting it without question until it does something that appears to be inconsistent with its principles. Proceeding in this way—only examining exceptions—is a perfectly rational decision rule for a voter who wishes to pursue his own interest, including the minimization of his information costs.

For the politician an ideology can serve to build a body of support that is sufficiently widely based and sufficiently stable to permit the exercise of leadership—up to the point where particularly unpopular decisions induce the party's supporters to re-examine their adherence to the ideology.

The ideology of a political party can also be looked upon as the terms of the agreement among the groups that form an existing coalition or the terms that a group (or a group of groups) is willing to offer to other groups willing to coalesce with it. While politicians are rarely able to create a complete consensus (except perhaps when there is a national emergency), they are constantly striving towards that unattainable goal and, through endless compromise, living with their inevitable failures. The best of them deploy the few inches of manoeuvering room they have fought to attain through compromise, promises, persuasion, log-rolling, and all the other tools of the trade, and put it at risk for a purpose that transcends their interest and the interests of their immediate supporters. Small wonder it is a rare man with a rare opportunity!

It is hoped that this chapter has served to suggest the environment within which the principal actors in the drama of politics play their parts. In the next chapter we shift to the presentation of a general conceptual framework. The purpose of that framework is to provide a consistent and explicit basis for examining what loosely might be termed the interest of an individual—any and all individuals: prime ministers and day-labourers alike. It will be recalled that it is one of our basic assumptions throughout that it is the well-being of *individuals* and only the well-being of individuals that ultimately matters.

REFERENCES

Bird, Richard M. (1970) *Growth of Government Expenditure in Canada* (Toronto: Canadian Tax Foundation).

Bentley, A.F. (1967) *The Process of Government* (Cambridge, Mass.: Harvard University Press).

Breton, A. (1974) *The Economic Theory of Respresentative Government* (Chicago: Aldine).

Buchanan, James (1975) *The Limits of Liberty: Between Anarchy and Leviathan* (Chicago: University of Chicago Press).

Buchanan, J. and G. Tullock (1962) *The Calculus of Consent* (Ann Arbor: University of Michigan Press).

Canada (1910) House of Commons. *Debates*, 11th Parl., 2nd Sess., April 12, pp. 6802-933.

Canada (1976) Interdepartmental Committee on the Organization of the Government of Canada *Organization of the Government of Canada 1976* (Ottawa: Supply and Services Canada).

Dahl, R.A. (1956) *A Preface to Democratic Theory* (Chicago: University of Chicago Press).

Downs, A. (1957) *An Economic Theory of Democracy* (New York: Harper).

Economic Council of Canada (1975) *Looking Outward: A New Trade Strategy for Canada* (Ottawa: Information Canada).

Gordon, Scott (1977) ''The Demand and Supply of Government: What We Want and What We Get'' Discussion Paper No. 79 (Ottawa: Economic Council of Canada).

MacAvoy, P.W. and R.S. Pindyck (1975) *The Economics of Natural Gas Shortage, (1960-1980)* (Amsterdam: North Holland).

MacIver, R.M. (1926) *The Modern State* (Oxford: Oxford University Press).

The National Finances, 1977-78 (1978) (Toronto: Canadian Tax Foundation).

Niskanen, W.A. Jr. (1971) *Bureaucratic and Representative Government* (Chicago: Aldine-Atherton).

Novick, Robert (1974) *Anarchy, State and Utopia* (New York: Basic Books).

Olson, Mancur, Jr. (1965) *The Logic of Collective Action* (Cambridge, Mass.: Harvard University Press).

Paquet, Gilles (1978) ''The Regulatory Process and Economic Performance'' in G. Bruce Doern (ed.) *The Regulatory Process in Canada* pp. 34-67 (Toronto: Macmillan).

Peltzman, S. (1973) ''An Evaluation of Consumer Protection Legislation: The 1962 Drug Amendments'' *Journal of Political Economy* 81: 1049-91.

Peltzman, S. (1975) ''The Effects of Automobile Safety Regulations'' *Journal of Political Economy* 83: 677-725.

Posner, R. (1975) ''The Social Costs of Monopoly and Regulation'' *Journal of Political Economy* 83: 807-27.

Rawls, John (1971) *A Theory of Justice* (Cambridge, Mass.: The Belknap Press of Harvard University Press).

Samuels, W.J. (ed.) (1976) *The Chicago School of Political Economy* (Lansing: Michigan State University, School of Business Administration).

Solo, R. (1974) *The Political Authority and the Market System* (Cincinnati: Southwestern Publishing).

Stanbury, W.T. (1977) *Business Interests and the Reform of Canadian Competition Policy 1971-1975* (Toronto: Carswell/Methuen).

Stigler, G.J. and C. Friedland (1962) "What Can Regulators Regulate? The Case of Electricity" *Journal of Law and Economics* 5: 1-15.

Trebilcock, M.J., L. Waverman, and J.R.S. Prichard (1978) "Markets for Regulation: Implications for Performance Standards and Institutional Design" in *Government Regulation: Issues and Alternatives* (Toronto: Ontario Economic Council).

Truman, D.B. (1951) *The Governmental Process* (New York: Knopf).

Wilson, G. (1964) "The Effect of Rate Regulation on Resource Allocation in Transportation" *American Economic Review* 54: 100-171.

Wilson, J.Q. (1963) *Political Organizations* (New York: Basic Books).

Chapter Two

A Conceptual Framework and Some Applications

Regulations are often proclaimed because they are said to be "in the public interest," as are the particular decisions (rulings) arrived at under them. What is that interest? To ask the question is to answer it, for the concept of "the public interest" is essentially meaningless except as a term that seeks to legitimize the promulgation of rules,[1] and the decisions made under such rules, that are ultimately and inescapably arbitrary—although not necessarily uninformed or capricious.[2] They rarely, if ever, would pass a unanimity vote test and, hence, involve a degree of coercion.[3] Evidence is rarely, if ever, advanced that purports to "prove" that the resulting overall gains (if any) will exceed the overall costs (almost always certain) beyond a reasonable doubt. Much less is it argued that those who will win are those who should win and that those who will lose should lose. And that is precisely where the public interest concept is so helpful as a legitimizing umbrella. In a theocracy the phrase "it is God's will" could readily substitute for the term "public interest." As we have stated many times before, *all* interpersonal changes in the distribution of income and wealth are, in a sense, inherently and inescapably arbitrary. As we have also stated, that does not mean that such changes are either good or bad, for their "goodness" or "badness" is inherently and inescapably a matter of normative judgment that can be more or less balanced and considered, or one-sided, or capricious.

"Justice is what the courts decide" has its counterpart: "The public interest is what the government of the day, through its ministers and appointed departmental-agency officials, decide." And these decisions are made under legislation that almost invariably provides the regulatory

---

[1] It should be recalled that the term "rule" in our context is a generic category, and includes statutes, rules, regulations, orders . . .

[2] Appendix D prepared by W.T. Stanbury of the Institute for Research on Public Policy and the Economic Council of Canada provides a number of definitions of the meaning of "the public interest" as seen by a wide variety of writers.

[3] It is almost impossible to conceive of an actual regulatory change or decision that has not had or will not have income/wealth distributive consequences. Needless to say, those who are adversely affected are rarely compensated, at least directly. Their votes will not be forgotten in putting together the party platform or policy package, however, as we will discuss later.

decision makers with a great deal more discretion than have the members of the bench and certainly not a parallel degree of independence (although judges too are appointed!), as discussed in a later chapter. We do not wish to be misunderstood by these flat assertions. They are not intended to suggest that all regulations are evil (although some are, in our eyes, certainly perverse), nor that arbitrary decisions can be avoided or that greater regulatory agency independence would solve the problem. Our point is rather the futility of any attempt to understand, much less assess, regulatory changes, decisions and processes in terms of the "public interest" concept. The concept is useful as a means of avoiding questions and, as such, is hardly likely to assist us in answering them.

To pre-emptorily dismiss the public interest concept in this fashion is one thing: putting something better in its place is another.

The selection of a particular framework undoubtedly significantly affects what one derives from an analysis based on it. And whether or not what one derives is "good" or "bad" depends, in the end, upon the purpose to be served. In our opinion the most useful purpose would be to suggest a framework for considering whose interests are served by alternative regulatory processes and how they are so served. All of the policy evaluation techniques, as discussed elsewhere, have a vital limitation—which is not to say they have no value. They do not provide a ready means of approaching the income/wealth distribution question, although competent analysts who use the techniques are well aware of the distributional implications and often explicitly discuss them. Both Waverman (1977) and Posner (1971) are agreed on the overriding importance of distributional considerations in government regulations. This is a view with which we are in complete agreement. The framework we suggest emphasizes those distributional implications of regulations, and other government policy instruments too for that matter.

The framework we propose is what, for want of a better name, might be called the "rule change investment" approach. By this term we wish to suggest that individuals, corporations, unions, and so on, have to decide, implicitly or explicitly, how much, if anything, to invest in obtaining a favourable change in government rules (or decisions reached under such rules), or to prevent unfavourable rule changes and decisions. In many respects, such a rule change investment can be appraised like any other although, as we will discuss later, there are some unique aspects of an investment in rule and ruling changes that need to be taken into account. The next section sets forth this framework.

2.1 THE CONCEPTUAL FRAMEWORK IN TABULAR FORM

The basic ideas that together constitute the conceptual framework are certainly not unfamiliar to economists although the manner in which they are assembled is novel. The reasoning can be briefly stated.

(1) Each individual plays eight roles, often simultaneously. These are identified in Table A.

TABLE A
THE ROLES OF THE INDIVIDUAL

As shown in Table B

I. Holder of rights and obligations
    A. Non-exclusive
    B. Exclusive and non-transferable
    C. Exclusive and transferable (marketable assets)

As shown in Table C

II. Receiver of benefits by virtue of I(B) and I(C)
III. Seller of own services by virtue of holding own human capital (I(B))
IV. Buyer of final goods and services for own and dependents use by virtue of I(B) (maintenance, ''pure'' consumption and leisure)
V.   Buyer of exclusive rights (including pension contributions) on own account to increase I(C)[1]
VI. Seller of exclusive rights on own account to decrease I(C)
VII. Taxpayer (including compulsory contributions) to reduce liabilities under I(B)
VIII. Investor of both time and money in increasing rights (and/or reducing liabilities) other than by V and VI, or both.

---

[1] Pension rights are rarely transferable but are included here for expository convenience.

(2) The first of those roles is as a holder of rights and obligations. These are shown as the *pro forma* Comprehensive Net Worth Statement of the Individual in Table B. Every individual has such a subjective Comprehensive Net Worth although the magnitudes (including zero) of some of the items contained in it differ enormously from individual to individual.

(3) By virtue of some of the rights and obligations contained in the individual's Comprehensive Net Worth, or as a result of playing the first role, if you will, there are *direct* flows of satisfaction derived from the very possession of some rights and there are flows of time and money generated and allocated with respect to the other seven roles. Table C shows for each of the seven roles a *pro forma* sources and uses of funds and time statement with respect to each of these seven roles of the individual.

(4) The basic information contained in Tables B and C can be recast in terms of a *pro forma* income-consumption-savings statement for the individual. This is shown as Table D.

(5) The final table, Table E, shows how the basic information contained in Tables B, C and D for *an* individual can be aggregated to provide a conventional Net National Product Account Statement.

The conceptual framework is set forth in terms of a system of interrelated accounting statements (if one uses the term ''accounting'' in the broadest possible sense!) because it ensures internal consistency and completeness. It also permits the presentation of a large number of concepts as simply and briefly as possible.

The roles identified, and the sources and uses of funds and time associated with them, purport to be exhaustive with two exceptions: private interpersonal relationships are almost completely ignored. Individuals and their dependents (if any) are, in effect, treated as one person. Secondly, gifts in the conventional sense are ignored. This has been done not because it would be difficult to include them conceptually but rather because it would add needless complexity and length for the purpose at hand.

The eight roles of the individual specified in Table A are best described in terms of the details given in the subsequent tables which are now considered in turn.

Table B: The *Pro Forma* Comprehensive Net Worth Statement: The Role of the Individual as a Holder of Rights

Each individual *at any point in time* holds certain property rights (net of obligations). This is his stock of wealth. As indicated before, this Table can be looked upon as a *pro forma* comprehensive wealth statement for the individual that includes, in principle, every conceivable type of right that an individual can hold. Needless to say, the rights actually held by particular individuals differ enormously. All individuals *necessarily* hold some of the rights (e.g., Item I(A) and Item I(B)(1)) but it would be a rare individual who simultaneously held some of each of the types of rights identified.

Three basic kinds of rights are distinguished: non-exclusive (i.e., collective, shared or communal) rights; exclusive but non-transferable rights; and exclusive and transferable rights.[4] Roughly speaking, non-exclusive rights are what have come to be termed ''pure public goods.'' Exclusive-transferable rights are the marketable assets with which everyone is familiar. The exclusive but non-transferable rights (Item I(B)) are, by definition, non-marketable and exclusive to the individual.

There are many advantages to be gained by considering individual wealth in property rights terms that cannot be elaborated upon here.[5] For our purpose, among those advantages are: the connection between the incentive

---

[4] This classification is taken from Dales (1975).

[5] For a useful compilation of some of the most recent literature on property rights see Wunderlich and Gibson (1972) and Furubotn and Pejovich (1974). Both volumes have extensive bibliographies.

TABLE B
THE *PRO FORMA* COMPREHENSIVE NET WORTH STATEMENT:
THE ROLE OF THE INDIVIDUAL AS A HOLDER OF RIGHTS

(Item I in Table A at Time t)

	Imputed Market Value	Present Value $	Psychic Income
I(A) Non-exclusive rights (net)			
1. collectively provided services (e.g., transportation and communication *systems,* defence, police and fire protection)		X	X
2. physical environment			X
3. interrelated legal/social/political/economic *systems* consisting of:			X
a) rules (including the rules concerning changing the rules) encompassing, *inter alia*,			
i) tax/subsidies (incl. transfers)			
ii) expenditure programs			
iii) regulations *per se* including prices, quantities, access and transactions (e.g., collective bargaining)			
iv) civil rights			
b) organizational structures and processes			
c) the incumbents of offices and employments in these organizations other than self			
4. prevailing conditions in these systems (e.g., unemployment-inflation)			X
I(B) Exclusive but non-transferable* rights (net);			
1. human capital (which is net of the present** value of the expected flow of non-discretionary consumption expenditures)		X	X
2. interpersonal relationships including family, friends and neighbours			X
3. social status			X
4. offices, employments, professionals licences and proprietorships		X	X
5. entitlements under annuities (incl. pensions and trusts)		X	
6. entitlements under transfer payment, social insurance and grant programs		X	
7. tax liabilities		X	
I(C) Exclusive and transferable rights (net) including securities, real property, copy rights, patents, machinery and equipment, and inventory of stock in trade	X		X
Comprehensive Net Worth	X	X	X

* Many of these rights are contingent.
** Of particular importance is the flow of time allocated in Table C.

systems (implicit or explicit pay-off rules) under which individuals seek to maximize their own satisfaction on the one hand and the institutional and organizational structures and the processes and rules in which those incentive systems are embedded on the other; the incentive for individuals, directly or indirectly, to invest in changing these structures, processes and rules (and decisions made under such rules) in order to increase their own satisfaction and sometimes also that of others. Another advantage of the property rights approach is that it highlights the vital role of the state as the ultimate rule maker and rule enforcer that can and does, by changing the rules, affect all of the sources of well-being of all individuals directly or indirectly, for good or for ill.

Because the types of rights encompassed purport to be exhaustive, and as stated earlier include many non-marketable rights, three distinct valuations are indicated in the columns of the Table: those that have a market value; those that have an imputed value that can be estimated more or less reliably in dollar terms, and finally those that have an imputed value that is entirely subjective (shown as "psychic income" in the column to the far right-hand side of the Table). The latter can best be thought of as rights that yield a direct flow of satisfaction (or dissatisfaction) to the individual. These direct flows should be kept in mind in interpreting Table C.

It should be noted that some rights are shown to have more than one valuation in the sense that there are two entries in the columns opposite the particular row. In the case of Item I(A)(1) and Item I(B)(1) the double entries seek to reflect the fact that while imputed dollar values can be estimated these cannot reflect even imperfectly the direct (subjective) satisfaction of the individual from the possession of these rights. Psychic income, in the form of pride and prestige, is an important direct source of satisfaction for some individuals from some of the rights they possess. This accounts for the double entries for Items I(B)(4) and I(C).

Because Table B is, in essence, a much expanded *pro forma* balance sheet, all of the non-marketable rights that yield imputed flows of benefits in cash or kind or direct satisfaction must be thought of in present value terms. The appropriate rate of discount is, in part, the subjective time discount rate of the individual concerned. The future flows of benefits are based upon the expectations of the individual at the relevant point in time. These expectations may be more or less reliable. Moreover, the degree of subjective probability attached to the expectations may be high or low. This can be thought of as the subjective risk discount rate that, together with the subjective time discount rate, when applied to the expected flows of benefits, yield the present values incorporated into the individual's Comprehensive Net Worth Statement.

This means that when the individual perceives, for any reason, that his expectations about future flows were too high or too low or that the risk has altered in either direction, his Comprehensive Net Worth (wealth) can be altered dramatically even though there is no tangible change in the individual's circumstances as seen by others. Not only will such changes result in changes in the level of satisfaction of the individual, as the perceptions change they are also likely to induce subsequent behavioural responses.

In a federal state each individual is simultaneously under the jurisdiction of a federal, provincial and local government. Many individuals are also members of one or more occupational, religious and social organizations that provide non-exclusive net benefits to those who belong to them. One should imagine the non-exclusive rights of each individual's Comprehensive Net Worth Statement as being the composite of these governmental jurisdictions and organizational memberships.

Table C: The Sources and Uses of Funds and the Allocation of Time by the Individual

The other seven roles identified in Table A are considered in Table C. This is done in the context of the sources of funds generated or applied by the individual with respect to each of them. It also shows those roles to which the time of the individual, which has its source in the individual's human capital $(I(B)(1)$), is allocated. The subcategories identified under each role included in Table C purport to be exhaustive, at least for our purpose.

As indicated earlier, all intra-family non-market transactions are ignored. *All* organizations (proprietorships,[6] partnerships, corporations, non-profit organizations *and* governments) are treated on a wholly consolidated basis with the result that all intra-organizational transactions are "netted out." The sources and uses of funds statement of the consolidated organizational sector is shown in the *pro forma* statement provided as an Addendum to Table C. The latter statement shows that only "tax and compulsory contributions" are unique to governments.

The individual as investor, Role VIII, is of crucial importance to our conceptual framework. What is usually called "investment," it is essential to note, has three distinct aspects in Tables B and C. The individual can be:

first — a holder of marketable assets (Item I(C));
second — a transactor (Items V and VI), which here means nothing more than the trivial matter of signing a sales or purchase contract or the informal equivalent;
third — Role VIII involves the individual as an investor of his own time and money (including fees paid to associations and for

---

[6] For the present purpose proprietorships and partnerships are treated as organizations and are treated as though they paid themselves for their services as employees and as managers of their own businesses (III(1) plus III(3)). The investment costs involved in deciding whether or not to set up such businesses and in directing themselves as managers are included under VIII(1).

professional services) in the expectation of increasing his Comprehensive Net Worth *other than by personal saving in the usual sense.* We can define this third—(Role VIII)—kind of investment in a slightly different way. By refraining from "pure" consumption expenditures and/or leisure, an individual can allocate the money and time thus "saved" to invest in improving his Comprehensive Net Worth (wealth) by means other than the acquisition of marketable assets (personal saving).

This seemingly neglected dimension of individual investment is defined more precisely in Table D and then elaborated upon in the subsequent discussion.

TABLE C
THE SOURCES AND USES OF FUNDS AND THE ALLOCATION
OF TIME BY THE INDIVIDUAL*

(Items II through VIII in Table A for time period t to t + 1)

	Sources and Uses of Funds		Uses of Time
	S	U	
Other Roles			
II. Net receiver of dollars by virtue of holdings of Items I(B) and I(C)	X		
III. Seller of own services by virtue of holding I(B)(1) *and* I(B)(4)			
1. office or employment	X		X
2. professional services	X		X
3. managing own business	X		X
IV. Buyer of final goods and services for own use by virtue of I(B)(1)			
1. non-discretionary (maintenance, including own time)		X	X
2. discretionary (pure consumption, including leisure)		X	X
V. Buyer of marketable assets on own account to increase Item I(C) (includes reduction in liabilities)		X	
VI. Seller of marketable assets on own account that reduces Item I(C) (includes increase in liabilities)	X		
VII. Taxpayer by virtue of obligations and compulsory contributions—Item I(B)(7)		X	
VIII. Investor increasing rights and/or obligations under Item I other than through Items V and VI			
1. optimizing transactions in marketable assets—Item I(C)—on own account, including information and bargaining costs		X	X
2. increasing human capital—Item I(B)(1)—through physical exercise and education		X	X
3. job search and career advancement other than by education *per se*—Item I(B)(4)		X	X
4. maximizing transfers and government grants under existing rules—Item I(B)(6)		X	X
5. minimizing tax liabilities under existing rules—Item I(B)(7)		X	X
6. maximizing the likelihood of favourable decisions under existing regulations or rules—Item I(A)(3)		X	X
7. securing favourable changes in the rules—Items I(A)(3) and I(A 4)			
a) voting			X
b) personal persuasion and lobbying		X	X
c) participation in association activities		X	X
Sum of the sources of $S equals sum of $U	X	X	
Unallocated time			0

---

* Illegal activities are excluded as are gifts intra-family non-market transactions.

ADDENDUM TO TABLE C
CONSOLIDATED SOURCES AND USES OF
FUNDS STATEMENT OF ORGANIZATIONS[1]

(Derived from Items in Table C)

	Sources of Funds	Uses of Funds
(1) Sales of final goods and services to individuals	IV	
(2) Payments for services supplied by individuals		III
(3) Net payments to individuals by virtue of their holdings of financial claims		II
(4) Net sales of marketable assets to individuals buying on own account (including loans and repayments)	V less VI	
(5) "Investment" expenditures of individuals (including fees and membership dues)	VIII	
(6) Taxes and compulsory contributions	VII	

Total equals Total

---

[1] Includes proprietorships and partnerships.

Table D: *Pro Forma* **Income, Discretionary Consumption, Investment and Personal Saving Statement of the Individual**

The purpose of this Table is to define what we have just termed the third type of investment as precisely as possible. It is Item 9 in Table D *plus* the investment of the individual that may be devoted to the same purpose.[7]

Several Role VIII kinds of investment by individuals are differentiated in Table C and, with one exception, there is no need to elaborate in the text on what has been specified in that Table. These kinds of investments by an individual are frequently observed. Witness the time and effort devoted by multitudes of individuals to "improving themselves" through night courses, correspondence courses, "working out" at the "Y", union, professional association and political party activities, not to mention reading the help wanted columns even when employed. In the same category are entertaining "the boss" or those with "connections," and climbing the "social ladder" through obtaining memberships and actively participating in social clubs— the more prestigious the better! Needless to say, discretionary ("pure") consumption expenditures and investment expenditures, in our sense, are often inextricably related. The allocation of the individual's time between leisure and investment (also in our sense) is, to some extent, a matter of the individual's attitude towards what he is doing. The motives of an individual who, for example, joins a service club or golf club or political party or a charitable association (and sometimes all four and more!), and perhaps eventually fills elected offices in them, are frequently "mixed," to put it mildly.

Attention is directed particularly towards the investments in favourable rulings from government agencies (VIII(6)) and in securing favourable changes in government rules themselves (VIII(7)) through voting, personal persuasion, lobbying and participation in association activities.[8] Although stated in positive terms, it is also true that similar investments can be made defensively—to protect an endangered advantage. In many respects, such rule change investments can be looked upon as the linchpin between the economic and political systems: the bridge between the interests of the individual and the rules and rulings of the collectivity.

It is important to recognize that because information, bargaining and influence costs are frequently extraordinarily high, the forces that interact in capital markets where workable competition exists do not obtain in the "market" for favourable government rulings and rules. As a consequence,

---

[7] This means, in essence, the time allocated to Role VIII in Table C. As we have defined it, the time of the individual can only be allocated to work [Role III] or self-maintenance [Role IV(1)] or to leisure [Role IV(2)] or to type three investment [Role VIII].

[8] Although we emphasize governments, the same applies to favourable rules and rulings of all organizations: of particular importance are the self-regulating professions and some labour unions.

TABLE D
PRO FORMA INCOME, DISCRETIONARY CONSUMPTION, INVESTMENT
AND PERSONAL SAVING STATEMENT
OF THE INDIVIDUAL

(period t to t + 1)

Income	Items in Tables B and C
1. Sale of own services[1]	III
2. Investment, annuities and transfers	II
3. Net gain on sale of assets	derived from VI
4. Net accrued gains on asset holdings	derived from change over period in some items included in I(C)
Less Expenditures	
5. Non-discretionary consumption (maintenance)	IV(1)
6. Net losses on sale of assets	derived from Item VI
7. Net accrued loss on asset holdings	
Income Before Tax	as in line 4, above
	VII
Less Taxes	
Net After-Tax Income	
Less	IV(2)
8. Discretionary ("pure") consumption expenditures	VIII
9. Expenses incurred for the purpose of increasing net worth (excluding purchases of marketable assets)	changes over period in Items I(B) and I(C)
Equals	
10. Personal saving (increases in marketable assets[2] and/or annuity rights)	0

---

[1] Includes business income as part of Item III(1) plus III(3). The proprietor is treated as though he paid himself a salary in Item III(1) and the net income from the business after the salary expense is included in Item III(3).

[2] Cash and bank deposits are, of course, the most marketable of all assets!

the rates of return on government rule change investments can be persistently high relative to those found in conventional financial markets. Investments of money in exerting influences can have a higher pay-off than purchasing securities with comparable risk. Moreover, those individuals whose net after-tax income is low (and who therefore have little scope for personal saving) and thus whose time is cheap, can sacrifice their so-called leisure time and invest it in obtaining increases in their Comprehensive Net Worth by engaging in what we have called rule change investments that can be more rewarding than "moonlighting."

Table E: Reconciliation of National Accounts with Conceptual Framework

"Reconciliation of National Accounts with Conceptual Framework," Table E, is provided to indicate that the conceptual framework we espouse for public policy decision analysis purposes is not inconsistent with the usual national accounts framework now embedded in conventional economics. It also serves to identify, of course, the flow over time of currently produced goods and services that is vital to the analysis of a multitude of macro-economic stability and growth issues. Many of the results of the rule change investments we have emphasized earlier have profound effects upon the changes in the rate of flow of current output—an issue briefly addressed at the end of this chapter.

TABLE E

RECONCILIATION OF NATIONAL ACCOUNTS
WITH CONCEPTUAL FRAMEWORK

(All Items are summed for all individuals over period
t to t + 1 and are measured in constant-dollar terms.)

Net National Product	*Item*
Personal consumption expenditures on goods and services	IV
Net investment (inventory accumulation and real capital expenditures less depreciation) by individuals and business	embodied[1] in net change in Item I(C) with some exclusions
Government spending including capital	current years spending[2] re I(A) not included under II and III
Exports minus imports	not included in framework
Equals	
Wages, salaries and supplements	III(1) & (2)
Net income of unincorporated business	III(3)
Retained corporate profits	embodied[1] in change in Item I(C)
Dividends, rents, interest, etc.	included in II
Transfers from government	included in II
Less taxes	VII

---

[1] Several complexities need to be noted: first: one man's assets are another man's liabilities. Thus, many financial transactions (Items V and VI) simply cancel out when summed over all individuals. Second, what remains should reflect, roughly at least, the increase in the net stock of real goods and facilities held by the private sector as *valued by the market*. Thus, the earnings retained by a corporation and "ploughed back" through capital expenditures in machinery, equipment, etc., are reflected in the increased market value of the shares of the corporation. These, in turn, reflect, again roughly speaking, the capitalized value of the flow of *additional* corporate net income to be derived from them. This *should* obviously exceed the purchase price of such assets but the market may underestimate or overestimate their potential contribution to future profits.

The net increase in the stock of corporate bonds also *should* reflect the value of the underlying fixed assets purchased with the proceeds, but will not do so precisely because bond prices will reflect current interest rate levels and the degree of risk involved in the particular issues, as seen by the market.

Finally, the increases in the stock of government bonds outstanding and in the money supply (primarily bank deposits) pose some conceptual problems. In principle, under our formulation these elements should be excluded from the change in I(C) for they are reflected in: (a) I(A) plus I(B)(6) minus I(B)(7); and (b) the net addition (i.e., after depreciation) to the stock of tangible capital goods (i.e., consumer durables) and facilities (i.e., residence) owned by individuals—including the facilities and stock in trade of proprietorships.

It should be recalled that our formulation is in constant-dollar terms where dollars are relevant. If this assumption were not made, the increases in the money supply that caused the general price level to rise (or at least accommodated it) would still be excluded from I(C). The government's proceeds from the issuance of non-interest bearing bonds—more money—would be an increase in tax liabilities (Item I(B)(7)) aggregated for all individuals. The distributional consequences are extraordinarily complex, needless to say, for they depend upon the portfolio of assets held by the individual and the market mechanisms that transmit the price changes at various rates through the economy.

[2] Item II includes servicing costs of the public debt, superannuation payments, and transfer payments. Item III includes wages and salaries paid to public servants and stipends paid to elected or appointed holders of offices and those paid under contract for services performed for the government.

2.2 THE ADVANTAGES OF THE FRAMEWORK FROM A PUBLIC POLICY DECISION POINT OF VIEW

The conceptual framework embodied in the foregoing Tables, together with the explanation provided in the text, has, in our view, several major advantages when examining government policies in general and regulatory policies in particular. Those advantages of the framework are now discussed.

(1) Our framework focuses attention on the individual. This is desirable for *four* reasons.

(a) Increasing the well-being of individuals (although certainly not necessarily all individuals!) is assumed to be the sole purpose of government policies.

(b) Only individuals, singly or collectively, make decisions and policy-making is, after all, a subset of all decision making.

(c) When we speak of individuals deciding (choosing) or acting in their "self-interest" this can be given content by defining an individual self-interest as the maximization of the flow of satisfaction from discretionary consumption, including leisure, and of his Comprehensive Net Worth as defined in Table B. To use some technical terms, the arguments in the individual's utility function are his current discretionary ("pure") consumption (including leisure) *and* his Comprehensive Net Worth as we have defined it.

It is important to note that in our formulation the pursuit of self-interest is *not* inconsistent with what is loosely called "charity." For example, it might well be in an individual's interest to support the adoption of a generous transfer system even though this would mean a net financial loss (i.e., the favourable change in Item I(B)(6) (an asset) was less than the unfavourable change in Item I(B)(7) (a liability)) if the result were a perceived improvement in the social/political environment (Items I(A)(3) and I(A)(4)). This improvement might be a "selfish" concern for the maintenance of civil order or the "unselfish" satisfaction (pride) derived from the individual's perception that he is a member of a more "just" society (Table B, column "Imputed Value—Psychic Income").

(d) Consequently, the Comprehensive Net Worth Statement provides as precise *and* exhaustive a definition of the word "interest" as we believe possible. Thus, when we speak about a policy change being in someone's "interest," we mean consistent with the maximization of the individual's comprehensively defined net worth as set forth in Table B. Obviously, because that statement includes a number of imputed values, and some that are so intangible as not to be susceptible to dollar value imputation, it is set forth not as a "fill-in-the-blanks" form. To ignore the rights that can not be valued in dollar terms would, however, ignore a vital dimension of public policy. Our civil liberties have no monetary value, but surely they are an important component of our "wealth" broadly conceived.

(2) By differentiating the decisions that one makes in his own interest and those that he makes by virtue of his holding of an office or employment (Item I(B)(4)), the relationship between the incentive system of an organization and the interests of the individual are made explicit. It is clearly in the interest of the individual to behave in a manner consistent with the organization's incentive system for not only does this mean more remuneration and prestige "on the job," it also means advancement through the heirarchy of the organization.

It is tempting to say that an organization's effective, as distinct from nominal, incentive system makes the "interests of the organization" and the interests of the individual officer or employee coincide. This is an acceptable shorthand when recognized as such, but it is fundamentally inconsistent with the framework forwarded here. *Only individuals have interests from our perspective. Thus, organizations are simply collectivities of individuals whose joint efforts affect the interests of the participants, of course, and the interests of others in the several ways we have discussed.*

The activities of a corporation, for example, affect, the interests of its shareholders, its customers, and its suppliers, in addition to the interests of its officers and employees. To the extent that the corporation's activities have effects not reflected in market prices (e.g., "externalities" such as pollution) the collective interests of individuals (Item I(A)(2)) are also affected by its activities. This interrelationship between organizational incentive systems and the pursuit of self-interest is particularly important in considering the roles of elected representatives, appointed officials, and journalists. It is pointless to enjoin them to behave in a fashion that is inconsistent with the incentive systems (reward/punishment system) under which they carry out their duties. To achieve a change in the behaviour of those holding offices and employments, it is crucial to change the incentives under which those who *select* them function *and* the incentives under which those who are appointed by them also function. This matter is explored in some detail in a later chapter.

(3) The framework throws into sharp relief the conflict between the extremists of the "growth-no-growth" points of view. Generally speaking, the advocates of "growth for the sake of growth" concentrate their attention on the *rate of increase over time* of "real" Net National Product as defined in Table E. In this formulation, the components of I(A) are excluded completely. A more sophisticated version is, in our terminology, an undue concern for the rate of growth in individual consumption (discretionary, non-discretionary plus leisure) (Item IV) summed over all individuals, where net investment (as per Table E) is correctly ignored because it is a *means* to the growth of individual consumption.

The "no growth" advocates seem to be advocating that the maximization of the Comprehensive Net Worth of individuals (Table B), aggregated over all individuals, is the more meaningful goal. In particular, they complain that the direct flows of satisfaction encompassed by all of the items included under I(A) in that statement are being ignored by the personal consumption (plus leisure) growth enthusiasts. Moreover, they are arguing that the benefits of greater individual consumption (Item IV) are being "bought" at the expense of a serious deterioration of the collective benefits of I(A), and, in particular, I(A)(2)—the deterioration of the physical environment.

If this is, indeed, the essence of the debate, it is hardly surprising that it is not "resolvable" in objective terms. As we have emphasized, all of the items included in I(A) have imputed values and only one of them can conceivably be valued in dollar terms (I(A)(5)). The "trade-off" between more personal consumption (the rate of growth of Item IV) versus the deterioration of I(A) and, in particular, I(A)(2), is therefore *inherently* incapable of estimation.

As in many such debates, there is some genuine misunderstanding involved. Some sophisticated "growth" enthusiasts intend that individual consumption encompass both I(A) *and* IV, the former being a direct source of satisfaction whereas individual satisfaction is obtained indirectly through the consumption of tangible goods and services in Item IV. There is a tendency for economists to use words like "consumption" as proxies for individual satisfaction *that would include* Item I(A), and certainly I(A)(2).

The quarrel *should be* with those who assert that individual satisfaction derived from Items I(A) *and* IV is of no concern and that *tangible output,* including consumer goods and services plus net investment (as per Table E) is "valuable" *for its own sake*—ignoring even the implications of considering those aggregates on a per capita basis.

The no growth enthusiasts should recognize that I(A) includes not only I(A)(2) (the physical environment) but also I(A)(4)—an item that would encompass the prevailing distribution of wealth.

One usually finds that those who are "growth" enthusiasts in the narrowest, "more tangible output" sense, wish to dismiss both I(A)(2) *and* I(A)(4), for they fear that a concern for the physical environment would bring about changes in the distribution of wealth that would be unfavourable to themselves. This matter is discussed again in Chapter 5 and another aspect of the "growth"−efficiency question is considered in Section 2.3.

(4) One of the virtues we would claim for our conceptual framework is the fact that it does *not* break new theoretical ground. To the best of our knowledge, *every* aspect of the framework is drawn from, and hence consistent with, conventional classical-neo-classical economics. The advantage of our conceptual framework is that it draws together many of the existing elements of economic theory in a mutually consistent manner. The categories purport to be exhaustive and all of the flows and stocks of time and money are accounted for. This is particularly useful with respect to the development of a public policy decision-making model. Moreover, our

formulation makes, we believe, many economic concepts readily accessible to non-economists.

(5) The ease with which the framework permits the transformation of flows (Table C) into stocks (Table B) is particularly helpful in analysing regulations because so many regulations affect flows over extended periods of time (e.g., prices and wage rates) and therefore have major *wealth* (a stock) *distribution implications.*

(6) Uncertainty is reflected in the framework, in principle, both in the rates at which flows of non-marketable items are discounted to obtain their present values and in the market values of assets included in Item I(C). In subsequent chapters we will discuss why investment in favourable government rule changes that are less prone to adverse change are particularly attractive for this reason—the rate of discount is lower and the present value of the enhanced flow thereby greater.

(7) By considering individual interests from the framework we have developed here, the interpersonal income/wealth distributional consequences of policy changes are highlighted *and the concomitant conflicts among the interests of individuals.* Indeed, our definition of a distributional conse-quence of a policy change is the disparate direct and indirect impact of that change on the current consumption (broadly defined) *and* Comprehensive Net Worth of individuals.

2.3 SOME DEFINITIONS AND AN EXPLANATION

Many public policy discussions are needlessly protracted and/or pointless because the protagonists use the same words but mean quite different things by them. To minimize this problem we will subsequently use the terms listed below in accordance with the definitions provided. These definitions are themselves based on the terms defined in our conceptual framework in Tables A through E.

- individual consumption = discretionary (''pure'') consumption, including voluntary = Item IV(2)
  leisure
- individual maintenance = non-discretionary consumption (maintenance) = Item IV(1)
- individual income = net after tax income = as defined
  in Table D
- national income[9] = aggregated individual income

---

[9] This is *approximately* equal to Net National Product as conventionally defined but see Table E and footnotes to that Table.

- individual investment = expenses incurred for the purpose of increasing net worth (excluding purchases of mar- = Item VIII ketable assets or the reduction of liabilities)
- business investment = as conventionally understood
- personal saving = purchases of marketable assets = as defined and/or annuity rights in Table D
- individual wealth = Comprehensive Net Worth = as defined
- national wealth = aggregated individual wealth in Table B
- growth = rate of increase of national wealth, as defined above
- efficiency gain = usually treated as the phased increase in the *level* of national wealth resulting from reductions in the market imperfections described in Appendix A. This might also be defined as a non-permanent increase in the rate of growth.

This latter concept is of such significance, yet is so controversial, that a comment seems required. The "classical" view is that the gain in the level of national wealth having been attained, the growth rate *may* reach a steady state unless individuals change their time preferences or their work (consumption)/leisure choices. The qualification "may" is introduced because it is conceivable that, as some have asserted, an economy without market imperfections may grow at an accelerating rate because "knowledge," one of the purest of pure public goods, would accumulate more quickly with unforeseeable implications for the rate of technological progress. Others, on the other hand, have argued that an economy without market imperfections would be *less* conducive to innovations because of the reduced incentives to take risks. Needless to say, the higher growth rate that *may* arise from the greater rewards for risk taking may not be costless. The resulting interpersonal distribution of wealth is almost certain to be less equal. This can have negative effects on the level of national wealth as we have defined it by virtue of the lack of pride associated with a society that is less egalitarian (Item I(A)(3) and (4)).[10]

For expository convenience (particularly in Chapter 4(a)), when we mean individual consumption or maintenance or incomes or investment or wealth, the qualification individual is to be assumed. In the same vein:

- appreciation = an increase in the wealth of the individual or the
  (or synonyms)   avoidance of a reduction that otherwise might occur without the investment of the individual;
- increase or = changes relative to what would have occurred in the
  decrease   absence of the regulation or ruling.

---

[10] As it applies to the condition of the social system.

REFERENCES

Dales, John (1975) "Beyond the Marketplace" *Canadian Journal of Economics* 8:4, 483-503.

Furubotn, Eirik G. and Svetozar Pejovich (eds.) (1974) *The Economics of Property Rights* (Cambridge, Mass.: Ballinger).

Posner, R. (1971) "Taxation by Regulation" *Bell Journal of Economics and Management Science* 2: 22-50.

Waverman, L. (1977) "Regulated Industries & The New Competition Bill" paper presented at the National Conference on Competition Policy, University of Toronto, May 13, 1977.

Wunderlich, Gene and W.L. Gibson, Jr. (eds.) (1972) *Perspectives of Property* (Institute for Research on Land and Water Policy, The Pennsylvania State University).

Chapter Three

The Principal Actors and Their Roles

An individual's Comprehensive Net Worth (CNW) constitutes his wealth at a point in time. His interest, to use the word in the more conventional sense, is to protect and enhance his CNW over time. This involves fending off the incursions of others, grasping those rare gains that can be obtained at no one's expense, and increasing his own interests at the expense of others where this is consistent with the law, social pressures, and his own conscience. Some individuals seem to find these constraints extremely flexible. Like a growing fetus pressing ever more strongly through the amniotic fluid against the inner walls of the uterus until birth, some individuals, undeterred by conscience and, indeed, glowing with pride, continue to press through the fluid of the legal and social systems against the yielding interests of others until death.

In the presentation of the conceptual framework in Chapter 2 we emphasized that one could consider the attempt to change government rules and obtain favourable rulings (or prevent unfavourable rulings) as a kind of investment by individuals in improving their wealth. We also sought to show just how significant the stakes could be—for winners and losers alike. In this chapter we consider the roles of individuals whose personal interests are served by pressing the interests of others—the agents of other individuals, so to speak—agents whose remuneration, in one way or another, constitutes the investment in changing the rules to enhance the wealth of other individuals.

To put the matter in a slightly different way, it is the basic perspective of this paper that the interests of *individuals* are all important. Here, however, we are considering those individuals whose interest (remuneration both pecuniary and non-pecuniary) largely depends on how well they play their parts in their own game—the several, simultaneous games that together constitute the collective decision-making system.[1] A few of the crucial roles are briefly described in this chapter to remind the reader about how the adversarial system of rule-making functions.

Each of the several games that are simultaneously in perpetual play, and in which the holders of the offices and employments we have just cited are

---

[1] For a general discussion of policy making in gaming terms, see Hartle (1976).

59

engaged, have unique sets of rules. These rules govern both the selection of the players and the incentives. These incentives determine the actions of the players in each game that are to be rewarded and those that are to be punished. These selection and incentive rules differ markedly from game to game. Coupled with the self-selection process by which, generally speaking, those who enjoy a role excel in it (and conversely), the differences in the behaviour of those who fill the several kinds of roles to be considered can best be explained by the major differences in the selection and incentive rules that apply in each instance. These rules are often at least partially implicit.

To emphasize the last point let us state most emphatically that we take the view—indeed believe—that in considering the players in the roles we are about to describe, the important differences among them arise from differences in the rules under which they are selected and the rules under which they are rewarded and punished. There are few, if any, significant differences among the games in the intelligence, integrity and public spiritedness of those who play them. Each game has a few players of whom the majority are proud and some others of whom they are ashamed.

Among the exclusive, non-transferable rights shown in Table B is that of "an office or employment held by an individual" (Item I(B)(4)). Some of these offices and employments involve, as one of the responsibilities of the incumbent and in some instances the principal responsibility, pressing special interests. For brevity and simplicity we designate them in this chapter as:

(a) corporate executives
(b) labour leaders
(c) association executives.

These are considered collectively to constitute what we term "Special Interest Group Leaders." Their roles are considered in the first section.

The second section is devoted to a brief description of the roles of those actively participating in the conflict resolution process by virtue of the fact that they are holders of offices (again Item I(B)(4)):[2]

(a) party candidates
(b) ministers
(c) deputy ministers
(d) regulatory agency heads.

They are considered to constitute collectively "The Conflict Resolving Group."

The third section considers the role of academics[3]—restricting our attention to those who actually or potentially are involved in fields that have a reasonably direct bearing on collective decisions. Although the subject of

---

[2] The role of the judiciary is not considered here because, although it is of great significance in the system, it is well known and separate from our subject at this point.

[3] Academics and journalists are also holders of offices and employments, (Item I (B) (4)). It is hoped that the point has been made and further repetition is not required.

freedom of information is of concern to all of the role players (one way or another!), that subject is broached in this section. The role of the academics as a special interest group is acknowledged here in passing. That aspect of their role is not unimportant—certainly not for them—but not central to the present expository purpose.

Because of the enormous importance of voter perceptions in the whole decision-making process, and the pivotal role of the journalist in interpreting to the voter what is transpiring in the public decision-making system, the final section discusses that role explicitly.

3.1 INTEREST GROUP LEADERS

The three roles discussed in this section have one thing in common—it is in the personal interest of the individuals involved to press the interests of others. Obviously the interests they press are, to a large extent, competitive with each other, although the corporate executives and some of the trade and industry association executives work in pursuit of similar, but not necessarily identical, interests. It is also true that there are associations included in Section 3.1.3 that would pursue interests similar to those of labour leaders—particularly consumer/safety/civil liberty associations—collective rights associations in our terminology.

The byzantine relationships are, we believe, best conveyed by Figures 2(a) and 2(b) which illustrate, in the former, the spots to which pressure (leverage) is applied and the major networks among them and, in the latter, the sources of pressure and the diverse routes by which it can be exerted. The permutations and combinations of all possible sources and all possible destinations and all possible routes is mind-boggling. If one were to add, as one should, the personalities involved and their interpersonal relationships, an understanding of how the influence system functions requires a substantial and continuing investment of time, effort and money. Needless to say, those who have made this investment and have access to the pressure points can provide a most valuable service and are remunerated accordingly, as some of the recently retired senior public servants and former ministers have discovered.

The two figures should be interpreted as though Figure 2(a) were at the centre of Figure 2(b). Could someone not devise a game, along the lines of "Monopoly," designed to both instruct and amuse, that captured this situation? The new game should combine the mixture of rules and chance that typify the game of bridge, but the number of cards dealt to each player at the outset should not be equal if a semblance of realism were to be retained.

3.1.1 The Role of the Corporation Executive

The chief executive officers of corporations are usually assumed to seek to maximize profits on behalf of the shareholders who hold him accountable.

In a widely held corporation the executive may be dismissed by the directors when he is perceived not to be able to "deliver" as well as another could. This is probably the most useful single generalization that can be made, although it is just that and there are important exceptions, one of which is mentioned below. From this perspective, seeking government intervention that would increase corporation profits, and battling government intervention that would reduce corporate profits, is one of the responsibilities of the executive office. Investing in manipulating government decisions one way or another, where the potential benefits are expected to exceed the costs, is just part of the job.

There are many routes that may be followed to this end. Take a bureaucrat or politician to lunch. Pay a professional lobbyist with the requisite "contacts" to do so. Write a letter. Appear before some tribunal. Call a press conference and issue a press release. Proceed through an industry association of which the corporation is a member. As indicated in the foregoing figures there are a multitude of ways and means available—some more efficacious than others in the particular circumstances.

For the chief executive officers of corporations in regulated industries (e.g., transportation, broadcasting, telecommunications, in particular), the situation is different in that "government relations" are the heart of their responsibilities. Because the largest of such corporations are usually so widely held, these executives are rarely held accountable by shareholders. The consequence is that they spend an enormous part of their time and energy in obtaining the "best deal" from the government system in large part for the kudos of the corporation's executive team.[4] Personal pride and prestige, as a winner in the "fight" with government and its many emanations, is an important factor. Entrepreneurship capacity is primarily directed toward devising the most effective strategies for dealing with government. "Softening up" the public that is believed to be irrationally hostile towards such corporations, in order that governments may more readily acquiesce in their demands (which may or may not be reasonable in the circumstances), is another important function these executives play.

---

[4] Because such corporations are often highly capital intensive, the judgments of the gnomes (and advisers to gnomes) of the financial market are of more than passing interest too.

Figure 2(a): **Major Pressure Points and the More Important Interconnections Among Them**

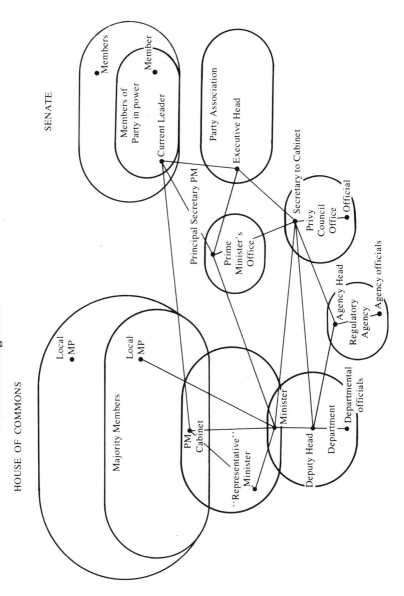

Figure 2(b):   **The Pressure Routes and Their Sources**

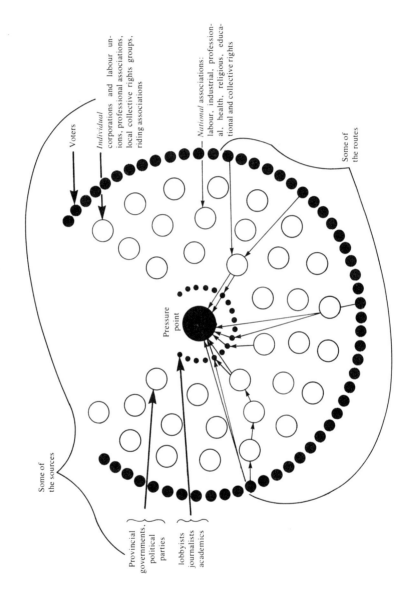

3.1.2   The Role of the Leaders of Labour

The heads of associations of labour unions (e.g., CLC) have inward-looking responsibilities that include, for example, resolving inter-union jurisdictional disputes and encouraging the member unions to finance the unionization of the unorganized. The vital responsibility is, however, to present a strong and united labour front (despite the realities) to the public and the government. Maintaining public sympathy, despite the costs the public has to bear as a result of strikes (the major bargaining weapon of labour), is crucial, for it strengthens the weapon. Concessions wrested from government on behalf of organized government employees, and the employees of firms under federal labour law jurisdiction, can be used as a basis for calculating ''relativities'' that are of assistance in bargaining in other sectors. Government policies that seem to help management and the wealthy must be attacked for symbolic reasons, if for no other. Holding the limelight and appearing militant and intransigent on behalf of the ''little man'' in pressing the government for policy changes is another crucial dimension of the job—maintaining the often precarious support of the member unions.

Unlike most association leaders, in the labour field the elected head and the executive head are usually one and the same man. However, he is supported by a substantial full-time staff.

3.1.3   The Role of the Presidents and Executive Officers of Associations

Typically, these associations have at the same time an elected head who is a prominent member of the association who serves for a short term and a continuing staff member who is its executive head. The former holds office in recognition of his ''great and lasting contribution to the profession''; the latter has a job. The former must, among other things, make an annual speech telling the government what it must do in the public interest to aid the members of the association. The latter, among other things, must rewrite the annual brief to government arguing for greater benefits for the members. It is obligatory that the incumbent of the executive office appear to be unreservedly in support of the members' interests and fascinated at the possibility of attending the many meetings that are involved in rewriting the same annual brief to government.

There are an extraordinarily large number of these associations. In the Ottawa-Hull telephone directory for 1978, for example, under a randomly selected column beginning and ending ''Canadian _____ (Association),'' 30 of them are listed. And there are approximately eleven columns of such associations!

All associations and their officers face the ''free-rider''[5] problem. The application of pressure in aid of favourable rule changes and rulings costs time and money, like any other investment. Organizations need offices, equipment, staff, and incur the expenses of gathering, preparing and disseminating information, entertaining politicians, bureaucrats, journalists and so on. These ''transactions costs,'' as they are dubbed in economics, are not trivial and they require that the members repay them through fees. But, if others are going to pay to advance your interests in pursuit of their own, why pay the fee? After all, the benefits flowing from influencing government rule changes and rulings are, in many instances, not exclusive to those who invested in obtaining them. Moreover, some corporations and unions may perceive that their special interests can most effectively be pursued by acting independently.

Where there is no possibility of ''free riders,'' the greater the potential benefit *per member* (where benefit includes costs avoided) the higher the organizational (investment) costs the members are willing to bear. However large the pot of aggregate benefits, with a large number of ''free riders'' the pot is divided so finely that the rational investment in obtaining them for the individual member approaches zero. This is the reason, of course, that the provision of basic collective services (e.g., defence) cannot be financed through voluntary fees. The larger the group affected by a particular kind of rule change or ruling (e.g., an industry such as clothing manufacturing), the more difficult it is to apply social or other pressures on non-members of associations to become members and bear their fair share of the investment cost in obtaining favourable policy changes (preventing unfavourable policy changes). This is a perennial problem faced by all pressure groups. The narrower the group with a common interest the easier it is to exclude free riders.

The more important a government policy is to the pursuit of a group's interests the more there is at stake to warrant a substantial investment in applying group pressure. This is the situation in regulated industries and highly concentrated industries (e.g., steel, aircraft, shipbuilding). At the other end of the spectrum are consumer, health, safety and environmental interests—our collective rights groups. Here ''everybody's interest is nobody's interest'' and association fees are correctly treated as a charitable contribution. These collective rights groups have, for obvious reasons, great difficulty in staying alive—despite the fact that they play an invaluable role. They are discussed again in Chapter 5.

There are undoubtedly many strong pressures constantly brought to bear on governments by interest groups to obtain favourable policies. No doubt these forces are, to a considerable degree, countervailing, as the so-called

---

[5] See Olson (1965) and Trebilcock *et al*. (1978).

pluralists would have us believe. But there is no reason to believe that the resulting equilibrium reflects much more than the resolution of the forces that are readily organized and already have a great stake in the outcome. One of the fundamental tenets of a democracy is "one man, one vote." Proceeding in parallel with, and greatly influencing the outcome of that relatively open system, is the much more closed interest group system where one interest does not exert equal pressure with another. Whether they should is, of course, a normative issue of the first order of magnitude. What does seem beyond question is that in choosing the instrumentality for intervention ministers are not unmindful of the fact that regulation, as distinct from tax or expenditure intervention, has certain political advantages when seeking to satisfy strong special interests. One of those advantages is that the regulatory route may proclaim the government's awareness of a problem of widespread public concern, yet not greatly damage the special interest group because it can marshall the resources (lawyers, accountants, experts) to protect its interest in a regulatory forum much more effectively than can those whose interests are nominally being served by the regulation. From a politician's point of view this is the best of both worlds: credit is obtained for acting "in the public interest" while, at the same time, not greatly hurting the interest that is ostensibly being damaged. We will return to this important issue in the next chapter.

Although associations make direct (although not necessarily open) representations to government, they also appeal to the public through the media. Here are some of the injunctions they must bear in mind in the attempt to gain public support or quiet public opposition.

(1) They must seek advantages in forms that disguise the magnitude of the costs and the allocation of the costs through the complexity of the instrumentality. Preferably the costs are indirect and widely distributed so that those who are damaged are largely unaware of the extent of the damage and are unable to organize opposition.

(2) If possible, they must disguise the concession as a benefit to a worthy cause that is either costless or large relative to the cost, or is a cost to be borne by those who, in some sense, *should* bear it because they are resented for some (probably silly) reason.

All of these strategems are in aid of facilitating the acceptance by the ministers of the special interest groups' demands, for it minimizes the political costs to them of so doing. Ideally, ministers should be placed in the position of appearing to be doing that which every right-thinking person knows to be "right, proper and long overdue." In other words, facilitate the politician's task of converting a necessity, as the politician sees it, into a political virtue, as seen by the voter.

However, when the "free-rider" problem is acute, do not be so subtle as to obtain a benefit or avoid a cost for which ministers can take *all* the credit, leaving members wondering what they are obtaining for their membership fees. Some bluster, particularly of the ''human interest'' sort, is a necessity.

3.2 POLITICIANS, MINISTERS AND OFFICIALS

The order in which the roles are discussed is roughly this: from member of Parliament to minister to deputy minister. The roles of the heads of regulatory agencies are then discussed.

3.2.1 The Role of Members of Parliament

As discussed in Chapter 1, the resolution of conflicting interests is the fundamental function of the political (and judicial) system. That function is performed directly by the Cabinet and the bureaucracy in a parliamentary system. But to a degree it is also indirectly performed by political parties that are able to elect the largest number of members of Parliament and thereby gain office and, in a minority government situation, subsequently make the requisite ''deals'' with one or more other parties to secure a majority vote on the crucial issues.

It is useful, perhaps, to think of each political party as a competitive supplier of what, for want of a better name, we will call ''policies.'' Each such supplier offers a full line of policies, or will add to the line if there is thought to be sufficient demand. At any point in time there are only a few suppliers of lines of policies (at least in Canada). Local party candidates can be thought of as retailers of the full line of policies offered by one of the few competing suppliers. This is the ''full-line forcing'' concept taken from the theories of industrial organization cited in Chapter 1. In some situations individuals seek the exclusive franchise of a particular supplier. In others, the supplier searches for the individual who is most likely to attract customers to its full line of policies in the particular constituency and/or whose acceptance of the franchise would bestow additional advantages on the supplier (e.g., represent an important interest or add prestige to the executive if the supplier were successful in gaining office).

If one treats party members as investors of time and money in a particular supplier, they, of course, will want some say in the line of policies the supplier offers and in the selection of the local retailer-franchise holder. Moreover, the local retailer-franchise holder will wish to influence the line of policies the party offers so that it *and* he will appeal to the largest number of ''customers''—voters—in his constituency.

Historically, political party organizations have played, at least at times, a significant role in resolving conflicting interests by hammering out platforms, selecting ''appropriate'' candidates and, of course, in selecting a particular party leader who can personify, to a degree, the resolution of at least some highly symbolic or high profile conflicts.

Although their roles are by no means unimportant, we will ignore here the role of party workers in general and the leaders of riding associations, and provincial-national party associations, and only make a few brief comments on the role of the elected members of a party that holds the largest number of seats in Parliament at a particular point in time. To simplify matters further, we will assume the government of the day has a clear majority.

Because in Canada party discipline in the House of Commons is so overwhelmingly strong (with some exciting but rare exceptions), the principal role of the franchised party member is to be an *elected* party franchised member! For with the largest number of such members the party's leader and his Cabinet then assume decision-making power—the essence of the political process. The individual holding the local party franchise, unless selected by the party leader for the Cabinet or a parliamentary assistantship or some other post, becomes essentially a member of a party caucus and an ombudsman for his constituents. The power of the caucus *vis-à-vis* the Cabinet seems to be highly variable. The weaker the prime minister relative to his ministers, the more precarious the position of the Government of the day relative to the Opposition and the more controversial the issue the greater the influence of the caucus is likely to be. Although the ultimate weapon in maintaining party solidarity in the House is the threat of withholding campaign funds from recalcitant elected members of the party, it is also true that the views expressed in the caucus must at least appear to be taken seriously by the Cabinet and the back-benchers must be convinced, again more or less, that the Cabinet's stand is a plausible resolution of the conflicts to be faced *and* in their long-run interest. The back-benchers of course, do not wish to be franchised sellers of a line of policies with little appeal in their own riding, relative to the lines being offered by the competing party suppliers and hence the lines offered by the competing franchise holders in the member's own riding. The elected members, therefore, can play a not insignificant role in the conflict resolution process—their significance depending upon the circumstances. It should also be mentioned that those members within the caucus who have a common local (urban-provincial) base, by meeting separately and devising proposals that would be particularly "salable" in their particular area, constitute an effective pressure group for the common interests of that area and thus can alter Cabinet decisions.

3.2.2 The Role of the Minister

To a considerable extent, the role of the minister is the point of resolution among all of the other roles and the forces they represent that we have described. However, there are some additional dimensions of the role that need to be emphasized. Ministers are, with few exceptions, simultaneously responsible for a particular department. The bureaucratic forces brought to bear upon them are discussed later in this section.

There is, however, one aspect of the ministerial role that is not defined by the other roles. That is the role of the minister as a member of a political party and, particularly, of a Cabinet. A minister is not a minister unless he is a member of the party holding the largest number of seats in the legislature. And with few and passing exceptions he is not a minister unless he is personally elected. The need for personal success at the polls is obvious enough. A few brief words perhaps should be said about the minister/prime minister/other colleagues aspect of the role, although this is largely by way of a reminder.

Ministers are selected in part because of their personal political clout (bargaining power), in part because of their intelligence and personalities, and in part because they actually or plausibly can reflect the most obvious interests of voters: language, religion, sex, region, province, urban-rural, occupation, industry, labour and numerous other interests. Aside from those ministers assigned portfolios in the areas of national scope (e.g., defence, external affairs, finance, treasury board), ministers are expected by their colleagues *and the bureaucrats standing behind them* to push those interests. The Cabinet works on an adversarial basis but with two vital provisos: Cabinet solidarity, as far as the public is concerned, on every Cabinet policy decision; no major policy decisions can be made by ministers without Cabinet approval unless the responsibility has been explicitly delegated to the minister by the prime minister or by Cabinet as a whole.[6]

There is a significant point that needs to be made about what constitutes a major policy question. The term "policy" is used extremely loosely by most of us, including the author. One can define a policy change as a change in a decision-making rule (which can be explicit or implicit) and a decision made in accordance with such a rule as a non-policy decision. This means that the area of discretion involved in the latter type of decision is sufficiently narrowly circumscribed by the rule that the judgment of those assigned the authority to exercise it will be accepted by those who promulgated the rule (or did not alter it when they had an opportunity to do so), *and* either chose the person given the authority or did not remove the incumbent for cause.

This is all well and good as far as it goes. But what about the frequent situation where the incumbent of an office who is making decisions under a policy rule promulgated by higher authority in turn establishes a set of rules as to how he intends to interpret and proceed under the overriding rule? For those affected by them, these subordinates' rules are policy decisions too. With the cascade of authority there also flows a cascade of ever more subordinate policy decisions. What constitutes a "policy" depends entirely upon where the observer cuts into the inevitable hierarchy of policies. The

---

[6] See Sharp (1976, p. 1). See also: Mallory (1977, pp. 3-19); D'Aquino (1974); Lalonde (1971); Smith (1974); Robertson (1971); McKeough (1969).

distinction between "policy and non-policy" is almost entirely in the eye of the beholder. A change in the coffee break rules goes unnoticed by the deputy minister and certainly the minister. It is a policy decision as seen by the clerks!

Furthermore, however thoughtfully a decision-making rule may be drafted it can only reflect a range of anticipated future circumstances. It cannot, unless it is extraordinarily vague, comprehend every eventuality. If it is too vague, it involves a greater degree of delegation than is intended. If it is too specific, it is impossible for the exercise of authority to be responsive to minor alterations from anticipated circumstances, with absurd results in some cases or with the rule maker having to make all the decisions himself for everything is an exception.

To compound the difficulty, what is construed as a major policy issue and a minor policy issue in the politician's mind may not be construed in that light by others. The materially trivial may be symbolically momentous. And how could the material/symbolic distinction be expressed in a formal rule that delegated authority? And the impossibility of so doing is one explanation for the fact that those at the pinnacles of a bureaucracy are unable to delegate as much authority as they might otherwise wish. A capacity to know the difference immediately is the mark of a professional bureaucrat!

But, if the delegation of authority question is so delicate, why should ministers be allowed to delegate authority at all? Time is one of the obvious answers. For if the "no delegation" argument is pushed to the fullest extent, *all* ministers would have to be involved in all decisions. And they can barely cope (some would say they now cannot adequately cope) with their work load despite the enormous degree of delegated authority that currently prevails.

The parliamentary system as a democratic form of government hinges on the ever-present opportunity for the government of the day to be defeated if it does not have the largest number of votes in the House and to be replaced by another. It is of the essence that the Cabinet take full responsibility for everything that transpires under its authority. To suggest that ministers are only responsible for those matters about which they have personal knowledge is not only ludicrous but extraordinarily dangerous. The concept of ministerial responsibility entails, among other things, responsibility for:

(a) establishing the rules (constraints) under which authority is delegated;

(b) ensuring that the quality of the incumbents of appointed offices warrants confidence in their judgments (within the authority delegated to them);

(c) monitoring the performance of those appointed; and

(d) changing (a) or (b) on the basis of adverse information under (c).

Having carried out each of these steps as conscientiously as possible under the circumstances, a minister (and hence a government) may still find himself (itself) in trouble in the House because of a decision made under delegated authority. Although perhaps most unfair in human terms, the minister's offer of resignation is in order if that would avert the defeat (embarrassment) of the ministry. Without this harsh consequence attendant upon an unavoidable "accident," in this hypothetical situation, ministers could deny responsibility for almost anything and the voter would have no redress except at the next election. And when casting his ballot the packages ("full lines") offered by the alternative parties contain innumerable items. Elections are not referenda on particular decisions.

The congressional system has built-in checks and balances that are operative between fixed and staggered elections. The parliamentary system, in essence, grants a majority government almost absolute power between elections (within constitutional limits) and, in the last analysis, the public is protected from the gross abuse of that power during that period by holding the ministry responsible for *all* of its actions on a day-to-day basis when the House is in session.

Cabinet members are equal in one respect—they are members of the Cabinet! However, there is, as one might expect, a status assigned to each portfolio. Ministers can, therefore, be promoted, demoted, shifted horizontally, and fired by the prime minister. Personalities and circumstances certainly alter cases but, as a reasonable generalization, the following proposition holds true: the portfolios that include regulatory functions reporting through the minister are not, generally speaking, the most prestigious.

What is often ignored, yet is vitally important in reality, is the distinction between "central agency" ministers and "special interest" ministers. The former include, under the present structure, in addition of course to the prime minister himself (and his own bureaucracy—the Privy Council Office), the Department of Finance, the President of the Privy Council (Government House Leader), the Minister of Justice, The Secretary of State for External Affairs, the Minister responsible for Federal-Provincial Relations and, to a lesser extent, the service departments—the Departments of Supply and Services and of Public Works. (The Public Service Commission is of great importance too as a "central agency" but the chairman reports directly to Parliament, although the PSC−Treasury Board relationship is, to say the least, complicated!) The portfolios of these ministers cut across special interest lines for they reflect the several dimensions of the *collective* concerns of the Cabinet. Their task is to ensure that, in so far as is possible, the *full* policy line of the party is both balanced and feasible given the immutable constraints. To acquiesce in the face of each of the narrow demands of ministers who pursue, as they are expected to pursue, the special interest of special interest portfolios would be to generate an unbalanced and/or infeasible policy package. In a sense, these collective interest portfolios, to a greater or lesser extent, can be thought of as emanations of the prime minister who is responsible for the overall reconciliation of particular interests. This does not mean, of course, that the ministers who bear the collective burdens of the Cabinet are emasculated for they are simultaneously representative of regional or other interests. Rather we wish to suggest that in their portfolios they are expected to suppress their narrow interests in favour of the overall interest of the collectivity of ministers.

We have tried to emphasize the role of politicians generally and of ministers particularly as the resolvers of conflicting interests. We have also tried to emphasize the inordinate difficulty of that task and, as discussed in Chapter 1, the constraints upon the exercise of leadership. In the next chapter "Some Political Axioms" are set forth. Those axioms are anticipated in the following hypothetical "injunctions" that ministers must follow in reaching "policy" decisions and in structuring the decision-making process. The "injunctions" might be thought of as what the minister(s) must bear firmly in mind when considering the way in which voters perceive structural— "policy"—changes.

The tone adopted in the "injunctions" is purposefully facetious and they are all overstated. This has been done to drive home the endless incongruities in the reality with which they must, of necessity, approach the impact of decisions on voter *perceptions*. These perceptions are based largely upon what journalists report. The reader should not infer that ministers are either more cynical or more opportunitistic than "your average man." It is simply that their task is unique. They should be judged in accordance with the demands and constraints of that unique task, not in terms of some other. With these important qualifications (including a reminder that the axioms on which they are largely based are considered in the following chapter), the hypothetical injunctions for ministers are as follows.

(1) Never do anything substantial when a symbolic gesture will suffice. Substantial actions cost money and voters do not like high taxes (exception: if an expenditure is to be made to reflect concern, ensure that the amount allotted appears to be sufficiently large that it cannot be treated as a token. The amount actually spent need *not* be equal to the amount allotted).

(2) Hidden costs are better than open costs and open benefits are better than those that are hidden. This proposition is subject to the qualification that, if the losers are unpopular, the costs must appear punitive and benefits provided the unpopular must appear to be given most grudgingly.

(3) Unpopular decisions must appear as inescapable and/or the fault of others. Popular and long-overdue decisions must be presented as voluntary, courageous, imaginative and bold.

(4) Carefully select, in so far as possible, the year, the season, the day and the hour of the day for the release of news in accordance with the need to trumpet it or suppress it. Use the rhythm of fading memories, seasonal preoccupations, weekends and publication deadlines to maximum advantage.

(5) Recognize the interest group leaders' necessity, because of their "free-rider" problem, of appearing effective to their members. If not too costly, when they are basically in a weak position, assist them in appearing *publicly* (i.e., at least to their own members) as more effective than they are. They thus become beholden to you and therefore less effective than they otherwise might be at a later date.

(6) Never admit that the government is powerless to do anything about the resolution of a problem *except* when facing up to it would create an even greater loss of support.

(7) Never appear unconcerned. Anything that is a matter of some concern to someone is a matter of some concern to you.

(8) Pressure groups whose members are involved for charitable motives have little staying power and can often be silenced by establishing prolonged and expensive procedures (e.g., commissions of inquiry) that will gradually weaken their voice because of membership attrition.

(9) Any information that will not obviously help the cause should be suppressed. It may later be used against you.

(10) Leak information on a "not for attribution" basis to the best (i.e., most dangerous) journalists. They are then less likely to be perspicatiously critical of you later for they would not wish to lose their "insider" advantage relative to their competition.

3.2.3 The Role of the Deputy Minister[7]

In most cases senior bureaucrats, like many politicians, sacrifice money income for perquisites, pride, and prestige. However, unlike politicians, bureaucrats generally settle for less of those benefits in exhange for much greater security of tenure. The most senior bureaucrats have career alternatives outside the public service because they have knowledge of how the system works, access to other bureaucrats and politicians, and a public image. Generally speaking, however, these alternatives are treated as fall-back positions. Relatively few bureaucrats enter the public service with the intention of obtaining qualifications or influence that they can subsequently sell.

Most senior public servants try to enhance the power and influence of their own departments or agencies. But they must also try to maintain and strengthen the power and influence of the public service as a whole. In part, this arises because protecting "the system" protects their own positions. They naturally believe that the system that elevated them to the top cannot lack virtue. Also, they are frightened by the retaliatory action of other public servants if they appear to be disloyal to the system.

---

[7] Some of this material is taken from Hartle (1976), pp. 71-74.

Senior bureaucrats are, in a sense, friendly adversaries. They compete for budgets, personnel, ministerial time, and appointments to offices of greater prestige. But they are friendly in the sense that they recognize the rules of the game that require that senior public servants not compete with one another at the expense of the system as a whole. Winning at the expense of the system is punished by other public servants—if not immediately, then at some time in the future.

Senior public servants punish other senior public servants by advising a minister to fight the proposals of the enemy's minister, withholding information, enticing away the enemy's most effective staff, withholding favours from the enemy (e.g., accommodation), and by social ostracism (not to be sniffed at in a small town like Ottawa).

Senior public servants do not have the power to fire subordinates, except under the most extreme circumstances. They have only limited scope for rewarding them through salary increases or other perquisites. Their main power lies in their ability to affect the rate of promotion. Those who are not anxious for promotion are almost impregnable. Zealots, those who pursue a course of action without regard to its effect on their careers, are perceived as a serious potential threat to the system and are rarely given positions of authority.

Those senior public servants whose role is largely advisory, as distinct from administrative, usually cannot communicate to their subordinates the "real" nature of the problems with which they are grappling. This is partly because of a shortage of time and partly because the issues or strategies are considered to be "too sensitive" (i.e., fraught with political consequence). As a result, their subordinates are often underworked or working on questions that no one is asking. This means that despite the large staffs supposedly supporting them, most senior public servants playing advisory roles, strangely enough, are playing by ear a large part of the time.

Senior officials who press for greater efficiency in their own departments are likely to be hurt because: ministers object to the public outcry from releasing redundant employees or from cancelling contracts with suppliers; subordinates retaliate by doing less or poorer work while not giving grounds for dismissal or even grounds for denial of salary increases or promotions; tight organizations are hurt most when across-the-board stringency is applied; the "savings" are not available to the senior official—they are appropriated by other departments or by the taxpayers; senior officials who are good administrators have less prestige than those perceived to be influential policy advisers, so that the time devoted to administration is at the expense of time devoted to the more prestigious functions; hard information is not available on which to assess efficiency, so that the tough senior officials appear arbitrary; and deputy heads who are perceived to be arbitrary find it more difficult to attract and retain competent subordinates.

Because of the short time-horizon of ministers—at the latest they require a pay-off before the next election—senior public servants are sorely tempted to propose short-term solutions to long-term problems. The public servant who is successful in devising and selling a facile ''solution'' will strive to move to another post before the limitations of his solution become obvious. If this strategem works, the failure will appear to be the incompetence of his successor.

Senior officials seek to gain monopoly positions to increase their prestige (perceived power or influence). They strive to acquire exclusive jurisdictions over the provision of advice to superiors, control of access to information by superiors, and the provision of an essential service (e.g., accommodation or recruitment). Three arguments are usually advanced for stronger monopoly positions: avoidance of duplication, the need for confidentiality, and the lack of accountability associated with shared responsibility. Monopoly positions are constantly under attack, however, by other senior officials, who of course do not wish to be indebted to a colleague.

Senior officials seek desperately to avoid losing the ''right'' to participate in the consideration of a problem. Capturing an interest in a problem is at least as important as finding a resolution to it, because influence, budgets, and staff often follow the allocation of responsibility for dealing with a problem. (This, in part, explains the enormous proliferation of interdepartmental committees, task forces, etc.)

With rare exceptions, career bureaucrats are not committed to particular parties or ministers but to the maintenance and strengthening of the bureaucracy and of their positions within it. Ministers who support their senior officials within the bureaucratic system can expect bureaucratic support in the political system, and conversely. This means, in effect, that ministers must accept the incentive system within which the bureaucrat works and not demand that he behave in ways that would damage his current or potential position in the bureaucracy.

Many senior bureaucrats have about as much power to reward and punish ministers as ministers have to reward and punish senior officials. Successful officials have a complex and extensive network of alliances: within the bureaucracy, with other ministers, with the prime minister (or members of his immediate staff), with journalists, and with interest group leaders. They can therefore conjure up or suppress information and support. They can also delay or expedite.

From time to time a minister can get rid of a senior bureaucrat. But this is relatively rare because the prime minister, who is responsible for these appointments, almost invariably has to find some other post for the official that is roughly comparable, at least in aggregate benefits (e.g., less prestige but more perquisites). These kinds of posts are always in scarce supply relative to the demand for them. The need to find a safe haven for the discarded bureaucrat probably arises from the pressures from other senior bureaucrats who find it in their interest to protect one of their own. Who knows who might be next?

The role of the senior official as seen in these terms understates the bureaucratic leadership function. There is such a function—a function too frequently unnoticed. There are some senior public servants whose quiet and persistent dedication to the continuing well-being of the nation is beyond reproach.

But does this entirely laudible bureaucratic leadership pre-empt the role of the minister? Under some circumstances it may when there is a weak ministry and/or a weak minister. Whether or not the senior official wishes to, some decisions *have* to be made and in the absence, physically or figuratively, of the minister(s). The deputy minister(s) must, perforce, make them although he is well aware that he is exceeding his authority. There are a few public servants at any point in time who, of course, would be willing to ''use'' ministers to further their own policy objectives. (We speak here not primarily of the attempt to change policy for personal advancement motives, but the two may coincide.) There are also policy issues that involve questions of such overwhelming technical complexity that it is virtually impossible to disentangle the advisory/decision-making roles—given the best will in the world on both sides.

It is widely believed and theories have been formulated on the assumption (Niskanen, 1971; Breton, 1974) that bureaucrats constantly press ministers for more and more government intervention—regulatory or otherwise. And that having once intervened the bureaucratic pressure is for even greater scope and depth in the breach made in the private sector. There is *some* truth in this general belief. But a qualification has to be made that is also true and perhaps even more important. The popular generalization applies at the bottom of the hierarchy. It applies less and less as one goes up the hierarchy. At the pinnacles it is almost invariably false. Indeed, the converse holds. The most senior public officials, particularly those who support ministers with collective responsibilities to the Cabinet as a whole, as discussed above, resist as strongly as their influence allows more government intervention. They feel that the burdens they carry are already staggering and they certainly do not welcome additions. The only exception would be those senior officials who, by and large, are the least senior of such officials and do so in order to enhance the relative prestige of their departments or agencies. By so proceeding such officials may greatly please their ministers, who also want the prestige (and public exposure) of a more powerful department or agency; however, they run the enormous risk of alienating the most senior officials upon whose regard the career prospects of the others may significantly depend.

In their dealings with journalists and academics, deputy ministers usually keep the following injunctions in mind.

(1) Reveal nothing to the media except those selected bits of information supportive of your minister and the government. Perhaps more effective still, flood the media with so much information that the significant is buried under the overwhelming trivia (this tactic provides evidence for claims of "openness").

(2) Make certain your profile does not compete with that of the minister.

(3) The only exception to (1) would be where there is open jurisdictional warfare with another department.

(4) Swallow your pride and accept the fact that you often must *appear* to be boring to the media and out of touch with what is going on inside the system.

(5) A hint of mystery is acceptable if not inconsistent with (2)!

3.2.4 The Role of the Head of a Regulatory Agency[8]

Appointments to these offices, like those of deputy ministers, are at the discretion of the prime minister (i.e., by Order-in-Council). The motives behind particular appointments, like the emotions of those who receive them, are, no doubt, mixed. For some it is the fulfillment of an ambition; for others it represents "the end of the line," and for still others, but rarely one would have thought, "another step along the way to . . . " The terms are long—from 5-10 years—and the grounds for dismissal so narrow as to give the incumbents great security.

Having been appointed, the office holder is faced with the task of fulfilling responsibilities that are often extraordinarily ambiguous in terms of the objectives to be served by the agency, although the procedures to be followed are usually painfully rigid.

A particular application or submission before a regulatory agency typically raises four types of questions.

(a) Is the subject within the jurisdiction of the agency?

(b) What is the appropriate procedure in this case—who should be allowed to appear and on what basis?

(c) What evidence is admissible?

(d) What staff work is required that can be carried out in the time and with the resources available?

Having studied the submission, the evidence, the supporting material, and the work prepared by the staff, the agency head (and other members) must reach a decision bearing in mind the following.

(1) What are the alternatives?

(2) Which of them is supported by precedent?

---

[8] Most of these agencies have several members who are also appointed by Order-in-Council. We do not consider the other members here. For an enlightening glimpse at some of the characteristics of these appointed officials, see Andrew and Pelletier (1978); also Doern *et al.* (1975), and Doern (1978).

(3) If yes, should the precedent be followed or should the agency's policy be altered?

(4) If the latter, on what basis?

(5) What are the likely implications for

    i) previous rulings?

    ii) future submissions?

    iii) government reaction, including proper ministerial intervention in one form or another?

Leaving aside those submissions dealt with on a "let the precedent stand" basis, where the precedent may be more or less in the minds of those who reached the earlier decisions rather than publicly stated, the agency head and the other members must, of course, weigh the effects on the several competing interests that will be affected, directly or indirectly. As we have seen, those effects may be more or less obvious and the degree of conflict among the interests more or less significant. When such conflicts are involved, the personal preferences of the agency head and his fellow members among the interests must prevail—taking into account the implications set forth above.

What are those preferences likely to be? Here again speculation is idle for they are, no doubt, as variable as those of other men. The only thing one can say is that in the selection of the incumbents their past behaviour is taken to reveal, it must be presumed, those preferences in the most general way. This does not mean, however, that the judgment of those involved in the selection process was accurate. Given a secure office and having reached a point where a career is likely to terminate, preferences may, in the event, be revealed that are quite surprising to the selector.

Whether the incumbents feel beholden to those who appointed them or resentful towards them because "better" appointments were denied, obviously, is impossible to say.

In the federal bureaucracy the heads of autonomous (statutory) agencies are thought to have about the same status as junior-middle rank deputy ministers. They are not thought to be in the bureaucratic race and, hence, not in competition with other bureaucrats except, possibly, with respect to territory in the struggle for influence in "policy" matters.

The heads of regulatory agencies would not deal with journalists or academics except, conceivably, on a descriptive-explanatory basis.

The relationship between the deputy minister of a department and the head of a statutory regulatory agency (the first reporting to a minister and the second reporting through the same minister we will suppose) deserves comment. Disregarding those situations, which occasionally occur, where their respective "territories" are unrelated, this relationship is, under the present system, enormously variable. It can run the gamut from friendly co-operation to blatant hostility. When these two officials both take the "that is my perogative"—"no it is my perogative" stance, the argument between them about who is responsible for "policy" is not resolvable in rational terms because the policy/non-policy distinction is meaningless, as we discussed elsewhere. When the word "policy" is used in these territorial squabbles it comes to mean "important" and "unimportant." Needless to say, no one likes to think of himself as solely responsible for the trivial. Emotions run high. At the other end of the spectrum is the "partnership" approach where there is a valiant effort made to resolve differences by negotiation and compromise, and only *in extremis* does the minister receive conflicting advice from them, (it being presumed that the deputy minister is the "policy" adviser to the minister and the agency head the commentator on that advice).

Because the "appropriate" relationship is undefined, the hostile arms-length relationship is a subject for gossip within the bureaucracy, but is not taken as catastrophic (except by subordinates) and the co-operative relationship is not considered improper and usually passes unnoticed.

The reader should *not* be left with the impression that we judge these relationships to be reprehensible, much less scandalous. Rather, what we seek to convey is that "independence" is not unambiguously defined (with one notable exception[9]). This ambiguous relationship is not of great importance because on many issues, the regulatory statute permits an appeal to a minister or to the Cabinet in any event, as discussed later. The result is that a wide range of relationships can and do exist that are not considered, by either those involved or by disinterested parties within the system, to be unethical. There is also a general attitude that: "We are all working for the government and let's do the best job we can collectively." When used in this context the word "government" means the continuing organizational entity, not the government of the day, and reflects a continuing concern for the institution and the country, as the parties involved see it. The roles of the two men, the deputy minister and the agency head, are not *structured* so as to be adversarial.

3.3 THE ROLE OF THE ACADEMIC

Academics are a unique breed. The audiences of academics are usually unique too: captive students and their peers in the same discipline (in their own field, in particular). The incentive system under which they carry out their duties is little understood. The first order of business is to secure an appointment, and then tenure, at a university (college). This usually requires academic (Ph.D. degree) credentials, a record of publications in prestigious professional journals, and a teaching record that is not entirely disastrous.

Excellence is judged primarily by the academic's peers and the standards applied are their standards. These standards need not encompass, much less

---

[9] A direct instruction issuing from a minister to an agency head.

put great weight upon, relevance to the day-to-day decisions made by individuals, collectively or singly. The fact that the standards of excellence in an academic discipline are invariably *and fortunately* international, coupled with the lack of available information in Canada about a wide range of social-economic-political phenomena, contributes to the apparent lack of responsiveness of some Canadian academics to uniquely Canadian issues (see Cairns, 1975).

It must be acknowledged, with regret, that the international standards of academic excellence in the social sciences and humanities, that are a crucial element in the incentive system under which most individual academics perform, often seem, at least at the present time, to be at variance with responding to the pressing problems that face the Western world. There seems to be a depressing tendency, supported by peer group appraisals, to invent more and more ingenious variations on an established melody rather than to reconsider whether the melody is to be an overture to an opera, a passage in a symphony or, indeed, whether what is needed is a new form of expression of which a particular melody is a relatively minor aspect.

The purists respond to the seeming disparity between demand and response by placing great emphasis on timeless, dispassionate rationality. They find the present cries for solutions to immediate problems as opportunistic calls that would, if answered, constitute a diversion from their ultimate responsibilities. Conversely, those with a longer historic time horizon probably believe that creativity, in all its forms, was usually a response of a few *individuals* to an immediate and pressing situation.

Two generalizations would seem to emerge: creativity is an individual not an institutional response; and most individuals respond to the incentive rules of the institutions upon which they are dependent. These rules generally reward conformity and punish creativity as, perhaps, the unconscious defensive mechanism of the institution. What seems abundantly clear is that, with the rarest of exceptions, to berate the members of an institution for their failure to act against the reward-incentive structure of the institution upon which they are dependent for their security is to cry into the wind. This, it seems to us, is the fundamental and inescapable problem. But there are others that are more amenable to change.

One is the fact that academics have become increasingly dependent upon governments both directly and indirectly, for their financial support. In some fields, particularly economics, government jobs in Canada have been available (at least until recently) that were, to say the least, highly remunerative relative to academic appointments. Government contractual work was available that offered generous per diems, but the results, unless favourable, were often suppressed and the quality of the work was not tested by peers. On the other side, research grants provided with no strings attached, of a substantial magnitude and covering a time period of sufficient duration to permit major projects to be planned and executed, were few and far between. The limited funds available for grants were spread thinly and widely (after all, we need some geographic balance in the allocation of research funds, do we not?) and were of a short duration. This precluded the support of sustained work on a major scale by the most promising. In Canada, private philanthropy, at least in support of the social sciences, has been trivial relative to that in the United States, on a per capita (or any other!) basis.

Government secrecy has been another serious problem and has had a *most* deleterious effect on the quality of research, journalism, and consequently parliamentary debate. It is one thing to say that ministers are accountable to the public through the ballot box. It is another to consciously keep those casting their ballots uninformed. The inordinate, indeed obscene, degree of government secrecy in Canada is one of the most pernicious and serious flaws in the Canadian political system. Canadians are suffering from a secrecy disease that, like a cancer of the collective brain, by its nature dulls the perceptive powers of the weakened victim to recognize its presence, much less seek treatment—a treatment for a disease that, unlike some cancers, is readily at hand and of proven efficacy.

Everyone likes competition for others but not for himself. Similarly, everyone likes accountability by others but not for himself. In a relatively atomistic economy with little government intervention, accountability for the effects of collective decisions is of no great moment. It is either demonstrable in the uses to which public funds are seen to be put and/or by their transparent sources—taxes. Such is not the prevailing situation. Yet the means of achieving accountability are grossly restricted by centuries-old parliamentary secrecy rules. They may well have been appropriate then in protecting an authoritarian monarch from his (or her) enemies both within and without (e.g., Elizabeth I). They are hopelessly inappropriate in a constitutional democracy where openly resolving the difference among "the enemies within" is the essential function of Parliament. If Parliament is becoming increasingly irrelevant, as some claim, the fault lies not in its cumbersome procedures and other such superficialities that could and would be readily reformed from within if the institution were faced with more substantive responsibilities *and more information* and some other reforms. This question of parliamentary responsibilities will be returned to in the consideration of so-called "independent" regulatory agencies.

3.4 THE ROLE OF THE JOURNALIST

Voters perforce cast their ballots on the basis of their perceptions of reality. And, in the political forum, these perceptions are, again perforce, largely based on the "information" supplied by journalists. Journalists, by the nature of their employment, are responsible for obtaining and reporting "all the news that's fit to print (or broadcast)" but with the vital proviso that the news must sell the vehicle that carries the advertising (See Winn and McMenemy, 1976, pp. 129-45). The potential profits from the sale of advertising space or time is the driving force behind the decisions of publishers and broadcast licence holders. Consequently, because the revenues from advertising hinge crucially on the size and composition of the audience, the owners are unwilling to invest more in better reporting and news analyses than the increased audience potentially generated is expected to yield in enhanced advertising revenues. (It was most appropriate that Vol. II of the Davey Report on the media was entitled, *Words, Music and Dollars*.)

There seemingly is an insatiable appetite for prurient and morbid detail, particularly if it concerns the famous. Beyond this desire for titillation, most individuals are generally unwilling to devote time, effort and expense to obtain information about matters that do not affect their own interests significantly and immediately (Simon, 1955; 1957). The more complex and subtle the subject, the greater the lack of general interest. Those journalists who wish to be prestigious (and hence well remunerated) must constantly wrestle with this painful reality for their current and potential employers will assess them not with respect to some abstract ideal but against the marketability of their output. Consequently, the rational journalist will invest little of his time and effort in the investigation of highly technical matters unless there is a reasonable probability of a pay-off to *him* commensurate with the cost incurred. Because of the voters' limited attention span, an ounce of simplicity, novelty and concreteness is worth a pound of complexity, profundity and abstractness. The best journalists are able to inject a great deal of the latter by making it appear as the former. They are the hard-working creative artists of the profession. (Geoffrey Stevens of *The Globe and Mail*'s Ottawa Bureau has done some remarkably good columns on government regulation, for example.) Needless to say they are as rare in journalism as they are in any other profession. The majority, through a combination of incompetence, a lack of curiosity, and a lack of in-depth understanding of difficult subjects, are easily conned by a superfluity of superficial press releases and by painful complexity that can be used to bury the significant.

These attributes of journalism have a major effect on collective decision making for, aside from the secrecy issue *per se*, there are a multitude of different perceptions of reality prevalent at any one time. All of the actors in the roles previously discussed are highly conscious of this phenomenon and take advantage of the weaknesses wherever possible in the pursuit of their divergent interests, as we have indicated.

REFERENCES

Andrew, Caroline and Rejean Pelletier (1978) "The Regulators" in G. Bruce Doern (ed.) *The Regulatory Process in Canada* pp. 147-64 (Toronto: Macmillan).

Breton, A. (1974) *The Economic Theory of Representative Government* (Chicago: Aldine).

Cairns, Alan C. (1975) "Political Science in Canada and the Americanization Issue" *Canadian Journal of Political Science* 8: 191-234.

D'Aquino, Thomas (1974) "The Prime Minister's Office: Catalyst or Cabal?" *Canadian Public Administration* 17: 55-79.

Doern, G. Bruce (1978) "Introduction" in Bruce Doern (ed.) *The Regulatory Process in Canada* pp. 1-33 (Toronto: Macmillan).

Doern, G. Bruce, Ian Hunter, Don Swartz and V. Seymour Wilson (1975) "The Structure and Behaviour of Canadian Regulatory Boards and Commissions; Multidisciplinary Perspectives" *Canadian Public Administration* 18: 189-215.

Hartle, D.G. (1976) *A Theory of the Expenditure Budgetary Process* (Toronto: University of Toronto Press for the Ontario Economic Council).

Johnson, A.W. (1978) "Public Policy: Creativity and Bureaucracy" *Canadian Public Administration* 21: 1-15.

Lalonde, Marc (1971) "The Changing Role of the Prime Minister's Office" *Canadian Public Administration* 14: 509-31.

McKeough, D'Arcy (1969) "The Relations of Ministers and Public Servants" *Canadian Public Administration* 12: 189-98.

Mallory, J.R. (1977) "The Two Clerks: Parliamentary Discussion of the PCO" *Canadian Journal of Political Science* 10: 3-19.

Niskanen, W.A., Jr. (1971) *Bureaucracy and Representative Government* (Chicago: Aldine).

Olson, Mancur, Jr. (1965) *The Logic of Collective Action* (Cambridge, Mass.: Harvard University Press).

Robertson, Gordon (1971) "The Changing Role of the Privy Council Office" *Canadian Public Administration* 14: 487-508.

Sharp, Mitchell (1976) "Decision Making in The Federal Cabinet" *Canadian Public Administration* 19: 1-7.

Simon, H.A. (1955) "A Behavioural Model of Rational Choice" *Quarterly Journal of Economics* 69: 99-118.

Simon, H.A. (1957) *Models of Man* (New York: Wiley).

Smith, Dennis (1974) "Comments on the Prime Minister's Office" *Canadian Public Administration* 17: 80-84.

Trebilcock, M.J., L. Waverman and J.R.S. Prichard (1978) "Markets for Regulation: Implications for Performance Standards and Institutional Design" in *Government Regulation: Issues and Alternatives* (Toronto: Ontario Economic Council).

Winn, Conrad and John McMenemy (1976) *Political Parties in Canada* (Toronto: McGraw-Hill Ryerson).

Chapter Four

Some Political Axioms

Much of what needs to be said under this heading has already been said, implicitly at least, in the discussions of the several roles of the principal actors. It is our belief that, although there is some pressure for increasing government intervention attributable to the bureaucracy's demands for great power, influence and remuneration, this is not the heart of the matter. Intervention primarily has taken place because it was thought to be expedient from a ministerial (political) point of view. To reiterate what we have already said, the most senior bureaucrats are usually opposed to increased government intervention because they already have all the power and influence they can handle and more intervention makes their responsibilities even more onerous—and they are ludicrously heavy.

As has been noted by others,[1] there is a kind of inherent escalation in effect involving, at the outset, demands for government action appearing in the media. This is followed by opposition party criticism and promises. Then there are ministerial statements of concern and rhetorical attempts at moral suasion. This is followed by more intense opposition criticism of the ineffectiveness of the government's efforts. This results in stronger and more specific promises. The ministry may then introduce draft legislation. The legislation, when passed, may be very specific, as needs be in a taxing or statutory subsidy scheme (e.g., family allowances) or it may have ample scope for ministerial (bureaucratic) discretion or for the exercise of discretion by a statutory agency established for the purpose where discretion in either form is granted by Parliament. Rules are then promulgated by the minister or the regulatory agency. These, in effect, make the intervention much more specific. Precedents are then gradually established with greater precision being achieved each time a decision is reached (hopefully!).

All of this seems to describe the usual scenario. But it begs the question: intervention yes, but why intervention by regulation? *The more useful question to put is the inverse: "Intervention yes, why not regulation?"*

Taxes have to be raised to finance some essential public services and to redistribute total income in a manner that cannot be realized by changing

---

[1] See references in Doern (1978) and Trebilcock *et al*. (1978) p. 28.

85

prices (including wages).[2] The level and structure of tax interventions in these instances is a matter of conscious decision but the instrumentality is not, to all intents and purposes.[3] When we push out from this tax-expenditure ''core,'' however, (and if one ignores the major differences in their real impacts), regulation is probably the first policy instrument that comes to the public mind and hence to the mind of the politician. ''There ought to be a law . . . .'' is such a ubiquitous statement that it is a joke—literally. What is meant is the demand for an enforced rule requiring that individuals or corporations or unions, or whatever, be compelled to stop doing something they are doing or start doing something they are not doing. The thought that the government, by changing the relative costs and benefits associated with alternative actions, thereby *induces*[4] changes in behaviour is simply not contemplated. Nor, of course, are the vitally significant behavioural changes almost invariably induced by prescriptive or proscriptive rules, as private sector decision makers continue to pursue their interests faced with a new set of costs and benefits (relative prices in the economist's terms) associated with alternative kinds of behaviour as a result of the rules. This lack of awareness of the indirect effects of rules is passing strange because all of us try to minimize our tax liabilities. This often involves not only altering the *form* of what we do but also what we do. Be that as it may, most people do not think about the indirect effects of alternative government policies like economists. (Do we hear ''Thank God''?) And the imperative rule is the most obvious form of government intervention, with the core exceptions mentioned above.

We emphasized earlier that one can analyse regulations by comparing them with tax/subsidy (capital levy/capital grant) schemes that would have approximately the same effects. This seems to us a most useful *analytic* exercise. But it ignores the *political* purposes to be served by intervention. When considering the alternatives to regulation from a political (voter acceptance) point of view, the following ''axioms'' appear to have some validity. Undoubtedly, the list of axioms could be extended, but our purpose here is heuristic. It should be pointed out that these kinds of axioms are meant to be generalizations applicable to any political party in a democracy.

---

[2] As emphasized earlier, many regulations have a major affect on individual income. But, they cannot explicitly be geared to the *total* income of the individual. Nor can they reflect differences such as the number of dependents of an individual or his age, or his sources of income. Many regulations introduced ostensibly to help the poor (e.g., poor farmers) in the event are of the greatest benefit to the relatively wealthy.

[3] This grossly over-simplifies the issue because governments can and do finance the types of expenditures just noted by borrowing and/or printing money. But in the absence of some taxation the bonds could not be sold—the ''purchases'' would have to be compulsory, and hence a form of taxation. Similarly, the money might well be unacceptable, and ''paying'' for goods and services would be tantamount to confiscation—another form of taxation.

[4] The reduced work effort often associated with higher marginal tax rates on additional earnings is an example of such an induced behavioural change.

4.1 THE SACRED NATURE OF HUMAN LIFE AXIOM

Voters will not accept any scheme that *explicitly* acknowledges that each human life is not infinitely valuable. It is transparent, however, that each human life is not in fact treated as such when policy decisions are made. If it were: why is there a single railway crossing? Why not overpasses on all crossings, including those in the most remote areas where traffic is infinitesimal? Why is there a ''shortage'' of dialysis machines? Why are new products allowed on the market after only a million clinical trials? Why not a billion? Why is there not a policeman constantly on duty on every block in every town every night? Why is the whole of our national income not devoted to cancer research? Implicitly, of course, risks inescapably have to be run and ministers and bureaucrats make decisions that indirectly result in death, injuries and illnesses. These are the agonizing decisions when they are consciously made in the full knowledge of the implications. This is probably the basic reason why politicians cannot seriously consider the proposal to abate pollution by means of selling pollution rights. Certainly, it would be a most *efficient* means of reducing pollution. But can the well-to-do be allowed to buy the right to make other people sick? Is that not how the headline would appear?

Ministers are in some ways like undertakers: they are paid to disguise what everyone knows to be painfully true. And those who can do a better cosmetic job and stage the most seemly show are likely to drive out the competitors, other things being equal.

4.2 THE VILLAINS AND THE HEROES AXIOM

The second axiom is that voters will not readily accept the decision to allocate what they perceive to be rewards to those whom they perceive to be ''the bad guys.'' As in western movies, the politician is left in no suspense as to who the voters believe to be ''the bad guys.'' Just as in the movies, ''the bad guys'' are invariably bigger than ''the good guys'' and, of course, are cruel and unscrupulous as they wield the overpowering forces in their attempts to take the patch of land ''the good guys'' have wrested from nature to add to their already enormous holdings. Politicians who fail to recognize that this is the classic plot that symbolizes reality—in the minds of many if not most—soon discover that voters flock to the box offices where their competitors' movies are being shown. These competitors have not forgotten that ''good guys'' are always rewarded and ''bad guys'' eventually punished.

Classics, whether they be Greek plays or Shakespearian dramas or western movies, are classics because they capture a universal aspect of life as a large number of people see it. They therefore have an intrinsic ''truth.'' The actors and the scenes change, but the fundamental plot remains the same.

As Scott Gordon has pointed out to the author in a recent letter: ''The reason for the popularity of the villains and heroes scenario is that we are partially civilized. There is a taste for violence in most people's utility function, but the veneer of civilization requires that the violence be justified, by being directed at villains. The chastisement of the wicked is the second most pleasurable activity of man.''

A unique feature of modern life is most significant within this context, however. For reasons that were cited earlier, the omnipresence of large corporations specifically, and large organizations generally (e.g., labour unions, bureaucracies), has made it difficult for voters to differentiate between a legal fiction, the corporation (a form of property right ownership) on the one hand, and the individuals involved in, and the interests affected by such organizations on the other. The more abstract the function performed by the corporation, the greater the confusion. The public's attitude toward insurance companies is a case in point. That the interest of other individuals (''good'' or ''bad'') are hurt by ''ripping off'' the insurance company never enters most minds. Ethical issues are not raised: just practical ones—will I be caught? What will happen if I am? In short, they do not ''look through the corporate veil'' and see the resulting adverse effects on the interests of other individuals. Thus, we find labour leaders castigating ''big business'' while the shares of such companies are often a major item in the portfolios of the very pension plans in which their members have a significant personal interest.

Whether or not voters *should* look through the corporate veil is not at issue as far as politicians are concerned. The fact is that most voters do not. And in formulating their policies the voters' *perceptions* of reality *are* the politician's reality. The ''bad guy'' image of the large corporation makes it extremely difficult for ministers to adopt a policy that involves a subsidy or capital grant to them. The recent large capital grant to the Ford Motor Company by the Government of Canada and the Province of Ontario was an exception that proves the rule. This involved the crucial question of the assignment of the political ''blame'' to Queen's Park or to Ottawa for the possible loss of the jobs had the grant not been made to counteract the competition of American State governments. One can be reasonably certain that the grant would not have been made by either government without federal-provincial *political* competition. This is the kind of situation that, under other circumstances, if anything were done, it probably would have been by means of a tax concession.

An important consequence of the common public perception of and attitude towards ''big business'' is the virtual political impossibilityof compensating the losers when rights are assigned *to those whose interests are being damaged* by corporations who are polluting the water or the air. Unable to sell a restricted number of pollution rights as a means of reducing pollution, for the reasons mentioned, what remains? The instruments of regulations and tax concessions for capital expenditures related supposedly to pollution abatement are all that are available.

When there is an intrinsically scarce resource to be rationed, for example, the carrying capacity of the airwaves, why not sell the right to the highest bidder *with the right carrying with it the contractual obligation to use the asset for certain purposes and not for others?* The reason: "the most wealthy and the most powerful could then 'buy' our collective right to cultural expression," would not some editorial writer trumpet in outraged tones? (Coase, 1959).

Politicians are faced with many triangular situations. On the one side there are the voters whose understanding of the consequences is limited and their "prejudices" almost unlimited. On another side are corporations crying wolf and threatening dire consequences unless preposterous concessions are made that are proportionate in size to the "giants" demanding them. Then there is the third side of the triangle. This is the "reality" side: where pandering to prejudice could yield short-run *political* benefits but ultimately hurt the longer run interests of those demanding them, although those prejudiced souls whose interests were damaged might never be aware of the source of their difficulties. Accepting the claims of the corporate side at face value would not only involve an inordinate political cost but, indeed, bestow some completely unwarranted benefits on corporate managers or the shareholders or employees of the moment, or both.

Objective economic analysis can assist ministers in wending their way through this minefield. However, it is obvious that, from a political point of view, a corporate tax concession is much more palatable than a subsidy of equal cost. (Research and development subsidies are an exception because the very name makes the "cause" virtuous to many eyes.) Furthermore, because the separation of fact from fiction is so onerous and so technical, and the voters' response sometimes so intense, regulations applied by an "independent" agency have much to commend them to ministers groping for alternatives. The creation of such a regulatory agency gives the appearance of ministerial concern yet, with any luck, will result in decisions that avoid dire consequences. Ministers are concerned about the concerns of the prejudiced—they *have* to be. They are also concerned not to create even bigger concerns later when, perhaps, output and employment fall as a result.

Those who claim that many regulatory agencies are "captured" by the regulatees[5] miss the rather obvious point: one cannot capture that which has already been surrendered. The decision to intervene in the private sector by an "independent" regulatory authority represents a decision to reject other forms of intervention that could be more or less stringent. For example, state ownership is available. Alternatively, a tax rate of 100 per cent could be imposed on profits in excess of y per cent of the shareholder's investment in corporations in designated "public service" industries. Leaving aside the

---

[5] Stigler and the members of the Chicago School cited in Chapter 1, see Samuels (1976).

rate structures of "utilities" *per se*, an issue on which we comment later, the result, in principle, would be much the same as those achieved by regulation except that the resulting confrontations about the "appropriate" tax assessment of such a corporation would take place between the tax department's officials and the corporation's professional troops behind closed doors, where the officials could be as tough or malleable as they thought expedient. The corporation's appeals through the courts would be interminable and the courts poorly equipped (staffed) to assist the judges in sorting through the mounds of technical evidence. "Standing"—the right to intervene would be less clear cut for third parties. Whether the courts would, in the event, be more or less generous than a regulatory agency is anyone's guess. But if the courts were to construe such a provision in a taxing statute as narrowly as they usually construe taxing statutes, more "capture" would be involved rather than less and the companies might well be better off than they now are.

Moreover, as discussed in some detail in the next chapter, it is by no means clear that under the parliamentary system the notion of "independent" regulatory agencies makes any sense. The "capture" notion makes some sense, in a "checks and balances" congressional system, however. But even in the United States "independent" regulatory agencies are being criticized because they cannot be held accountable (Cutler and Johnson, 1975).

Closely related to what has just been said is the rate structure question. Voter concern is not solely with the inordinate profits (in their minds at least) of unregulated public service corporations, but with the discriminatory "charge what the traffic will bear" pricing policies they would adopt. Taxation of "excessive" rates or returns on investments would, however, preclude government intervention for the purpose of setting rate structures that have *buried in them complex tax/subsidy systems*. These systems approach taxing "what the traffic will bear" in those instances where those who are being taxed (by charging rates well above the marginal cost of the service) are, in the voters minds, and hence vulnerable in political terms, thought to be the fatter of the cats ("business" and long distance telephone calls, for example). The "tax proceeds" are then used, in effect, to subsidize those whose political voices are loudest (individuals generally and rural individuals especially with respect to telephones). It would be inordinately complex and politically unpalatable to achieve the same net effects through an explicit tax/subsidy system (see Posner, 1971).

The complex tax subsidy arrangements built into rate structures (postal rates are another example) illustrate another "axiom" that is too obvious to warrant discussion: rural votes carry a disproportionate weight because the number of rural ridings is greatly in excess of the number of urban ridings on a proportionate representational basis. Obviously, "buying" rural voter support is thus "cheaper." Moreover, is not farm life virtuous by definition? Surely also, have we not all watched "the bad guys," in hordes, descend on horseback through the dust to dispossess the tanned, handsome, virile young homesteader—backed by his attractive but demure wife who is invariably carrying a baby in her arms. The family farm is sacred. Period.

4.3 THE ADVANTAGES OF STEALTH AXIOM

One final generalization can be offered concerning the selection of regulation (or perhaps the rejection of alternatives!) as the mode of government intervention. The beneficiaries of a concession prefer to obtain that benefit through regulation or a tax concession rather than by means of subsidy for the painfully obvious reason that the costs are thereby hidden. *Everyone* shudders when a headline appears such as "Dairy Farmers to Receive One-Half Billion Tax Dollars This Year" or "Mining Interests Rip-Off Treasury to the Tune of $_____." The taxpayers/voters shudder because they ache in their wallets: the recipients shudder at the image created which, of course, they believe to be completely erroneous (except possibly in their heart of hearts that remain outwardly mute!). "After all," the beneficiaries tell themselves, and one another, "This isn't a handout. It's what we rightly deserve." Whether or not their pride is hurt, all can agree that with such headlines appearing annually proclaiming such forthright subsidies, the subsidies are much more vulnerable to criticism and consequently present tempting targets for expenditure cuts. Supply limitation regulations that have roughly the same affects on net income are more discrete, more complex, and much less likely to be criticized and therefore removed.[6]

Because the political purpose is to gain votes, why not buy it with the consumer's money through higher prices? It pleases the beneficiaries. It is largely not attributed by consumers to the source of higher commodity prices. It leaves no odious tracks in the annual expenditure budget for egg storage facilities! "Doing good by stealth," the purest form of charity, would aptly describe the essence of this exercise if it were not that the donors of the benefactions are not let in on the secret either and thus denied the inner glow of self-satisfaction!

4.4 SOME IMPLICATIONS AND INFERENCES

The foregoing generalizations about the politics of regulation will no doubt be construed by some as cynical. This, in our opinion, would be to misconstrue what is implied. The *Concise Oxford Dictionary* defines cynical as " . . . incredulous of human goodness; sneering . . . " What *is* implied is that we believe that many humans are, indeed, credulous. There is *no* justification for the inference that we believe they are lacking in "good-

---

[6] Government price supports through stockpiling have also been known to smell like rotten eggs—and in a starving world too!

ness.'' Nor is it valid to infer that we are ''sneering'' at humans generally and/or politicians in particular. Credulity is not a vice, it is the consequence of being uninformed or misinformed. Our sneers are reserved for those who are either by choice. As far as politicians are concerned, they too are only judged harshly to the extent that they make self-seeking decisions when they have a choice. Consciously opting for a short-run personal advantage (we mean here power, not affluence) at the expense of the long-term well-being of those who can least afford to lose anything, to say the least, is hardly admirable. As with so many ethical problems, however, the situation is rarely that straightforward if one ignores the out-and-out dishonest politicians who constitute no larger a proportion of the members of the political profession than do the dishonest men in any other.

The politician's *rationalization* can be readily captured in syllogistic form; he might readily say the following:

1. Most people (voters) are misinformed (prejudiced).

2. But they are the only people (voters) we have.

3. In formulating our policies and our platform if we do not take into account (pander to) these realities about people the other political party(ies) will.

4. We (I) will be defeated (not form a government) (no longer be a minister).

5. Then the deserving (deluded) voters would be hurt more.

6. It is better for them that we fool them a little now to save them from their own ignorance which would lead them to vote for the other party.

7. The other party(ies) would *really* hurt them.

Many politicians, who are not noted for their credulity, can firmly believe this line of argument to be absolutely true and therefore can proceed, with a perfectly clear conscience, to try to carry out what non-politicians would almost certainly judge to be a gross public deception. Here too, there is no reason to believe that politicians are more subject to self-deception than any other group.[7] But to use one of the lines in the syllogism, ''they are the only people we have.''

Political leadership could perhaps be defined as the demonstrated capacity to induce voters, through informing them and persuading them, without inflaming base prejudices, to accept, perhaps even insist upon, a political decision despite their narrower prejudices and despite the fact that it does not appear to them to be in their short-term personal interest. Political courage lies in the attempt to do the same thing, without taking advantage of ignorance or by pandering to any prejudice (much less inflaming it) in the

---

[7] We have yet to observe *any* occupational group that was unable to rationalize the self-seeking behaviour of its members with some laudable purpose. Only those who push a good thing ''too far,'' and threaten the representation and self-image of the others are admonished. Even organized crime can be justified as ''all in aid of the family.''

knowledge and fear that the probability of failure is extremely high.[8] Once again, one would expect that leadership and courage to be as rare in the political forum as they are in any other. But neither characteristic is unknown in politics nor in other areas of human endeavour. The pessimist will be depressed by the infrequency of the occurrences of leadership and courage. The optimist will be elated at the seeming miracle that they ever occur!

There are four inferences we *do* want drawn from this discussion of the political forces.

First, objective analyses of the impact of regulatory policies would greatly increase the set of feasible alternative policies political parties could place before the voters. It would also minimize the opportunities that now exist for the well-informed, well-to-do and powerful to take advantage of the uninformed, the misinformed, the poor and the powerless.

The inherent conflicts among the interests of individuals and groups of individuals would not be removed. Indeed, they probably would be more obvious and consequently more intense. The resulting escalation of conflict would seem to be a price that must be paid if the present imbalances are to be at all ameliorated. This would make more difficult the difficult task of the politician regardless of party affiliation.

Second, lowering the existing secrecy barriers that now deny the relevant information to the journalist and the analyst is a necessary precondition. Secrecy is often rationalized as being "in the public interest." Nowhere is that meaningless phase more meaningless—to state a logical absurdity for emphasis. It serves the interests of the few only. By the same token, it cannot be claimed that openness is in "the public interest" for more openness is in the interest of the many and not in the interest of *all*, as the transparent reluctance to introduce freedom of information legislation attests. In Canada, it is demonstrably easier for ministers and the responsible officials to draft a War Measures Act *that is acceptable to them* than it is to draft a Freedom of Information Act.

Third, to assess existing regulations in terms of the degree to which they effectively achieve their *stated objectives*—statements that usually are designed to persuade or obfuscate—relative to alternatives would be largely a waste of time. To take these statements at face value would be to "prove" that ministers collectively, of either of the "old line parties," are either fools or knaves or both, which would be neither true nor fair. Such assessments would implicitly assume either that none of the "political realities" discussed (or others of a similar nature) are "real" or, if they are "real," *should not* be taken into account by ministers and officials in formulating their policies.

---

[8] The political demagogue blatantly exploits ignorance and purposefully inflames the basest of prejudice, sure in the knowledge of success and elated with the achievement. But even these odious individuals usually seem to be able to rationalize their behaviour in terms of the benefits being bestowed on "the nation" or the "Aryan race" or whatever.

The latter assumption implicitly assumes that a political party could survive (much less elect members) that proceeded as though most voters were fully informed and without "prejudice" in our sense. It ignores the competition for office in which, in the struggle for votes, those that "take into account" what voters know (do not know) and what voters believe (hate) are elected and those that do not are not.

Such far-fetched assumptions about reality would assume away the problem and neither address it nor help in resolving it. In many ways, to proceed in this manner would involve pandering to the popular prejudice that all politicians are fools or rogues all of the time, a prejudice which in *part* explains the politicians' frequent resort to subterfuge. On the other hand, of course, most politicians are followers rather than leaders and opportunists rather than courageous like the rest of us. And some of them, hardly surprisingly, are as prejudiced and misinformed as those they represent. Neither hatchets nor whitewash brushes are in order.

Fourth, we would suggest that the most constructive and fair approach to take in seeking to analyse objectively particular government regulations, or other government policies for that matter, would be to seek to "answer" as reliably as theory, the data and quantitative methods would allow, four questions.

1. "Who benefits and who pays"?

2. What tax/subsidy or capital/levy system (or systems) would give approximately the same results?

3. What are the likely consequences (if significant) in terms of the level and rate of increase of national output over time? (The allocative effects.)

4. What are the *implicit* mechanisms (even explained in crude terms) in the political/economic decision-making systems that "explain" this result?

The "answer" to the second question would *not* be to find a feasible alternative to the regulation. That vital issue could be faced more squarely later. At the outset, administrative and/or political feasibility considerations would be *explicitly* ignored. Rather, the purpose would be to drive home, *in the minds of the voters*, "a way of looking" at regulations that could drastically alter their understanding of the significance of alternatives.

In our view, explanation of the underlying processes and estimates of the direction and magnitude of the distributional/allocative consequences would be more eloquent, without the introduction of an endless flow of "tut-tut" assessments. The first order of business is to increase the understanding of others of the impact of the basic alternatives. After that step has been taken, the consideration of the relative merits of the alternatives, that would take into account all of their implications, would be more meaningful.

REFERENCES

Coase, Ronald H. (1959) "The Federal Communications Commission" *Journal of Law and Economics* 2 (October): 1-40.

Cutler, Lloyd N. and David R. Johnson (1975) "Regulation and the Political Process" *The Yale Law Journal* 84: 1395-418.

Doern, G. Bruce (1978) "Introduction" in G. Bruce Doern (ed.) *The Regulatory Process in Canada* pp. 1-23 (Toronto: Macmillan).

Posner, Richard A. (1971) "Taxation by Regulation" *Bell Journal of Economics and Management Science* 2: 22-50.

Samuels, W.J. (ed.) (1976) *The Chicago School of Political Economy* (Lansing, Mich.: Michigan State University, School of Business Administration).

Trebilcock, M.J., L. Waverman and J.R.S. Prichard (1978) "Markets for Regulation: Implications for Performance Standards and Institutional Design" in *Government Regulation: Issues and Alternatives* pp. 11-66 (Toronto: Ontario Economic Council).

Chapter Five

The Argument Assembled and Some Illustrative Cases

This chapter attempts to pull together the elements of the argument developed in the preceding several chapters and apply the approach that we have developed to some illustrative types of regulations. For brevity the argument will be set forth as a set of point-form propositions.

Inescapably, the propositions are put in less qualified terms than the earlier text and should be read with the qualifications given there in mind. In a few instances some implications, not elaborated earlier, are drawn.

1. Individuals seek to maximize their current (pure) consumption (including leisure) *and* their Comprehensive Net Worth (Table B, Chapter 2).[1]

2. Leaving aside windfall gains and losses, an increase in a CNW can be achieved by first foregoing current "pure" consumption and then by adding to personal saving *and/or* by investment (Table C, Item VIII, Chapter 2).

3. One form of investment involves an allocation by the individual of time *and/or* money for the purpose of obtaining favourable changes in government rules and/or favourable decisions under such rules.

4. This can be done by voting, making submissions, lobbying and participation in association activities.

5. We emphasized in the discussion of the CNW in Chapter 2 the wide range of interests that a particular individual may hold at a point in time and the enormous variation in the magnitude and composition of the interests of individuals. Given these wide disparities in the package of interests held by different individuals, there are perpetual conflicts among them when they seek to enhance their interests, if needs be at the expense of others.

6. This is not to say that individuals do not share some interests, but rather to recognize that many vital interests are in perpetual conflict.

7. The policy decision-making process can best be thought of as a conflict resolution process. This is the essence of the political system.

---

[1] Hereinafter, the Comprehensive Net Worth of an individual will be designated by CNW and the plural will be shown as CNWs, meaning the CNW of two or more individuals.

8. The political system as a whole can be thought of as three closely interrelated systems.

a) *The party system* whereby candidates are elected, ministries (the government of the day) created, and statutory rules are promulgated by a majority vote in Parliament.

b) The *ministerial-bureaucratic (executive branch) system* that proposes rule changes to Parliament and, under the rules approved by Parliament, makes further rules and/or issues rulings. Generally speaking these subordinate decisions are made by the Cabinet, particular ministers and/or deputy heads of departments and/or the heads of regulatory agencies.

c) The *special interest group system* through which individuals, and the executives of corporations and associations (including labour), seek to obtain favourable changes in rules or rulings (where "rules" include statutes). By the term "favourable" we mean rule changes and rulings that increase the CNWs of the individuals with the special interests that are being pursued. "Favourable" also denotes defensive moves against rule changes or rulings that would damage the special interests involved.

9. In order to obtain favourable rule changes and/or rulings (henceforth called policy changes), the special interest system encompasses the following.

a) The exercise of persuasion on all of the actors involved in the electoral system and the subordinate decision-making system. This encompasses the electorate, members of Parliament, the Cabinet, deputy heads and regulatory agency heads and their subordinates. This, of course, requires the investment of time and/or money.

b) Coupled with (or instead of) persuasion, special interests may invest both time and/or money on a *quid pro quo* basis. The most vulgar form is bribery. More sophisticated forms also abound. These involve providing benefits in kind to those whose decisions or influence are crucial. Benefits in kind can also take the form of "saving the pocket" of those whose favourable decisions and influence are sought by, in effect, absorbing costs (time or money) that otherwise would have been borne by those from whom the *quid pro quo* is sought.

c) When the policy decisions are to be made by a regulatory agency that has relatively elaborate procedures, substantial investment costs often are involved in the preparation of submissions and in appearances at hearings. These usually entail costs to the applicants and the intervenors in the form of professional fees (primarily lawyers and accountants).

In short, participation in the special interest system involves investment costs (time and money) that can be deployed in one or all of the three ways we have indicated.

10. The very existence and the degree of pressure that can be exerted by organized special interest groups is dependent upon two factors:

a) the first is the magnitude of the benefits (whether tangible or intangible) at stake in influencing policy decisions;

b) the second is the extent to which those who would benefit from the favourable policy decision can be induced to bear their proportionate share of the investment costs entailed in obtaining it. This is the so-called ''free-rider'' problem. To put the issue in a slightly different way: those interests that are most widely shared are least likely to be formally organized and well financed. Although the potential *aggregate* benefits are conceivably enormous, many potential beneficiaries will make no investment in attaining them in the expectation (hope?) that they will share in the benefits without having to share in the costs.

The most public of ''public interests'' are therefore grossly inadequately represented in the interest group system, relative to special, narrow interests.

11. By definition, politicians gain office (an exclusive, non-transferable right distinguished in Table B, Item I(B)(1) of Chapter 2) upon winning in the endless sequential competitive struggle for votes, both at the constituency level and at the national (party) level. Having attained office, the politician has two responsibilities:

a) pursue shared interests;

b) reconcile conflicting interests in such a manner as to least damage (forgo ?) (a) while, at the same time, maximizing the likelihood of his re-election and the attainment of the largest number of seats for the party of which he is a member.

The political process is more readily understood when looked upon in terms of the adversarial nature of both the competitive electoral process and the resolution of conflicting interests—interests that seek policy decisions that provide some interests with benefits.

12. We emphasized in our conceptual framework the investment expenditures (both time and money) that are devoted to obtaining an office or employment—an exclusive non-transferable right. Clearly, the investment required in obtaining the temporary right to an elective office can be, and often is, extraordinarily high. These costs must be borne by the candidate himself and/or by ''contributions'' to the candidate directly or to a political party that provides support (again in time and money) to the candidates.

To the extent that such contributions to candidates and parties are made in the expectation of a potential benefit that would be widely shared, they may be thought of as ''charitable.'' To the extent that they are made on a narrow *quid pro quo* basis they are analogous to an investment in a risky marketable asset; that is to say, in the expectation of a potential gain that would be exclusive to the contributor.

13. Given the competition among politicians and parties, one would anticipate an escalation of the investment costs of electoral office to rise as the extent of government intervention increases. Because of the ''free-rider'' problem, the *relative* importance of charitable contributions would tend to

fall. Moreover, one would also anticipate the contributions of the less affluent would take the form of time rather than money.

14. Spurred by the competitive bidding for electoral support by political parties, the demands for government intervention escalate. Leaving aside the public acknowledgement of concern and exortation, the government of the day may decide that it must be seen to be "doing something." This raises the question of the selection of the *mode* of intervention.

15. We have emphasized that the mode of intervention selected will be dependent upon a number of complex, interrelated factors that simultaneously seek to resolve the conflicts among the two responsibilities of politicians identified in point 11, together with the campaign financing costs discussed under points 12 and 13.[2]

Of enormous significance are voters' *perceptions* of the consequences of particular policy decisions. The voters' perceptions of reality are the politicians' reality. Among the more important determinants of voter perceptions are the following:

— the powers of a ministry to suppress information (i.e., secrecy);
— the particular incentive systems under which academics and journalists pursue their careers;
— the "rules of thumb" adopted by voters to screen the flood of information that engulfs them (bounded rationality);
— the symbols they adopt, largely unconsciously, to distinguish between "good" and "bad."

The first of these determinants is, with a few important exceptions, the result of political expediency. The second is partly laudible, partly inherent, and partly unfortunate. The last two are, in part, perfectly rational from the individual's point of view, partly inescapable (generic limitations), and partly open to improvement through more and better education and improved family or social environments that would provide greater equality of opportunity for those of equal capacity.

16. As a consequence, politicians generally and ministers particularly are able to conceal "real" costs and magnify "real" benefits *or* magnify "real" costs and conceal "real" benefits. Is this, "good," "bad," or inevitable and hence not an ethical issue? As we stated in Chapter 1—it all depends . . .

Having summarized our line of argument, the following sections apply the framework to some hypothetical cases for illustrative purposes. The cases selected do not purport to exhaust the possible types of regulation, nor do the

---

[2] Politicians, like other individuals are assumed to seek to maximize their Comprehensive Net Worth. In our discussion of the role of the politician we have only considered the benefits of the elective office *per se*. Clearly, under some circumstances, the attainment of elective office can be thought of as an investment made in contemplation of indirect benefits. These may include illicit bribes to gaining public recognition that can later be "capitalized" upon in other offices or employments (e.g., directorships, law partnerships, etc.).

analyses purport to be more than sketches, nor is the order of any particular significance. We have, however, tried to draw out, where applicable, implications with respect to:

1) income/wealth distribution effects
2) resource allocations effects
3) growth effects.

The reader is asked to recall the definition of terms provided in the final section of Chapter 2 in interpreting the cases presented in the balance of this chapter.

5.1 CASE ONE: AN EXCLUSIVE LICENCE WITH RATE REGU-LATION

This case seeks to illustrate some of the principal effects of the regulation that are most often loosely called "natural monopolies." These are usually thought to encompass public utility-like corporations offering communication, transportation and energy services. The words "natural monopoly" are used loosely because the situation is often one of degree rather than of kind. Furthermore, some of the bundle of services supplied by such corporations might be open to competition if government protection, in the form of exclusive licences, were narrower in scope. Now the hypothetical illustration.

The regulatory agency, after receiving many submissions and after lengthy hearings, grants an exclusive licence to Corporation X to operate a cable TV network in an area previously not served by cable. Assume that it is common knowledge that this would increase the corporation's future profits, but that because of the uncertainty about the agency's final decision, X's share price did not reflect this fact prior to its announcement. Assuming the corporation is widely held, the market value of its shares rises sharply and immediately. (This is particularly plausible because cable licences are not subject to rate of return regulation.) Those who held the shares just prior to the announcement obtain an immediate and substantial capital gain. Their wealth, in the CNW sense and in the usual accounting sense, is increased.[3] Does the capital gain to the shareholders mean a net gain or loss to others?

If, as we have supposed, there is a great jump in the value of the corporation's shares, we can be reasonably certain that the cable services are to be sold (or more precisely are expected to be sold) at a price that provides a supra-normal rate of return on shareholders' equity. The shareholders at the point in time when the licence was issued obtain the capitalized value of these supra-normal profits—the stream of expected rents in the terminology of the economist. These rents constitute the prices charged for the service over and

---

[3] Should those shareholders realize the gain by selling their shares, a subsequent revocation of the licence would impose a capital loss on those who held the shares at the time of revocation.

above the opportunity cost of the resources employed. The subscribers are worse off to this extent (which is not to say they are worse off than they would be without the service) and it will be reflected in their reduced future levels of consumption and/or a reduction in their personal saving and/or a reduction in their investment in enhancing their CNW in other ways.[4]

The effects of the rent component in the cable subscription price may not fully accrue to the licensee's shareholders. The officers of the cable company, and their professional advisers, may well be able to obtain some of it in higher remuneration in one form or another. So might a powerful union or a monopolistic supplier of equipment. As far as the effects of the cable licence on the allocation of resources is concerned, only the rent implications need concern us here. By changing the distribution of wealth, the proportion of current earnings saved may be altered (less for the subscribers than it otherwise might be and more for shareholders, officers, etc.), probably with an overall increase if the latter are more well-to-do than the former. To the extent that the flow of rents to the licensee is not distributed by way of dividends and/or rewards to management and professional advisers, business saving will be increased if the cable company retains more profits than would the firms in other industries that contract slightly. The composition of consumption and the composition of the uses to which business savings are put also might change. These allocative effects are, however, trivial in importance relative to the effects on the distribution of wealth. For it is difficult to see why the resulting allocation of resources would be better or worse—just slightly different except, possibly, that, *depending upon the basis on which cable rates are established by the regulatory agency*, more might be spent by cable corporations on facilities and equipment relative to what would prevail under normal circumstances.[5] This misallocation of business capital will have adverse economic growth consequences for the economy as a whole. These consequences may not be insignificant if the regulated sector's capital expenditures are an important component of national capital expenditures.

Another way to consider the effects of granting such a property right as an exclusive cable TV licence is to think of the licence as the government assignment of the power to *tax* cable subscribers in a particular area, at a rate contingent upon the regulated rate structure, to a particular corporation (see

---

[4] As stated earlier, to avoid the repetition of the phrase ''relative to what it otherwise would be'' the reader should assume this qualification when changes are discussed unless otherwise qualified in the text. The reader is also reminded that ''investment'' in this chapter means the expenditure of time or money by an individual with the expectation of realizing an increase in his Comprehensive Net Worth other than by acquiring marketable assets. The latter, acquiring marketable assets (net), is termed personal saving here.

[5] Rates are frequently established by regulators on the basis of providing a given rate of return on invested capital. The corporation can therefore increase its cash flow by adopting the most capital intensive methods and highly sophisticated equipment and facilities, and by maintaining excess capacity. All of these outlays are inefficient in terms of opportunity cost—see generally Averch and Johnson (1962). Cable is not subject to rate of return regulation, however.

Posner, 1971). If the corporation is widely held, this contingent taxing power can be bought or sold in the market through trading in the shares. If the allowed rates only permit a normal return on assets to the shareholders, and assuming that only necessary costs are incurred, the taxing power as such is valueless and the shares will sell at prices that reflect the going rate of return on businesses of equivalent risk. The converse will hold if the regulated rates are higher.

The impact of the tax on subscribers, if there are rents incorporated in the rates, are about the same as any other tax except, of course, that the revenues of government taxes are usually used to finance government services or transfer payments whereas in the licence case the proceeds of the tax are reflected in an increase in the value of the marketable assets of a few. No small difference!

Some regulated rate *structures* (although not for cable TV) require rates to be set so that some subscribers do not pay the full cost of the services they obtain while others pay more than that cost. Under these circumstances, the corporation is the government's agent by which the former are given a subsidy that is financed by a tax on the latter. This, we will argue later, is a most important aspect of rate regulation. When the service supplied is necessarily a natural monopoly given the state of technology and factor prices at the time, the corporation, in the absence of licensing and regulation, will set its own rates and maximize the rents, as we have called them, by discriminatory pricing—rates that cover marginal cost *plus* what the traffic will bear given the circumstances of the particular subscriber. In other words, there will be a complex rate structure where the "tax revenues" that can be obtained from each class of subscriber are maximized. There will be no subsidization, for obvious reasons. The main *ostensible* purpose of rate regulation is to prevent this kind of discriminatory pricing and to eliminate overall rents.

Still looking at the matter from a tax/subsidy point of view, granting a licence where the regulated rates *overall* do not effectively eliminate the rents is tantamount, in wealth distribution terms, to bestowing a *capital grant* on the shareholders at the time the licence is issued and simultaneously imposing a capital levy (to be paid over time) on the subscribers who pay more than marginal cost of the services and conferring a capital grant on those who pay less than that cost—where the capital levy to some subscribers is roughly equal to the sum of the capital grants to the shareholders and the subsidized subscribers. The effects on the allocation of resources of the capital grant/levy will be roughly the same, we might suppose, as those of the licence and tax/subsidy rate structure approach, but with one crucial difference. The former approach converts a contingent redistribution of capital into a certain redistribution.

One thing does seem perfectly clear, however. The investment of time and money in obtaining a licence can yield extraordinarily high returns. We will have more to say about this later.

The obvious alternative to licensing in these "natural monopoly" circumstances would be for the government to *auction* franchises with the conditions to be met by the successful bidder clearly spelled out in advance, including provisions concerning rate structures and provisos concerning the government's right to change the level of rates charged by the franchise holder based on stated criteria. Such a system would capture the rents for the public because the competition among the bidders would be such as to accord a rate of return on investment (in the usual sense) consistent with returns available elsewhere in the economy involving the same risk. If nothing else, this would eliminate the socially unproductive costs now involved in preparing expensive submissions and in participation in hearings. Some[6] have gone so far as to argue that, because of the competition for the licences, these application expenses are so high that the rents are essentially captured by the lawyers, accountants and consultants of one kind and another who participate in the licence allocation process, with the result that the "winner" only earns a normal rate of return on investment or on the licence obtained.

Another alternative is public ownership where, *in principle*, either the service is provided at cost or the "profit" reverts to the treasury to be used for public purposes. As is well known, this "solution" presents its own problems. If the government enterprise is operated inefficiently, there will be no rents (except for inputs that are paid too much for too little!), but there will be a waste of resources. The unnecessary resources, if deployed elsewhere, could increase total output and hence higher aggregate consumption and/or increase the collective capital stock—the source of future consumption.

Considered from a vote maximization point of view, rate regulation has some extremely attractive features.[7]

1. It serves a laudible "public interest" purpose: the elimination of exhorbitant profiteering and discriminatory—"charge what the traffic will bear"—rates.

2. The villains are punished: giant corporations and, in the case of telephone rates, business subscribers.

3. The heroes are rewarded; in the case of cable subscribers these are the residential subscribers. (If we had been using telephone rates as an example, the vitally important rural vote is "purchased" by providing hidden subsidized services to remote, low density subscribers.)

4. Appointments to regulatory agencies can provide a quasi-senate reward for benefits received if needs be. With any luck in the appointments, "sensible" decisions, from a political point of view, are likely to emerge from the regulatory agency.

---

[6] Posner (1975)

[7] We ignore government ownership here. It possesses many of the same political advantages as those described for regulation.

5. Egos being what they are, with the Damoclesian sword of Cabinet override on regulatory decisions hanging over the proceedings,[8] the regulators are not likely to step too far out of political line too often if their wrists are slapped occasionally by way of a Cabinet intervention, as a reminder of who is in power.

6. Of great importance, when politically unpopular decisions are "necessary," the Cabinet can hide behind the illusion of regulatory agency "independence," wringing its collective hands with frustration in self-imposed impotence. This is discussed at length in Chapter 5.

7. The tortuous and prolonged procedures ensure that all but the most stout of heart or most generously remunerated fall by the wayside, thus exploiting the "free-rider" problem and an "invisible shield" against those who might intervene on behalf of the rights of the collectivity (i.e., the buyers of the regulated industry's output).

8. The extraordinarily high costs of the submissions to and appearances before regulatory agencies are well hidden. The corporate regulators can, of course, deduct the expenses incurred as a business expense so that, with a corporate tax rate of about 50 per cent, the general taxpayer bears half of their costs immediately. Secondly, such expenses are looked upon by the regulator as perfectly legitimate operating costs when considering rate increase requests and, in all likelihood, they are built into the subscriber (or other) rates approved. The fees charged by counsel and other denizens of the *demi-monde* of "regulatory experts" are raised to the point that their after-tax incomes can nicely accommodate the personal income tax—that is to say, that part that cannot be avoided by a host of stratagems. The level of remuneration (in all forms) of the executives of regulated corporations speak for themselves. These are expenses recouped in the rate structure. Thus, as Aesop might have concluded one of his fables . . .

5.2 CASE TWO: A FLOOR PRICE FOR LABOUR SERVICES—A MINIMUM WAGE

The introduction of a minimum wage law changes property rights in the following manner.

— A contingent right is created by the state. After a certain date, all hourly paid employees are to be paid at least $m/hour, we will assume, for their time on the job.

— By the creating of this contingent right for employees, the employer's right to hire labour at any rate he chooses to offer is implicitly reduced because a wage rate floor has been created.

— The worker or would-be worker does *not* acquire a right to a job and the employer's right to dismiss and/or hire employees is not affected.

---

[8] The subject of Chapter 6.

In essence, the individual's right to enter into a contract of service with a potential employer at a wage rate below the minimum is withdrawn.

In effect, the employer is being required to pay a *subsidy* of x¢/hour—the difference between the market clearing wage rate for a particular type of worker in a particular labour market, $w/hour, and the minimum wage, $m/hour,—for each and every worker who, before the introduction of the regulation, would have been paid the lower figure had he been on the pay-roll. The minimum wage regulation does not set forth, of course, how the employer is to finance this subsidy and it can be looked upon as a pay-roll tax on the employer equal to the subsidy to the employees who receive it.

It is obvious that the employer can avoid the tax by laying off all employees to whom the subsidy would be payable. However, minimizing the tax is not necessarily the same as maximizing profits (or minimizing the loss), the presumed overriding objective of the employer. Depending upon a whole concatenation of circumstances (e.g., technology, labour market conditions, the cost of capital, the sensitivity of the demand for the output to price changes, and so on) one would expect employers to do one or all of the following when confronted with the new, higher price (from the employer's point of view) of the least skilled labour:

— substitute labour-saving equipment;

— substitute more skilled workers whose wages become *relatively* lower than they were;

— raise output prices and, depending upon demand, thereby reduce output; and

— cease operations.

The efficiency effects, as defined in the last section of Chapter 2, are perverse.

Who benefits and who pays? Clearly, those workers who, after the introduction of the minimum wage, receive the $m-w/hr subsidy are better off, as are more skilled workers generally. Producers (including some workers) of labour-saving equipment, and those producers of goods and services that are less dependent on the least skilled labour also benefit. And so do the consumers whose tastes and preferences run to the types of goods and services produced by the latter. Those who are worse off are, first and foremost, the workers who become virtually unemployable at a wage of $m/hr because their productivity is too low at this wage. Employers are hit who have relied heavily upon such workers and who, for technical reasons, can make few of the substitutions mentioned above. Particularly hard hit among employers are those who face a significant proportion of buyers who are highly sensitive to price increases: consumers who are able to substitute other goods and services less dependent upon "cheap" labour. Restaurants provide a good example. Dishwashers, but not waiters, can be replaced by machines.[9] Many buyers can choose to eat at home if the price of restaurant meals is "too high" so that restaurants can "price themselves out of the market."

The Comprehensive Net Worth of the least skilled individuals (the uneducated, the young, the old, the disadvantaged) in our society is reduced. (Note, this is often the group the minimum wage policy was supposed to have helped.) The same is true for the weakest members of the business community. The converse also holds both with respect to the labour force and the business community.

Looked at from a politician's point of view the minimum wage issue is straightforward.

1. Raising the minimum wage is a clear demonstration of the hero-villain axiom. The many thousands of "little men" are the heroes and the exploiting or "sweating" businessmen are the villains, as the vast majority of voters see the plot.

2. Organized labour that, with a few exceptions, does not encompass the least skilled, by pushing for ever higher minimum wages can appeal to its own members who almost unanimously believe in the plot, *and* simultaneously serve the narrower interests of the membership at the expense, in large part, of the weakest members of the labour force and of the business community.

3. Those who hurt the most, the least skilled members of the labour force (who may well be pushed onto welfare or be truly exploited by those who illicitly hire them) have almost no political voice. They are unable to organize. Small businessmen who are dependent upon unskilled labour services also find it difficult to organize because they are so numerous and geographically dispersed.

5.3 CASE THREE: REGULATIONS THAT RESTRICT ENTRY AND CONFER BARGAINING POWER

Let us now consider two hypothetical regulations simultaneously: the first requires employers to hire all of their workers from among the existing membership of the appropriate industry or craft union—the closed shop universalized. The second precludes employers, by regulation, from bargaining on an industry-wide basis with unions. *These hypothetical regulations are most extreme but serve a heuristic purpose.* Suppose that, as a result, union bargaining power greatly increased, in part because the union could create an artificial scarcity of some kinds of labour by refusing to admit to membership many who were willing and able to work at (or below) the going union bargained rates. Higher wage rates, more overtime at even higher wage

---

[9] Automats and self-serve food establishments can "escape" and hence become more competitive relative to more traditional restaurants.

rates, and richer fringe benefits would result. The pool of unorganized workers would grow and their average compensation would fall.

The distributional consequences are clear. The earnings of union members would rise and so would their consumption outlays and/or their personal saving and/or their investment would pay off with other improvements in the Comprehensive Net Worth of the members. The opposite would occur for non-union workers. Shareholders in firms that employed a preponderance of union labour would sustain capital losses except where the higher labour costs would be passed on entirely in higher prices without offsetting reductions in sales (a price inelastic demand for the firm's output).

In tax/subsidy terms, the union members are given a right to tax their employers and retain the proceeds. To the extent that the employers cannot pass the tax onto buyers or back to suppliers, shareholders sustain a capital loss. Ignoring the backward shifting, the consumers are taxed by the amount of the price increases they face. Non-union workers denied membership in the union are taxed by the difference between the wages they would have obtained in a competitive labour market and the wages they actually earn. Because they have little, if any, bargaining power, by definition, they are unlikely to be able to shift the tax forward to employers who, in effect, are subsidized by the resulting lower wages paid unorganized workers. The taxed workers can only shift the tax backward by paying less for what they buy. This will, to some extent, have the effect of reducing the subsidy to the employers of non-union labour and will squeeze the shareholders of the employers of union labour still more. The union members are subsidized even further by the resulting lower prices for the goods and services they buy.

If, as one might suppose, any attempts to escape the tax by the employers of union labour through the introduction of more capital intensive methods were thwarted by wage increases that offset any potential gains, the rate of capital expenditures in the unionized industries would be permanently reduced. However, because the wages in the non-union sectors also would be permanently lower, the inducement for capital outlays there would be reduced too unless the cost of capital were also reduced commensurately. This would seem to suggest that the long-term consequence would be an overall reduction in the return of personal saving generally. Whether or not this would reduce the *rate* of saving is a moot point. If it did, the rate of growth would fall because of the decline in the growth of fixed assets as well as because of the misallocation of those assets between sectors.

This raises an interesting issue that cannot be explored here. Because of these potentially serious long-term consequences, the effects on the distribution of wealth on an intergenerational basis would be extraordinarily complex. If the union workers who obtained the bargaining power by the hypothetical regulations could grant to their progeny the right to union membership, we would have a new exploiting class in the Marxian sense—organized labour![10]

To be less dramatic, if there were a minimum wage in effect at the same time as the extraordinary bargaining powers were assigned to union members, the more successful the unions were in restricting entry the larger the pool of unorganized workers over time and the higher the unemployment rate of such workers. If these workers were supported by welfare payments financed from income taxes, the union members, the employed non-union members and, to a lesser degree, the shareholders of non-union labour would then be subsidizing the unemployed workers. This would be an indirect method of shifting the tax on non-union members to union members. Whether or not the union members would invest heavily in rule changes to avoid this eventuality can only be a matter of speculation.

The full consequences of the hypothetical regulations we have discussed are difficult to see. But it is not difficult to understand why union members would invest a great deal in obtaining the rule changes we have assumed! Nor, indeed, for other rule changes of a much more modest kind that increase labour's bargaining power.

To illustrate the application of our conceptual framework in approaching the analysis of this kind of a problem, the following observations are in order. Most of what has been said about minimum wage regulations also applies to other kinds of labour regulation. Here we have hypothesized extreme situations to make the point that when a group of individuals obtains sufficient bargaining power to be able to tax the rest of the community, some of the income thus generated can readily be invested in changing the decision-making rules in order to protect and enhance that taxing power. Many members, yet no "free-rider" problem, an identification with the hero symbol (both by the members themselves and many voters), and an income flow that is more than adequate to fund investment in rule changes constitute an extraordinarily potent combination of factors in political structure terms.

To disabuse those who have already consigned us to the fervent "anti-labour" group (in the hope that a few may not have stopped reading long before this!) may we add that the "capitalists" did precisely the same thing when they had the opportunity, as did the land-owners who preceded them. Moreover, one could make a convincing case that the professions are acting this way today.

To drive the point home, if the business community were able to obtain deregulation with respect to labour legislation, the extreme results hypothesized here would, no doubt, be completely reversed. The essence of this "case" could well have been set forth as the business community's demand for deregulation in the field of competition policy.

---

[10] This situation has indeed occurred in some instances, at least in the United States.

5.4 CASE FOUR: AGRICULTURAL PRODUCTION QUOTAS

Consider a particular agricultural product X the demand for which is price inelastic (e.g., the greater the supply, the lower the price *and* the lower the net revenues of producers). With low prices, producers' incomes are low so they increase output to increase their incomes but, because they all do the same thing at the same time, the result is even lower farm income from the production of X. One possible "answer" is the introduction of a regulation assigning each producer a seeded acreage quota for the coming year equal to, say, 50 per cent of the average acreage seeded over the preceeding five years. To keep the matter simple, suppose that the acreage quotas are *not* marketable except as a right attached to the transfer (sale) of the land itself. Suppose further that there is a ban on imports.

One might expect as a consequence a dramatic increase in the price of commodity X and an even larger increase in the earnings of its producers. This permits an increase in their consumption and/or an increase over time in their rate of capital accumulation and/or greater investment for the purpose of increasing their CNWs in other ways. Moreover, these farmers will now be able to sell their quota-carrying acres for a greatly enhanced price so that their wealth increases immediately. Because we can assume that the consumption of product X is a trivial part of the producer's own consumption expenditures, the quota regulation is, to all intents and purposes, a pure gain to them both in income and wealth terms.

The situation faced by consumers is the opposite: the higher price of X means higher non-discretionary consumption outlays.[11] The result is a reduction in their discretionary consumption and/or personal saving and/or investment.

Looked at as a tax/subsidy scheme, the quota system is approximately equivalent at the time that it is announced as a capital grant to *former* producers of X financed by government borrowings which are repaid by a special sales tax on commodity X, with all the consequences that entails. However, the tax would linger on, unless the quotas were withdrawn, in perpetuity. The distribution effects are enormously important to the producers of commodity X, however, and not of great significance to most others because their losses are spread so widely and hence thinly. However, once again, those with the lowest incomes, who face increased maintenance expenses, suffer a significant drop in their CNWs. The once poor producers of commodity X have gained but, in the process, the poorest urban workers have probably suffered the greatest loss in relative terms for they are likely to be the largest consumers of X.

---

[11] An inelastic demand for an agricultural product would suggest that it is a "necessity."

The potential forces at work are hardly mysterious. Rural votes carry more weight than urban votes because of the disproportionalities in the number of constituents per riding. The elected rural constituency politicians represent interests that are much more homogeneous than do those representing urban ridings. Thus, they can avoid most of the conflict resolution problems of the latter. Their representatives can speak with assurance on one issue and enter coalitions that cross party lines. In a sense, this greatly reduces the farmers' "free-rider" organizational problem from the outset. However, when it comes to particular agricultural commodities, the "free-rider" problem emerges if the commodity is not produced in a relatively specialized geographic area.

The sanctity of the family farm, the gnarled hands, the weather-beaten face, the lonely dirt road provide all the symbols behind which some extremely affluent entrepreneurs (net worth expressed in any sense!) are able to assist the politicians in imposing the vote-getting regulations required to enhance their net worth. That the poorer farmers—the reality from which the symbols were drawn—benefit much less than the wealthy farmers from such regulations hardly needs to be said.

What we wish to suggest is that agriculture has had to face, and may still have to face, some unprecedented problems of adjustment to a series of rapid, dramatic changes that have caused a great deal of suffering for marginal farmers. That they have needed some help and still need it is not in question here. Rather we wish simply to suggest that the policies adopted have mercifully slowed the adjustment process but, unfortunately, have protracted it. And, as is so often the way, those who least needed the help gained the most and those who could least share the burden had their burdens increased ("them that has gets, while them that hasn't, doesn't . . . .").

5.5 CASE FIVE: ENVIRONMENTAL REGULATIONS

Some of the regulations we have discussed heretofore would bestow a large benefit on a few at a cost that is allocated so broadly that it is small to those individuals who bear it. Environmental regulations are just the opposite. To illustrate, consider the hypothetical case of a corporation considering an investment in a pulp mill before environmental regulations with respect to effluent standards are contemplated, much less introduced. The corporation, in competitive bidding we will suppose, acquires timber rights in perpetuity on a large tract of Crown land. In making its successful (the highest) bid the corporation calculated what it could afford to pay for the timber, given the expected market for pulp and the optimal current technology and expected prices of all inputs, in order to make a slightly greater than normal profit with good luck and good management. Obviously, no allowance is made for the cost of the capital equipment needed to keep the effluent above some standard. The mill is built, workers are employed, and the shareholders earn a very respectable return on their investment. But there is only a small ''rent'' element in the corporation's profits—most rent having been secured by the government (taxpayers) in the realized auction price of the timber rights.

Suppose, however, the effluent has extremely adverse downstream consequences that mean, among other things, that owners downstream suffer a loss in the value of their real property. The downstream property owners who are numerous but not multitudinous have lost and the other taxpayers who are much more numerous have gained. (At least, in the limited sense that the timber they owned collectively is now indirectly being used, after being converted into cash, to finance new public facilities elsewhere, one might suppose.) Let us assume that the downstream property owners complain and the government refuses to compensate them. Instead, let us further assume that it passes a regulation establishing stringent effluent standards. To comply would entail a capital outlay by the corporation of $X million. These costs are so great that the firm's profits, after paying the interest costs incurred to finance the equipment, fall precipitously. As a result, the shareholders sustain a capital loss as the value of the corporation's shares tumble. The property owners (other than those poor souls who sold in the interval) are made whole as market values are gradually restored as water quality returns to its previous level. Under this scenario, the shareholders are, in effect, hit by a capital levy in the form of the effluent regulations.

As far as the allocation effects are concerned, we assume that there is a world competitive market price of pulp at any point in time, and that the output of a particular mill can have no impact on it. Had the effluent standards been in effect prior to the auction of the timber rights, the prices bid for timber rights would have been substantially lower and the mill probably would have been proceeded with on that basis—unless pulp production were not profitable with zero-priced timber rights! Had the government raised less from the lease of the rights, it is difficult to say whether or not the public facilities they financed would have been financed in some other way—that would, in turn, have distributional-allocative effects.

The loss to the downstream real property holders (temporary as it turns out under our example) would change their consumption patterns as a consequence, but these hardly seem of great moment. The wealth effects are the heart of the matter.

There are, of course, a multitude of alternative scenarios. But the one that makes the most important point from our perspective is the situation, which is not uncommon, where the losers number in the millions. Such a necessarily amorphous group, the members of which having nothing much in common except their geographic location, finds it extraordinarily difficult to find a vehicle for organizing themselves to invest in putting pressure on governments for stringent effluent regulations and their enforcement (or compensation).[12]

To consider the situation from a slightly different perspective, at the outset the Crown timber rights, until they are sold or leased, represent a marketable asset held by the taxpayers collectively. These taxpayers also may think of the water of a given quality as a non-exclusive right (Item L(A)(2)) they hold, although it is of greater purport in the "portfolios" of those in the immediate vicinity of a particular river or lake or ocean. The value of the latter right cannot be valued in money terms except most arbitrarily. Under the worst of all possible scenarios, and it is not far from being the situation in some instances in the past, the timber rights are literally given to a group of shareholders and there are no effluent regulations to prevent "the corporation" from polluting the water. That is to say, the costs of the reduction in water quality are not borne by the shareholders *or* the buyers of the output. Suppose that the output is exported and sold at world prices that reflect *not* the situation just described but rather the auctioned sale of timber rights and high effluent standards in other countries. Assume further that the domestic workers engaged in production of the exported product, who otherwise would not have been employed in the pulp mill had the same timber-water cost situation prevailed domestically as elsewhere, would have found employment in other industries. Under these circumstances the shareholders who obtain the timber rights obtain at one stroke, so to speak, a capital grant (increase in their marketable assets in their CNWs) that is essentially a capitalization of the once collectively held marketable assets (timber) and the non-exclusive right to unpolluted water. The voters thereby suffer a decline in their CNWs on all counts, for even the domestic price of pulp is not reduced! Foreigners, as buyers, gain nothing either. But they certainly do if they are the shareholders who obtain the timber rights at gift prices. In essence, under these conditions, they have been given two public assets for their own benefit. Some great fortunes, both domestic and foreign, have been made in precisely this way.

Our example, therefore, illustrates not only the effects of environmental regulations but also the great significance of regulations governing the terms on which the alienation of Crown lands and natural resources occurs. If natural resource rights are allocated "by regulation" it is painfully obvious that a large investment in obtaining a favourable "ruling" can, to say the least, be well warranted!

In the case hypothesized, in which timber rights were fairly auctioned, those taxpayers who enjoy the benefits of the facilities financed by the proceeds gain (higher CNWs) at the expense of downstream taxpayers who

---

[12] The valuation problems involved in compensation are horrendous. Witness those encountered with respect to land expropriation for the ill-considered Pickering airport.

suffer a capital loss as a result of the decline in water quality. Shareholders and workers may gain a little if their returns and wages are slightly higher than they otherwise would have been. The imposition of the effluent standards imposes a substantial capital loss of the shareholders and the workers are little affected if the mill continues to operate. Thus, as we have said, the shareholders, in the second round, in effect, suffer a capital levy to finance the facilities enjoyed by others.

It is not immediately obvious that the failure to have effluent standards in the first instance resulted in an inefficient use of resources if a conscious decision was made to "deplete" a river through pollution. After all, mining also depletes minerals. It should be remembered that, bearing all the costs and benefits in mind, the optimal level of pollution is not zero. What seems to have happened in fact is that the value assigned to water of high quality has risen as it has become more scarce, with the result that the "real" decision now seems a "mistake." The same, of course, can occur, in either direction, with respect to the depletion of any resource. Where the pollution of a stream is irreversible the river has essentially become a non-renewable resource and, like the case of minerals, "errors" are irreversible.

Looked at from the "mode of government intervention" (after the deterioration in water quality) point of view, as we stated earlier, probably the most efficient way to control effluent is through the sale of "pollution rights"—the volume of rights corresponding to the self-renewing capacity of the river. However, as is also indicated by our "sacred nature of human life axiom", it is virtually impossible for a politician to auction off, to the highest bidder ("the villainous rich"), the right to pollute the water and thereby endanger public health—as it will be claimed even though falsely perhaps.

Compensation of downstream losers raises horrendous valuation problems. Each will claim that they value their property more highly than any reasonable assessment of its fair market value.

In our example we have supposed that the effluent standards are effectively enforced to the serious detriment of the shareholders. One might suppose, however, that in reality the situation will not be so clear cut. The *announcement* of the effluent standards will satisfy some (at least temporarily). However, if they are not effectively enforced the politician can, in a sense, leave the shareholder's whole without losing too many votes. As the downstream losers become aware that the effluent standards are not being enforced, the battle will become protracted and expensive. All but the most hardy supporters of collective rights will give up. The government of the day buys time, day by day.

5.6 CASE SIX: HEALTH, SAFETY, DISCLOSURE AND "TRUTH IN ADVERTISING" REGULATIONS

These regulations and rulings pose some unique analytic problems because of the probabilistic nature of the situation. First of all, there is the question of the uncertainty concerning whether or not a particular new product creates potential health and safety hazards. If such hazards do in fact exist, what is the probability that the untoward consequences will occur: more than one in a billion? More than one in a million? More than one in a thousand? More than one in a hundred? More than one in ten? Could it be one in one? What is the severity of the adverse consequences likely to be? Who will bear those consequences? What would be the benefits provided by the new product in those instances where the adverse consequences did not occur? Who would obtain them?

To all of these questions another has to be added. Are we speaking of a hazard that should not be recognized by a reasonably informed and reasonably prudent man? Or should we think of the hazard to an uninformed and/or imprudent man? Do we have to be concerned about only the former? After all, even (especially?) a kitchen stove is a hazard to some.

These both interesting and difficult questions cannot be explored here. Suffice it to say that at the one extreme one can imagine unscrupulous individuals offering products on the market that, purchased by ignorant or imprudent people, will bestow little *tangible* benefits on them, but will impose a substantial risk of a cost, including the user's life itself. This is tantamount to robbery *and* murder on a Russian roulette basis. At the other extreme, to require by regulation that each new product undergo hundreds of thousands of tests so that the probability of an untoward eventuality occurring, even in the hands of an ignorant *and* imprudent person, no more than once in a billion times of use would mean that virtually no new products could be introduced. The cost of testing would mean that to recover that investment alone would require astronomic prices for the product that was finally marketed. Products that were infinitely safe would be infinitely priced, hence unavailable to all but the very rich. Under sufficiently stringent regulatory standards it would not have been acceptable for the caveman inventor to barter that strange new product we now call a wheel for a sharpened stick. All products, old and new, inescapably pose *some* risks.

The rate of technical change is now so rapid in some fields and the consequences of new products and production methods so complex and, in some instances, so adverse (irreversible), that it is extraordinarily difficult to see any ready answer other than some regulations governing the introduction of new products. ''The reasonable man'' cannot be expected to anticipate the potential hazards involved.

Although hardly a complete ''answer'' it would seem that the most sensible course would be the following.

a) Impose stringent information *disclosure* regulations for new products and hazardous ''old'' products.

b) Where there are no external risks (e.g., damages to others) involved by the use of a product, and the information is comprehensible to the "reasonable man," then the decision to use the product should be left in his hands.

c) Where the information requires interpretation by those with specialized knowledge (e.g., medical knowledge), then potentially hazardous products should be available only on prescription, or on passing certain tests (e.g., extension of the automobile, pilots and firearms licensing procedures).

Analytically, what is involved in prior testing (or the equivalent) is the imposition of a tax on new products that *must* eventually be passed on in higher product prices for the products eventually marketed if innovation is not to cease. It is simultaneously a subsidy of unknowable size to those who, on a probabilistic basis, otherwise would have borne the burden of the hazard. Obviously, a tax/subsidy system is not a feasible alternative to regulations in this case. The *form* of the regulation is the issue.

Minimizing health and safety hazards through regulations is not itself without hazard, it must be remembered. Among the hazards are those included below.

— Benefits are denied to those who would gain from the introduction of new products/services. A terminal cancer patient, having tried "everything," has little to lose by taking a chance with a new, untested product if he so desires.

— Excluding or delaying the introduction of new products protects the producers of existing products. It is quite conceivable that some of the products currently being sold could not pass the same tests as are applied to new products. Here we have some important income/ wealth distributional effects.

— Rulings under regulations are almost bound to be biased. The approval of a product that causes unanticipated damages, however rare, will subject the regulator to intense, after the fact, criticism. The rejection by the regulator of a product that could have provided benefits is unlikely to be attacked with the same vigour.

Another partial "solution" would be to require bonding of the suppliers of new products so that compensation, if needed, could, in fact, be paid. The present barriers to class action could be lowered.

The improvement in general education levels undoubtedly increased the demand for more consumer product information. Because the costs of obtaining the relevant information are so large for the potential individual consumer and so trivial when spread over all potential consumers, (particularly when it is often already in the hands of the producers!), the collective advantages of disclosure regulations are enormous. Here a lump sum tax is imposed on the producers (particularly purveyors of brand-name foods and drugs involving heretofore unknown ingredients) and a significant subsidy (in opportunity cost terms) is given to potential buyers. Here too, a tax on non-disclosure is not a feasible alternative to standards regulation.

Leaving aside hazardous goods, greater disclosure should improve the efficiency of the market process and remove some of the rents generated by brand names (e.g., increase competition).

All in all, regulations *of the appropriate type*, in the matters under consideration in this case, increase the CNWs of the many at the expense of the few *and* contribute to the efficient allocation of resources. However, there would seem to be an unfortunate tendency to adopt prohibitions rather than to seek ways and means to provide adequate consumer information, advice, class action opportunities, lower legal costs for small actions, and bonding. The possibilities of irreversible collective damages and of external risks pose the most serious and inescapable problems.

Because the benefits flowing from regulations in this case are so widespread and the costs so narrowly distributed, the "free-rider" problem is extremely serious in organizing pressure for appropriate regulation *and* ensuring its enforcement. The potential losers can spend large amounts to fight against effective regulation while the vast majority of potential winners are reluctant to make a significant investment.

From the political point of view, weak regulations weakly enforced have the virtue of appearing to be on the side of the angels while quietly protecting the devils. Protracted and expensive proceedings provide an effective barrier to effective regulation. This issue is discussed in the next chapter.

5.7 CASE SEVEN: PATERNALISTIC REGULATION

Little can be said that is not obvious about regulations that purport to protect people from themselves. Regulations concerning prostitution, sexual "deviance," obscenity, alcohol, tabacco, "mood" affecting drugs generally, and gambling, constitute, in the minds of some, important bulwarks against the forces of evil. They maintain a "decent" social environment, the contemplation of which is a source of satisfaction to some individuals (a non-exclusive right!), even though some of those who derive this satisfaction may surreptitiously break the law themselves. They suffer when their sensibilities are openly offended. One is inclined to be either cynical about the hypocrisy involved or indignant about the infringement on individual freedom of choice entailed. However, it must be admitted that a community's view of itself is not a trivial matter, as witnessed by the great interest in intercity, interregional and international athletic and other competitions. One can imagine the inward joy some may feel in boasting (with any luck only to themselves!) of the superior virtue of their community relative to others they may visit. If only they could confine their attention to intercommunity competitive sports. In any event, community pride is at stake and it commands prices—those mentioned above.

There are two other arguments often advanced in favour of paternalistic regulation. The first is certainly paternalistic in the true meaning of that term.

It is claimed by some that the *open* presence of the "evils" listed above can exert a deleterious influence, by demonstration, on the young and impressionable. This can lead to: "If they can do it, so can I" or "That seems like an easy way to make a few bucks" or . . .

The second argument is much more pragmatic. Some of the "evils" can cause serious health problems such as alcoholism, drug addiction, veneral disease, lung cancer, and so on. In a society that cannot allow people to die in the streets in significant numbers, the costs of maintaining and caring for the wrongdoers are ultimately shifted to the prudent taxpayers in the form of bills for hostels, hospital beds and welfare payments. Therefore, public virtue can be viewed as a means of protecting the pockets, not the morals, of the prudent citizenry.

Regulations prohibiting or controlling any of the items mentioned above have substantial wealth redistributional effects that can be highly advantageous for those who are willing to run the risk and break the law by offering for sale that which is prohibited. Illicit goods and services command high prices. The semi-voluntary victims of this "extortion" bear the tax as does the community that pays the enforcement officers to stop the trade. Corrupt politicians and enforcement officers share in the proceeds of the unintended tax on the illicit trade through the acceptance of bribes. Leaving aside the latter, for one or all of the reasons advanced above, the CNWs of the majority are increased slightly, those who pay the extortion suffer significant declines in their CNWs, and those engaged in the illicit trades enjoy bounteous increases in their CNWs.

From a vote maximization point of view, paternalistic regulations are a clear instance of the heroes-villain axiom. Those in favour of "vice" find it difficult to organize. However, as the community has become less homogeneous, more impersonal and less attached to formal religion, and better educated, it has perhaps become more tolerant. Consequently, the "gay liberation" movement and the soft drug liberalization movement are political forces to be reckoned with in some localities. Whether tolerance will recede with affluence remains to be seen.

It is undoubtedly true that the "sacred nature of human life" axiom is involved in the case of paternalistic regulation. And, as indicated earlier, to a considerable extent the politician is put in the position by the competition for votes of playing the cosmetician. Appearances are his reality.

REFERENCES

Averch, Harvey and Leland Johnson (1962) "Behaviour of a Firm Under Regulatory Constraint" *American Economic Review* 52: 1052-69.

Posner, Richard A. (1971) "Taxation by Regulation" *Bell Journal of Economics and Management Science* 2: 22-50.

Posner, R. (1975) "The Social Costs of Monopoly and Regulation" *Journal of Political Economy* 83: 807-27.

Chapter Six

Regulatory Agencies: The Independence-Accountability Issue

We have previously discussed some of the pressures that push or pull ministries to intervene in the economy. (The economic stabilization question has, of course, not been considered in this paper.) We have also commented upon some of the reasons ministries select, perhaps as the least of the evils, regulation as the mode of intervention. In this chapter we wish to consider a crucial issue related to the basis of that regulatory intervention when statutory agencies are the chosen instrument.

The question addressed here is, in our view, of the greatest significance for the Canadian political system. The existing situation is, also in our view, deplorable. The question of the degree of independence of so-called "quasi-judicial" agencies is certainly not the only issue in the structure of the regulatory process, but it seems to us to overshadow all others at this time.

The heart of the matter is the situs of statutory authority, and the powers of ministers individually or collectively to override the decisions of statutory agencies with regulatory authority. This ministerial "override" power is usually dignified by the phrase "the right of appeal to the Minister or the Governor in Council." The non-ministerial rights of appeal now provided with respect to regulation are complex and vary widely from statute to statute. A brief summary of them is provided in Appendix C[1] and they are not pursued in this chapter. Because it is so inextricably related to representation before regulatory bodies, we also briefly consider in this chapter some aspects of the financing of "public interest" groups. To keep the terminology uncluttered, we will discard the phrase "right to appeal to the Minister . . . ." and substitute the term "ministerial override."

To pursue the subject of this chapter in any meaningful fashion, a few vital distinctions must be made concerning the alternative ways in which

---

[1] In recent years, the *Federal Court Act* and the *Statutory Instruments Act* have generally strengthened rights of appeal, fortunately (see Appendix C). One significant area as yet remains untouched and untouchable—equally unfortunately: the decisions made by a public servant pursuant to a statute granting regulatory authority to a minister that are deemed to be of an administrative nature: airworthiness, drug safety and efficiency, health of animals, etc. This issue needs to be tackled. It is, in many ways, the bailiwick of an "ombudsman."

regulatory authority can be vested and some of the constraints on that authority other than the rights of appeal in the usual (non-ministerial) sense. The principal alternatives are roughly as follows:

The Vesting of Statutory Authority:

1) Governor in Council (i.e., the Cabinet)
2) Minister
    a) upon the advice of statutory agency
    b) upon the advice of designated officials
3) Agency
    a) upon the approval of the Governor in Council
    b) upon the approval of the minister
    **c) under statutory authority *qualified by* Governor in Council or ministerial directives as provided for by statute
    **d) under statutory authority
4) Deputy minister
    a) upon the approval of the minister
    *b) under delegated authority from the minister
5) Officials designated by the deputy minister
    a) upon the approval of the deputy minister
    *b) under delegated authority from the deputy minister

It is immediately apparent that only those regulations and rulings issued under the categories marked by a double asterisk have any semblence of "independence" from ministerial discretion and those marked by a single asterisk are only "independent" to the extent that the minister chooses not to intervene and can do so behind the scenes at any time and on any basis he should choose. These single asterisk situations are not discussed here.

The current legal-political debate centres primarily around the situation 3(c) and 3(d)—the double asterisk situations. What the foregoing list does not show is that the regulations and rulings issued under these kinds of authorities are now subject to *after the event* Governor in Council (Cabinet) intervention that may take a variety of forms depending upon the wording in the particular statute: veto, hold, amend, . . . The differences among the words actually contained in the particular statutes are of uncertain significance. The reality is that the Cabinet can and does impose *its* decision of choice on a wide range of regulatory issues entrusted to regulatory bodies with statutory authority.

One can argue, as has Hudson Janisch (forthcoming), that some of the words used in the various statutes giving override power to the Cabinet are active while some are passive, and that some are positive powers while others are negative powers. It is also true that the Cabinet cannot override some kinds of decisions. Generally speaking, it cannot reverse a negative regulatory decision (e.g., a decision to reject a licence application or, if it were to occur, revoke a licence). Certainly it cannot, in its overrides, go beyond the powers conferred by Parliament. Nevertheless, the reality is that it is not difficult for a minister to conjure up a supplicant and thereby convert the passive to the active. And one might suspect that there are ways and means of letting it be known that a particular negative decision would not be forgotten when, at some later date on a different issue, a positive Cabinet action might be required. In short, as every politician knows, it is not the isolated event, but the balance of rolling compromises that is of importance. In this sense, the precise words used in a statute tend to lose their meaning. Those who have the wit to know where ultimate power lies can learn to anticipate punishment and thus act so as to not invoke it.

Situation 3(c) is relatively new. Provision was made in the *Broadcasting Act* of 1967 for the Governor in Council to have the authority to issue *directions* to the regulatory authority (now the CRTC) on some limited aspects of broadcasting (foreign ownership primarily) coming within its purview. This authority was subsequently exercised and two directions were issued. Of greater significance are provisions contained in Bill C-14, the *Nuclear Control and Administration Act*, that, if passed, would replace the *Atomic Energy Control Act*; Bill C-33, *An Act to Amend the National Transportation Act;* and Bill C-24, the *Telecommunications Act* (which would replace the *Broadcasting Act*, the *Radio Act*, the *Telegraphs Act*, and the *CRTC Act*). If these Bills were passed as tabled, the Cabinet would, to all intents and purposes, have the authority to issue directives on any significant matter over which the regulatory authority had jurisdiction.

It is important to bear in mind that the government, in seeking parliamentary approval for authority to issue directives, is not proposing that this authority be granted in lieu of its current "override" authority but in addition to it. Given that the Cabinet already has all the power it could possibly require to impose the decisions it deems "appropriate," what conceivably would be gained by the ministry should the authority to issue directives to statutory agencies be granted? Or more fundamentally, what are the pros and cons of conferring the Cabinet override power at all? This is the "independent regulatory authority" issue to which we have already alluded. Let us explore that question first and then return to the directives issue.

6.1 INDEPENDENT REGULATORY AGENCY VS. MINISTERIAL RESPONSIBILITY

The terms "independence" and "responsibility" are hardly normatively neutral in most of our minds. The first conjures up visions of impartial justice (where even the word justice is loaded!) as contrasted with capricious and/or malevolent and/or servile arbitrariness. The second connotes thoughtful and/or conscientious and/or balanced behaviour as contrasted with behaviour that is careless or wilful or unmindful of the consequences— particularly the adverse effects on others. All those in favour of the antonyms of independence and responsible regulatory decisions please stand up!

Although put in facetious terms here, the debate between those who espouse the two approaches to regulation is, of course, not light-hearted and certainly raises some extremely significant issues.

In many respects, considering the independence-responsibility debate allows us to highlight one of the points in the earlier chapters. That point is neither more nor less than that the existing Canadian political system, in a multitude of ways, quietly serves many, often competing, special interest groups remarkably well without any one individual or group deliberately setting out to achieve that end, either now or in the past. Whether the Canadian situation is worse or better in this respect than the most obvious alternatives—the American and British systems—we are not prepared to say. Our argument is that the Canadian system could be better than it is and that some changes in present regulatory process would constitute such an improvement. A set of proposals to this end are advanced at the end of the chapter.[2]

Those who advance the criticism in respect to the Cabinet override on the regulatory decisions of statutory agencies seem to have in mind, though not always explicitly stated, the American regulatory model as the ideal. As Hudson Janisch (1978) has pointed out from a legal point of view, and as confirmed by American economist Paul MacAvoy (1978), the American regulatory system is currently undergoing some remarkable changes both with respect to the scope and depth of regulation (the general pressure for deregulation) *and* with respect to increasing pressure for greater accountability on the part of the so-called independent regulatory agencies. Much of the enthusiasm in Canada for greater regulatory independence seems to reflect a desire to see Canada emulate what the American system once was rather than what it is becoming. Leaving aside the regulation-deregulation aspects of the changes in the United States, informal commentators on the American system have been highly critical of the fact that appointed officials have had the authority to make decisions that, these critics were convinced, *should* be made by elected representatives accountable to the voters. Those who claimed that these independent regulatory agencies were often (always?) captured by those they regulated (Bernstein, 1955; Stigler, 1975), in essence were arguing that it was greatly in the interest of some groups to be regulated because they could obtain advantages (avoid disadvantages) from appointed regulators that the Congress would have rejected had the decisions been in its hands. Be that as it may, as we have previously stated, the notion of the "capture" of a regulatory agency in Canada is surely inappropriate, given the Cabinet's authority to override most of the crucial decisions of these agencies. What is to be gained by "capturing" a regulatory agency when the

---

[2] It is our suspicion that the Canadian parliamentary system lacks some of the vital accountability features of the British model. This needs explanation.

resulting favourable decision can be overturned by ministers who can choose not to acquiesce in the capture? Would it not make more sense for the regulatee to seek to "capture," one way or another, the "sympathy" of a few ministers? Better still, why not proceed on both fronts simultaneously? The statutory regulatory agencies frequently are classified as quasi-judicial agencies. Some of the advocates of greater independence read this as now being "QUASI-Judicial" and demand that they be made "Quasi-JUDICIAL." Their model is, in other words, the ideal judicial system with all the virtues that one associates with its best manifestations. They want not only natural justice but the formal safeguards of due process and, more importantly, decisions based on explicit publicly available rules (e.g., the equivalent of statutory rules) and firmly based on converging precedents in order that the regulators not be in the position where they *make* the "law" but rather *apply* the existing "law" to the particular case, in as objective a manner as intelligent, well-trained, well-intended human beings are capable. While not wishing to denigrate the judicial system in any way, the "apply the law not make the law" distinction is not entirely the way it is. Those who sit on the bench were not hatched from eggs and brought up in incubators in the basement of the court house. Moreover, the law is not always clear-cut, to say the least, and reasonable men can reach different conclusions about the facts in a case, again to say the least. A degree of judicial discretion (particularly in certain aspects of the law) is inescapable and, as is well known, by precedent, new law is made. However, if one looks at the situation as a difference of degree rather than of kind, as we do, the degree of discretion legitimately exercised within the judicial system is certainly much less than in the ministerial system. Furthermore, and of equal or greater importance, the tenured appointments to the bench, as contrasted with the electoral uncertainties facing ministers, undoubtedly make an enormous difference to the decisions reached by the incumbents of the two kinds of offices. Another important distinction has been that between the political and judicial systems. Putting aside constitutional questions, ministers, *with the approval of Parliament*, can override judicial decisions by statute. The converse does not hold, of course. Except on constitutional questions, where civil rights based in common law are considered part of the Constitution, the courts do not have the authority to override statutes. In essence, the independence advocates who have the judicial model in mind seek, *in effect*:

(a) regulatory *statutes* that set forth the rules the agency is to follow in reaching its decisions with the clear understanding that that which the rules do not preclude defines the *intended* range of discretion;

(b) that should the ministers decide that they wish to change the resulting decisions they should table a bill amending the statute and thus only be permitted to override a regulatory decision retroactively *with the approval of Parliament*; and

(c) that such a statutory change would, unless explicitly restricted (which of course .would be debated in the House), constitute a "permanent" change in the range of discretion within which the agency would henceforth reach its decisions.

In essence, adoption of this approach, or some variant of it, would constitute a major reduction in the ministerial prerogative *vis-à-vis* Parliament. It might be likened to the great restrictions placed on the royal prerogative that resulted, in considerable measure, from Sir Edward Coke's influence, through his opinions, decisions, and writings in the reign of James I.[3]

Those who push for responsible regulation do not want the inverse of the version of independence of the judicial variety just sketched. Rather they decry, and rightly so, the present situation where ministers can, at their convenience, pretend that the decisions of the statutory regulatory body are "independent" and thereby escape (minimize) the displeasure of the voters, when such decisions are unpopular. Although the ministerial override is often ready and waiting, a fact that makes the independence of statutory agencies largely mythical, ministers have been known to express deep anguish that although their hearts are firmly in the right place their hands are not: their hands are firmly tied. Canada has a system of discretionary accountability.

In Britain, regulatory agencies, to a much greater extent than in Canada, report (most frequently on an advisory basis) *to* particular ministers and hence to Parliament and not *through* ministers to Parliament. It is important to note that in Britain, decisions carrying Cabinet approval (Orders-in-Council) are much less common than in Canada. To that extent, ministers in Britain are, therefore, more accountable to Parliament, and hence the electorate, for regulatory decisions in a way that can be readily circumvented in Canada. Those in favour of greater ministerial accountability desire to see the Canadian system move closer to the British in this respect. Perhaps, indeed, they would want Canada to go even further than the British in ensuring ministerial accountability.

The adoption of such an approach would have a great deal to commend it. Three observations are in order, however.

(1) It would be essential that the advice or recommendations emanating from statutory regulatory bodies and submitted to particular ministers be made public. If confidentiality were to prevail, these agencies would, in essence, be indistinguishable from traditional government departments.

(2) The volume of regulatory decisions is so large relative to the capacity of opposition members or the media to evaluate them critically that one would be surprised if the level of public awareness were greatly increased *except in as much as the information that a minister rejected the advice*

---

[3] "The King hath no prerogative but that which the law of the land allows him." The Case of Proclamations, 12, Rep. 74, as quoted in Birkenhead (1926, p. 39).

offered or had decided to accept a controversial recommendation would signal the existence of an issue worth pursuing. This is not an insignificant exception!

(3) Voters choose among the candidates of political parties. To the extent that votes are cast for competing political parties rather than for the particular candidates as individuals, they are choosing among the alternative *bundles* of the past decisions and promised decisions that each party places before the electorate. The extent to which increasing ministerial accountability in the manner just indicated would alter electoral outcomes is a moot point. Nevertheless, to assert that the electorate would ignore the additional information or be unaffected by it, or that regulatory decisions would not be significantly altered thereby, or that ministerial involvement might be misinterpreted, are completely and utterly unacceptable. They are at best paternalistic, and hence patronizing. At worst they are frighteningly authoritarian.

Ironically, those urging greater independence along the lines we have sketched above (the judicial version), and those urging greater ministerial accountability (the "British" version) are both putting forward sets of proposals either of which, if adopted, would be substantially superior to the existing situation.

6.2 THE PROS AND CONS OF ISSUING MINISTERIAL DIREC-TIONS TO STATUTORY REGULATORY AGENCIES

From the perspective of the previous section the reader can no doubt anticipate the purport of this one.

From the ministry's point of view:

Pros:
(a) Narrow the range of discretion within which statutory regulatory agencies can make decisions. This may reduce the frequency with which Governor in Council overrides have to be invoked that can be embarrassing.
(b) No parliamentary approval is required for stated "policy" statements embodied in "directives."
(c) The continuance of the ministerial override authority means it would be unnecessary to declare government "policy" when it is expedient to remain silent in order to avoid controversy.
(d) Provincial governments could still be accommodated through the overrides, thus avoiding the extreme annoyance of provincial governments, forced to intervene before federal regulatory agencies on the same basis as private organizations.

Cons:

(a) Why stir up *any* sleeping dogs? These include the dog of regulatory independence and the dog of explicit policy on all matters falling within the purview of the statutory agencies.

From the point of view of interest groups:

Sophisticated and well-financed interest groups are not likely to take ministerial directions seriously. Anything the ministerial directions are likely to state will already be well known to them one way or another—such as past ministerial overrides. If anything, they will strengthen their previous efforts to obtain the support of a few ministers who might affect the content or the directives or influence the Governor in Council overrides.

Less-informed and less well-organized interest groups may be delighted by the clarification of the government's policy stance (if it is favourable to them) or have an explicit target to attack. The latter groups will face the problem that the directions may undercut the basis for their interventions, with the result that they will not be heard in these forums at all.

From the point of view of the appointed members of statutory agencies:

One would expect a wide range of reactions. Some will be relieved that an impossibly wide range of direction has been narrowed to more manageable proportions. Those with delusions of grandeur will consider the ministerial directions as an unwarranted reduction in their authority.

From the point of view of the opposition parties:

One might expect that the directions would not provide them with a basis for criticism on their content because they will be carefully worded to be platitudinous (obvious) or obscure. *The fundamental point that, if the government has now decided to make policies explicit, they should be embodied in bills to amend the relevant statutes, is unlikely to be newsworthy.*

From the point of view of the media:

The directions by and large will appear to them not to be newsworthy because the exciting stories will lie in what is *not* included in the direction(s)—a more abstruse topic that can only be addressed after a great investment of time and effort on their part.

A balanced assessment of the ministerial directions issue is almost impossible because what constitutes "balance" hinges almost entirely upon the position of the photographer and the camera angle, lens opening, and the shutter speed he selects. From either the "independence" perspective or from the "accountability" perspective, as discussed in the last section, the pursuit of statutory agencies *without reducing in any way the current ministerial override prerogative*, approaches, if it does not reach, the point of being scandalous. Its adoption would extend ministerial prerogatives, not curtail them, although those prerogatives are inordinately wide-ranging at the present time.

From another perspective, the expedient in the past, as reflected in the attempt to slough off responsibility through the creation of seemingly "independent" agencies with inordinately vague terms of reference, may visit costs on the present. The authority conferred on the National Energy Board is a case in point. In the past the energy issues were of enormous private interest significance but were, rightly or wrongly, not seen as of great public consequence. Then came the OPEC-induced oil crisis. What were once viewed as narrow, technical-special, interest group interests became instantaneously and, of course, unexpectedly, of national interest. Although the applications to the Board for export licences may take the same form and the decisions may be based on the same considerations, the consequences of the decisions are perceived universally to be of an entirely different order of significance. Because the basis for granting export permits is, as a matter of "policy," dependent upon the NEB's estimates of the extent of the existing stock, these estimates are, of necessity, highly speculative. To allow the NEB to continue on a "business as usual" basis is, to say the least, anomalous. It is like setting up an "independent" municipal Public Health Commission to direct and control the health department in its day-to-day operations only to find that the Commission alone can decide whether or not unprecedented steps should be taken when hundreds of citizens start dropping dead in the streets. For the Municipal Council to intervene, contrary to the advice of the Commission's expert opinion, poses some peculiar problems. However, if the Council finds the Commission's response inadequate in some sense, because it adopts a different view as to what is most important and what is less important in terms of the risks to be taken, should the Council sit idly by while the Commission's expert knowledge, inextricably interwoven with the inherently subjective judgments of the members, prevails?

This analogy presents the Municipal Council's apparent dilemma in such stark and simple-minded terms in order to make a point. The fact that it was expedient yet not unreasonable to create an independent Commission in the past does not excuse the Municipal Council from responsibility to intervene if it perceives that the Commission's decisions have a significant non-technical judgment element on a matter of pressing community concern. However, assuming a snap decision within the hour is not necessary, it would be irresponsible to ignore *technical* advice and superimpose uninformed political judgments. What would seem to be called for is that (hypothetical) Council require the Commission to provide, under the special circumstances, not a decision but rather a *set of alternatives* for Council decision, based on the best technical advice that the Commission can muster and including the

Commission's assessment of their relative merits with stated reasons. In the absence of unforeseen circumstances, *as so deemed by the Council*, the Council should abide by the decisions of the Commission if they are within the range of authority accorded to the Commission in the terms of reference approved by the *Council* as a whole in the usual way (e.g., *not* by the executive committee of the Council). Should the Council find it inexpedient to clarify in those terms of reference what it really wants the Commission to decide in particular kinds of situations, then it must later live with the embarrassing consequences. On the other hand, if it is too fearful of these future embarrassments relative to the current benefits of delegating responsibility, let it retain experts on its staff to provide technical advice and take the day-to-day criticism surrounding particular decisions.

Statutory Agency vs. Departments:

From still another perspective, the statutory regulatory agency has a useful function to perform in our society in providing a continuing *public* forum in which relatively technical issues can be considered and conflicting viewpoints (interests) can be presented before a group of appointed individuals who, in their questioning, are supported by a technically competent staff. In a sense, such agencies can be looked upon as continuing Royal Commissions of Inquiry in specific areas of public concern.

As Trebilcock *et al.* (1978) and others have pointed out, and as stated in our earlier discussion, it would be a mistake to romanticize about the "right to be heard" aspect of the regulatory agencies. Like the courts, although individuals are presumed equal before the law, their differences in income and status certainly do not provide them with equal access to the law. This is a most serious problem and one not easily rectified, although the relatively recent legal aid programs and new bail provisions go some distance in the right direction. This problem of "equal access" is particularly acute when one considers the statutory regulatory bodies, for the costs of all but the most perfunctory representations, coupled with complex procedural hurdles, are extremely high.

As far as collective rights groups are concerned, token steps have been taken through small grants of public monies to the Consumers' Association of Canada and similar organizations. Ministers put themselves on the side of the angels by supplying enough wing feathers to sustain a semblance of life, but certainly not enough to permit angelic flight. Even this nominal support was put in jeopardy as an "economy" measure. One cannot help but speculate whether this new found drive to "spare the purse" was not also motivated by a ministerial desire to placate the interest groups who were irritated, to put it mildly, by those striving for stronger collective rights.

Ameliorating the gross imbalances that prevail in the *demi-monde* of interest groups that so profoundly affect the outcome of the political system is both of vital importance and of enormous difficulty. The lasting and fundamental solution to the problem of the under representation of collective rights in the regulatory field, primarily because of the "free-rider" problem described earlier, is to reform and strengthen Parliament *vis-à-vis* the executive branch. The Canadian political system as a whole not only permits but, indeed, one could go so far as to say readily accommodates and even say encourages those narrow interests that have much to gain at the expense of the many (Trebilcock, 1978; Stanbury, 1976). They are able to obtain decisions, in one way or another, that would not be made if the issue were put to a vote in Parliament—a Parliament consisting of members elected on a proportionate representation basis: members whose campaign costs were so low and whose financial position so assured that anyone could afford to run; members who were nominated on an unrigged basis; members unfettered by undue executive branch secrecy.

Until some progress is made in reforming the political system in all of the foregoing directions a majority government can usually dismiss Parliament as inconsequential even though it is supposed to be the bastion of our liberties. Partly for historic reasons, partly as a consequence of a succession of short-term partisan advantages over the decades, partly because our courts have been so compliant, partly because governments have become so overwhelmingly large, complex and all pervasive, and partly because Canadians have treated their rights with such complacency if not indifference, we now have an executive branch of frightening power that is effectively unaccountable in vast areas of decision. It is not a matter of blaming particular institutions or political parties or individuals. Nor is it a matter of some conscious conspiracy. The causes of the problem are much too complex and, therefore, much more difficult to resolve than the identification of "the enemy." Within the narrow compass of this paper and our competence, all we can offer is the following concrete proposal that although extremely modest given the magnitude and multidimensional nature of the overwhelming problem we have just discussed would, if adopted, at least constitute a step in the right direction. Some other, again modest, suggestions are given in the final chapter.

6.3. A MODEST PROPOSAL FOR STRUCTURAL CHANGE

To examine in detail the pros and cons of all of the alternative structural changes that might be made in the approach to statutory regulatory agencies would take us too far afield. The proposal sketched below seems to crystallize our position and perhaps will help to focus the debate. That the existing approach is worse than unsatisfactory is, we hope, now accepted by the reader (although acceptance of even that proposition is unlikely to come from those who benefit so greatly from the current arrangement in so many, often unobtrusive, ways). The "free-rider" problem applies to regulatory reform as to other public policy issues.

1. Assuming that it would be impracticable to amend each statute(s) that establishes the authority of each statutory regulatory agency, an omnibus bill should be tabled in the House that established two distinct types of regulatory agencies: (i) *advisory agencies* and (ii) *decision-making agencies*. The bill should specify, for each existing statutory regulatory agency, whether it would henceforth be an advisory agency or a decision-making agency.

2. As the term suggests, the authority of each designated advisory agency would be restricted to the provision of advice or recommendations to the minister or the Governor in Council. This advice (recommendations) would be based on public hearings and staff or commissioned studies. The advice (recommendations) would be released simultaneously to the public. It would then be a matter of ministerial or Cabinet responsibility to accept or reject the advice.

In essence, the agencies so designated would become continuing Royal Commissions of Inquiry into policy matters of continuing concern, with the important qualification that there would be no authority for ministerial-Cabinet intervention concerning the publication of an agency's advice or recommendations. To ensure the independence of these advisory agencies it would be important to ensure that such agencies could not be quietly throttled by budgetary and manpower restrictions. (Their estimates might be reviewed by an all-party committee, chaired by an opposition member.)

3. Those statutory regulatory agencies designated as decision-making agencies would retain, with certain important provisos to be set forth later, their existing statutory authority and, indeed, could have that authority clarified in terms of the government's policy intent at any time by the Governor in Council in the form of published "directives." Indeed, a minister or the Cabinet could refer particular issues to the decision-making agency with a request for advice or recommendations. In short, the decision-making agencies could, from time to time, be required by the government of the day to perform public advisory functions. Now for the vital provisos.

(a) The present power of the executive branch to override the decisions of these agencies, except by the tabling of a bill in Parliament, would be abolished.[4]

(b) At any stage of the proceedings prior to *the agency's decision* on any matter, the government of the day could declare that it deemed the particular decision to be of such significance that it would treat it as a *government* policy decision. Consequently, the decision-making powers of the agency would thereby be withheld in the particular case and the agency's conclusions, whether in the form of a draft decision or advice or

---

[4] Some provincial regulatory agencies already have this power. Their decisions are appealable not to the provincial Cabinet, but only to the courts, and only on matters of law, not fact or opinion.

recommendations, would be treated as such, and the final decision would be announced by the responsible minister as a government policy decision debatable in the House of Commons.

To be fair to the participants, the executive branch would make its intention to shift the agency from the decision-making role to the advisory role in a particular case at the earliest opportunity. The appropriate point in time, in most instances, would be shortly after all submissions in a particular case had been received.

4. The omnibus bill would also include provisions that ensured that a significant flow of funds would be available on a continuing basis to finance what we have termed collective rights groups to appear before both types of agencies and that they would be allocated by Parliament (through a committee, also chaired by an opposition member) and not by the executive branch alone.

This set of proposals would, it seems to us, have some notable *advantages*.

1. The degree of ministerial accountability in significant regulatory matters would be greatly increased without burdening them with an overwhelming flow of routine decisions.

2. It would help to alert the opposition parties and journalists to situations that warranted probing. The flow of regulatory decisions is overwhelmingly great. No person or group of persons for that matter can possibly keep track of what is transpiring in all regulatory areas on a day-to-day basis. What is needed is a *process* that facilitates separating the crucial from the trivial. Adoption of our proposal would assist in this selection.

3. The ''capture'' of regulatory agencies by regulatees that is considered to be such a serious problem in the United States with its ''independent'' regulatory agencies would be averted. When a ministry wanted to intervene it could intervene—but it would be required to take full responsibility for the consequences.

4. The most desirable features of ''independence'' could be attained because executive branch intervention would be public and regulatory decisions, once made, could only be overturned by Parliament. This would be rare, given Cabinet government, but being held accountable might well change the decision!

5. A public forum for the discussion of continuing and frequently complex policy matters could be not only retained, but strengthened by ensuring the financial support of collective rights groups and continuing the requisite staff support for those appointed to regulatory bodies—a staff support that the traditional courts do not provide those appointed to the bench.

REFERENCES

Birkenhead, Earl of (1926) *Fourteen English Judges* (London: Cassel & Co.).

Bernstein, Marver (1955) *Regulating Business by Independent Commission* (Princeton: Princeton University Press).

Janisch, H.N. (1978) "The Role of the Independent Regulatory Agency in Canada" *UNB Law Journal* 27: 83-120.

Janisch, N.H. (forthcoming) "Policy Making in Regulation Towards a New Definition of the Status of Independent Regulatory Agencies in Canada" *Osgoode Hall Law Journal* 16.

MacAvoy, Paul W. (1978) "The Present Condition of Regulated Enterprise" Series #5, Working Paper, Yale School of Organization and Management.

Stanbury, W.T. (1976) "The Consumer Interest and the Regulated Industries: Diagnosis and Prescription" in Karl M. Ruppenthal and W.T. Stanbury (eds.) *Transportation Policy: Regulation, Competition and the Public Interest* pp. 109-55 (Vancouver: University of British Columbia, Centre for Transportation Studies).

Stigler, George J. (1975) *The Citizen & The State: Essays on Regulation* (Chicago: University of Chicago Press).

Trebilcock, M.J. (1978) "The Consumer Interest and Regulatory Reform" in G. Bruce Doern (ed.) *The Regulatory Process in Canada* pp. 94-127 (Toronto: Macmillan).

Trebilcock, M.J., L. Waverman, and J.R.S Prichard (1978) "Markets for Regulation: Implications for Performance Standards and Institutional Design" in *Government Regulation: Issues and Alternatives* pp. 11-66 (Toronto: Ontario Economic Council).

Chapter Seven

Conclusion and Recommendations

The Western world is in serious economic difficulty and Canada is no exception. Moreover, there seems little grounds for optimism in the years ahead. If anything, the general prognostication is that the more developed industrial countries are likely to be buffeted even more heavily. The omnipotent, benevolent image of government seems to have fled with the buoyant optimism and confidence of the post World War II period. It has been replaced by disillusionment, suspicion and hostility. Unrealistic expectations about what governments could accomplish have been replaced by equally unrealistic criticisms.

Many voters are treating the government like a spouse who, though seemingly passionately devoted, has been discovered to have been carrying on a series of clandestine love affairs all the while. Separation is out of the question because of financial dependence and responsibilities towards the children. But all the old grievances and slights are vividly remembered and the times of joy and contentment have vanished from memory. Recriminations abound, and the guilty party's attempts at reconciliation and pleas for forgiveness and promises of reform are cast aside with disgust: just further signs of weakness. "Well, if we *must* live under the same roof I can tell you the situation is going to be different. You're going to move into the small guest room down the hall. What's more, I am withdrawing everything from our joint bank account and furthermore . . . " For some, the demand for "deregulation" is just a completion of the "And furthermore . . . " sentence. When the hurt and rage subsides to a degree, these kinds of statements are usually recognized as unreasonable and more moderate conditions are imposed, if any. In considering "deregulation" let us transport ourselves to that more thoughtful state of affairs.

As we have tried to explain in the first section of Chapter 1, there are some aspects of regulation that could be having deleterious effects on the Canadian economy. But it would not only be surprising, it would be astounding if those effects were of great consequence unless one were to think of regulation much more broadly and generally than those who call for "deregulation" seemingly have in mind.

The word "regulation" is synonomous with the word "rule" (except in the narrowest legal senses) and rules are ubiquitous in all continuing societies and organizations. Tribal societies have rules that are every bit as real as those voted in a legislature. The feudal period had a plethora of rules, many of a traditional nature. The Roman Catholic church has, as it must, an enormous number of rules. Bell Canada has rules galore, as do other large corporations. Families have rules. In short, rules are an inherent dimension of all continuing collective endeavours. Those calling for deregulation obviously do not mean rules in this general sense, but rather *some* rules promulgated and enforced by government.

Even if we restrict ourselves to this relatively narrow subset of rules, which alone contain an untold (and untellable!) number of rules, the cries of anguish are, one can assume, not directed towards the rules governing electoral procedures, parliamentary procedures, court procedures, and administrative procedures, among others.

We might also suppose that they are not thinking of the rules that govern the military, the RCMP, the Penitentiary Service or the *Criminal Code* itself. Nor, just to drive home the point if that is necessary, do they have in mind the endless rules made under the following *kinds* of statutes (which are rules in themselves!):

— immigration
— taxation
— transfer payments
— regional development subsidies
— research and development subsidies
— research grants.

It is less clear whether there is concern about the rules, also made under statutes, concerning such matters as:

— food and drug safety and efficacy
— health of animals
— air safety
— nuclear safety
— industrial safety.

Are the proponents of deregulation thinking of the abolition of· the regulation of freight rates, telephone rates, cable TV rates, and several others?

What about the rules governing the allocation of the radio spectrum? What about the licensing of professionals (e.g., medical doctors, dentists, lawyers and accountants)? And what about the control of natural gas exports?

Perhaps agricultural products marketing boards (of which there are over 100) fall within the ambit?

Could it be that all labour legislation is to be included? Things such as union recognition, the right to strike, and, of course, the minimum wage?

What about financial disclosure rules, and the *Canada Corporations Act?* Patents, copyrights and trademarks perhaps?

Or is it only the rules involved in competition policy (the *Combines Investigation Act*) and consumer-environmental protection that should be withdrawn?

We have gone through this tiresome litany to establish three points the advocates of deregulation should bear in mind.

First: the very term deregulation is meaningless because no one in his right mind could possibly contemplate the removal of all rules, and ''regulation'' is just another word for ''rule.''

Second: immediately the particular rule(s) to be eliminated is (are) identified, it will be apparent that every rule (regulation) that has an unpleasant cutting edge also has its supporters.

Third: and more generally: each of us would be better off, in the narrowest sense of that word, if we had the power to remove those regulations that constrain us and at least retain, if not make more stringent, those constraining others.

This is *not* to say that the existing set of rules (regulations) is without many serious defects. Nor does it imply that the processes by which they were decided nor the decisions (rulings) made under them are without need of major overhaul. We do wish to emphasize, however, that in Canada the term ''deregulation'' expresses a state of mind, not the result of a conscious mental process. The situation in the United States is significantly different: witness the degree of deregulation being implemented by the Civil Aeronautics Board there.

7.1   SUNSET PROVISIONS

Perhaps before leaving the realm of fantasy, ''sunset provisions'' can also be disposed of at this point, in order then to turn to the enormously important issues that need to be addressed. For those fortunate few who have not heard of the idea, if it can be so dignified, the notion is that each statute (?), rule (?), regulation (?), order (?), and ruling (?) would be required to contain a provision that, beyond a stipulated date (fixed? appropriate?) it would no longer have force or effect unless formally reaffirmed by the authority under which it was issued.

There are some immediate and obvious mechanical difficulties that hardly need to be mentioned. First, given the enormous ambiguity of the term ''regulation'' itself, and the multitude of available synonyms, and the mind-boggling range of governmental rules (instruments?), it would be virtually impossible to draft an omnibus bill that would neither catch everything from whales to plankton within its net or would not have loopholes so large that the catch would be zero. Furthermore, even if the gauge of the net were ''just right,'' in some sense, how would the various decision-making bodies find the time to rethrash old straw when they can barely cope with the current crop?

Both of these difficulties could be readily avoided if, instead of an omnibus sunset provision bill, such a provision were added *on a highly selective basis* to some existing statutes, like those now contained in the *Bank Act.* An admirable idea, but hardly novel. Opposition parties could press harder for sunset provisions in bills that are tabled. But this opportunity is available to them now, and is no doubt raised as an amendment from time to time. Public pressure may induce a ministry to consider such provisions in draft bills more seriously in the future—an excellent idea. But these courses of action are not panaceas whereby, with the passage of but another rule, all "bad" and "superfluous" rules come to an end after a few years.

The notion of sunset provisions in the "regulatory" field is precisely the same as the notion of "zero-based budgeting" in the expenditure field. In the latter case, each year the budget was to be critically approached as though everything were possible including, of course, spending nothing on each and every program. This is roughly equivalent to asking a family to sit down each Saturday morning and seriously discuss whether or not its food budget for the coming week should be zero when the "serious" question the grocery buyers wrestle with is whether they should splurge and have a steak on Sunday and compensate by having macaroni and cheese on Tuesday and Thursday or . . . If the opposition members of the Public Accounts Committee of Parliament could select each year a few major programs for in-depth analysis by the department together with some outside (largely university) independent experts, I believe a great deal could be accomplished. To critically appraise each program each year is ludicrous. Enough said. If this study has conveyed the impression that the question of government intervention is immensely more complex than these types of travelling medicine man nostrums, something has been accomplished.

7.2 COLLECTIVE RIGHTS REGULATIONS

The regulations that seek to protect our collective rights have had the shortest history and, unless they are defended with vigour, will be the first to be attacked by the deregulation enthusiasts. Without wishing to appear to be defending their present form, or the manner of their enforcement, these *kinds* of regulations are part and parcel of the *minimal* role of government. Just as defence and police services protect our tangible collective and exclusive rights, enforced collective rights regulations stand guard for the intangible but vital rights we cannot protect individually.

7.3 THE ROLE OF GOVERNMENT

In the Introduction to this study it was stated that government regulation, if one defines the term to mean rules of all kinds as we do, is, we are convinced, the most general policy instrument of government. Taxation and expenditures, rather than being the main policy instruments, are essentially special cases that attract much more attention because their *direct* effects are so manifest because they leave dollar tracks on the books for all to see.[1] It is precisely because regulations do not leave these obvious tracks that they are often introduced rather than taxes or subsidies.

Therefore, when considering the "appropriate" role for government regulation, we are in effect considering the "appropriate" role of government itself. Disillusioned by government, frightened by current and impending problems, frustrated by seemingly endless government constraints that take an almost infinite variety of forms, there appears to be a growing demand among voters for much less government in any and all of its manifestations.

The times are evocative of those that prevailed at the time of Adam Smith when in 1776 he wrote his panegyric treatise to market competition and his vehement protest towards suffocating government intervention. Hardly surprisingly, the views of those economists whose ideology is closest to that of Adam Smith (the so-called Chicago School) have been accorded increasing favourable attention in recent years. The themes of individual freedom and reward for individual initiative are most persuasive. The notion of harnessing, through untrammelled competitive markets, self-interest to the benefit of the totality was a clarion call then and beckons seductively now.

If one were to make a predicition it would seem plausible that the demand for minimal government has not yet run its course. Nevertheless, surely it would be a grievous error to forget the dreadful faults of the minimal government system in its heyday and the unique circumstances of that time, both in Britain and in the rest of the world. Some of those unique circumstances are briefly described in Appendix A.

The fact that these too are troubled times calls for an Adam Smith of our unique times, but not a return to Adam Smith's prescription for his unique times. His insights about the pursuit of self-interest and incentives are as valid today as they ever were. But the size and strength of institutions, the state of knowledge and technology, the world balance of power are all so utterly changed that it is idle to pretend that what was "good enough for Adam Smith is good enough for us."

It is much beyond the compass of this paper to try to delineate a sketch of a sketch of a sketch of the new conceptual framework that someone, someday, may develop. But we would have thought that it would take into account, among a host of others, the following factors.

(1) The ever-receding range and significance of competitive open market decisions. That is to say, so many crucial decisions are now made *within* organizations of increasing size. Moreover, the conflicts between and

---

[1] Even pure public goods (defence, police services, roads, etc.) can, in principle, be accomplished by regulation and, indeed, have been in the past: conscription and confiscation carried out in the name of the Prince.

among such large organizations more and more are resolved at the bargaining table, not in the open market (i.e., they are resolved in political markets).

(2) It is impossible to conceive of the corporate-labour giants becoming small competitive microcosms, particularly when so many are international in scope. Can one imagine the professions not battling their respective para-professions for territory?

(3) It is also inconceivable that the income/wealth (as broadly defined in Chapter 2) that would emerge from a minimal government approach would, in the longer run, gain adequate voter support in a nation with a semblance of democratic government.

(4) Minimal government, in the sense of minimal government intervention in markets, where workable competition can prevail coupled with some form of guaranteed annual income scheme tax reform system might be devised. However, such a combination would remove one of the most important rationales for government intervention that *purport* to assist the disadvantaged, but in fact provide much more assistance to the advantaged. Would those strong interest groups that have been able to parade under false colours of government intervention for an ostensibly laudible purpose, in order to achieve inordinate benefits for themselves, readily acquiesce in such a scheme? To ask the question is to answer it.

(5) What the conceptual scheme must avoid is some kind of shadow government with all the major pressure groups represented that relies for its effectiveness on the prerogative powers of a ministry under a bundle of statutes that, by their vague wording, are essentially enabling statutes. This would make a mockery of Parliament and any notion of real political accountability would be completely lost.

The assertion "if you don't like what we are doing you can vote us out of office at the next election" has little if any meaning when "what we are doing" is, to a significant extent, embodied in many, many thousands of obscure Orders-in-Council and ministerial orders, the contents of which are known only to those immediately and directly involved.

The inordinate rise in the use of Orders-in-Council and ministerial orders, coupled with the secrecy provisions of other statutes together pose of serious threat to representative government. This statement holds without regard to political party or to the particular incumbents of ministerial and prime ministerial offices at any point in time.

In this light, we would recommend that serious consideration be given to the proposals advanced for discussion purposes at the end of Chapter 5. These proposals call for the withdrawal of the authority of ministers and the ministry as a whole to dispose of the decisions of so-called "independent" regulatory agencies *at will* under the euphemistic term "right of appeal to the Minister or Governor in Council." Instead, we would strongly suggest that a minister or a ministry be empowered to declare, in advance of a decision by a statutory regulatory body, that it deemed the matter of such general concern or importance that it would consider the agency's recommendation, but would take ministerial responsibility for the decision. If a ministry wished to declare that one or more particular regulatory agencies henceforth would play an advisory role only, so much the better.

The provision of a continuing open forum, through open regulatory agency hearings in specialized subjects of continuing and general concern, is most valuable. However, some means must be found to finance adequately what we have called "collective rights" groups. The ideal financing method would be by public subscription. This route should be pursued more systematically and aggressively. Despite the "free-rider" problem, much has been accomplished in the United States: witness Ralph Nader's success. In the meantime, pressure should be put on governments to fund such groups out of general revenues. The attempt to reduce such funding as an "economy measure" is outrageous, given some of the other expenditures that have not been touched—for example, the budget of the Prime Minister's Office.

Ultimately what is required, over and above the foregoing, is to increase the authority of Parliament *vis-à-vis* the executive branch in general and the Cabinet in particular. In Canada the executive branch has always been strong as compared with the British executive branch. As the extent and depth of government intervention has increased the dangers of excessive executive prerogative powers in Canada have grown commensurately. This danger is increased when individual ministers are weak *vis-à-vis* the prime minister and the bureaucracy, with its continuing concern for the maintenance of "the system," is relatively weak *vis-à-vis* the Cabinet.

7.4 SECRECY AND ELITISM

We have emphasized again and again in this paper the desperate need for an immediate and dramatic reduction in government secrecy. When the electorate and Parliament are effectively denied access to the essential information on which to base decisions, or that information is so inaccessible as to be beyond the reach of all but the well-placed, the liberties of the many are on the sufferance of the few.

In the past, Canadians have been fortunate that, for the most part, a benevolent elite has seen fit to do "good works by stealth." Perhaps, in the short term, the elite does, as it claims, know best. How could it be otherwise? Its members have, by definition, garnered to themselves the knowledge, experience and security of position that make their prognostications about their superiority of judgment relative to that of "the little man" self-fulfilling. However, as the overly protective parent stifles the fulfillment of the child's potential so does a knowledgeable and well-disposed elite stifle the maturation of the vast majority of Canadians.

More ominous is the vulnerability of an immature people to an elite that is sufficiently knowledgeable to gain and retain power by tyrannical methods if necessary—all rationalized, of course, as being in the interests of "the little man'' who cannot be trusted to know his own ''true'' interests. The time for change is now.

7.5 AN APPROACH TO RESEARCH ON REGULATION

The whole purport of this paper is that the existing regulatory process can be explained, to a depressingly high degree, by the lack of public understanding of the direct and indirect impact of regulations on the distribution of income and wealth (as defined in Chapter 2). Many regulations also have highly significant effects on the allocation of resources. These also need to be examined and the results made available to the public. What we would emphasize, however, is that the distributional effects have, in the past, tended to be downplayed relative to the allocative effects, and that this imbalance should be corrected in so far as possible.

Economists have been trained not to inject their subjective values on distributional questions into their work under the cloak of ''analysis.'' This is a sound professional principle that must be retained. What we are suggesting is not that analyses of regulations contain any judgments about the fairness or unfairness of the distributional effects. Rather, we would urge that such analyses simply set forth the distributional effects as clearly and precisely as the available data and analytic techniques permit. Let such results speak for themselves, in so far as the normative assessment of them is concerned.

Let us emphasize also that regulations often fly under colours that bear little if any relationship to their actual effects on the distribution of income and wealth or on the allocation of resources. Thus, statements of intended purposes or stated objectives, formal or informal, should not be taken at face value for analytic purposes. All that needs to be done is to place in juxtaposition these kinds of statements and the estimated actual distributional/allocative effects.

The earlier discussion of the effects of different kinds of regulations made it clear that some, and indeed many of them, bestow some gains and some losses on the same individual. Obviously, it is the net gain or loss that is relevant. Because each individual holds a bundle of interests, could one conceive of the net gain (or loss) to the individual of the whole package of existing regulations (and, presumably, all past rulings under regulations)? The answer is clearly no. For if there were no regulations there almost certainly would be some taxes and/or expenditures in their place. Only a speculative comparison of alternatives would be sensible. Without a mix of some regulations, some taxes, and some expenditures there would be no society. The only sensible analytic questions to ask are the following.

(a) What would be the impact on the Comprehensive Net Worth (as we have defined the term in Chapter 2) of a particular change in a particular regulation on individuals with certain attributes relative to the alternatives— including the abolition of the particular regulation, of course? The impact of a change on other individuals and on the system as a whole would also have to be considered if the analysis were to have much meaning.

(b) What are the estimated effects of the particular regulation on the allocation of resources, compared with the alternatives?

(c) With these ''facts'' in hand, alternatives (including, of course, the abolition of a particular regulation) could then be analysed. In conducting such assessments the stated objectives of the government of the day, because they are invariably cast in rhetorical terms, would not be of much value. It would be necessary, in my view, to adopt the traditional objectives such as reducing income/wealth inequality (interpersonal, interregional, interoccupational, intergenerational, and so on); greater equality of opportunity for individuals of equal capacity; a more efficient allocation of resources (including public versus private sector, current versus future, human versus man-made capital, etc.); and a rather vague objective of maintaining and strengthening Canada as our country. Are there not better ways of achieving these objectives?

The volume of regulations extant is overwhelmingly large—so large in fact that if all the competent analysts in the world were to work diligently for a decade, they could not seriously consider them all. Indeed, unless the flood is stemmed, such a group might well lose ground in terms of the work to be done relative to that accomplished with the passage of time. A highly selective research approach is therefore imperative. In some instances the research work should be directed towards areas where it seems possible to devise acceptable alternatives. In others, perhaps what is called for are ''debunking'' analyses—analyses designed to show that ostensible purposes are being subverted by seemingly laudible regulations. In still others, there is a desperate need for more information on which to make more informed judgments about where to proceed, either with respect to further investigations or in devising alternatives.

While not wishing to suggest that we have attempted to devise any overall research plan the issues listed below seem to us particularly to warrant attention. The order is of no particular importance and does not purport to be exhaustive.

(1) In terms of *effective* as distinct from nominal industrial regulation, how does Canada compare internationally, particularly with respect to the United States, Japan and West Germany?

(2) The Canadian pulp and paper industry seems to be in fundamental difficulty. What has been and is likely to be the relative importance of environmental protection measures as a contributing factor? Are there alternative ways of ''cleaning up,'' at least to some reasonable degree, the environment that do not make this industry unable to compete in international markets? What are the trade-offs?

(3) Regulatory compliance would appear to be particularly onerous for *small* businesses relative to larger enterprises. To what extent? Is this true? What could be done to ameliorate the situation if there is, indeed, a problem?

(4) Have regulations that conferred significant bargaining power on some labour, professional and occupational groups, or have been instrumental in raising some factor and product prices been a significant factor in making it increasingly difficult to attain reasonably full employment with increases in the general level of prices not accounted for by international forces?

(5) Federal-provincial jurisdictional questions in the regulatory realm are incredibly complex. The water quality regulations of the two jurisdictions exemplify many of the difficulties. An in-depth, multidisciplinary case study could prove most illuminating.

(6) Many statutes confer regulatory powers on ministers who in turn delegate, in most instances, the responsibilities to their officials. It is important to investigate, again in-depth, how these powers are exercised and their effects. Are the officials involved inordinate risk averters, as one would expect? Does this forestall innovation? The problems are particularly acute when a high science-technology component is involved in regulation. The realities of the applications of the *Food and Drugs Act,* would provide some needed insights into an aspect of the regulatory world that seems largely a "black box" except to those immediately affected. In particular, what are the rights of appeal against the "opinions" (that are, in effect, decisions) of scientific and technical bureaucratic "experts" who have every personal incentive to be cautious and no incentive to count the social cost of inordinate timidity?

(7) Is there any reason why broadcast frequencies, cable territories and satellite channels could not be sold or leased on an auction basis with the contractual conditions applicable to the successful bidder clearly set forth? This need not conflict with Canadian content objectives. Indeed, it could provide additional funds for cultural purposes.

(8) In the field of transportation, have we fully explored the possibility of establishing only maximum rates and opening all routes to competition, with the stipulation that a corporation, having once begun a particular service, could neither drop the service nor raise the rate for a significant period of time?

Appendix A

Welfare Economics

A.0 PROPERTY RIGHTS AND THE MARKET ECONOMY

Where a particular kind of asset, or the services of a particular kind of asset, are voluntarily exchanged for a *quid pro quo* on a continuing basis (but sometimes an infrequent basis), a market in that asset or service is said to exist. The sum of all such markets constitutes the market economy. The purpose of this appendix is to explore those aspects of the market economy, and only those aspects, that are particularly germane to the consideration of government regulation.

As we stated earlier, assets are defined for our purpose as a bundle of property rights.[1] A necessary condition for the existence of voluntary exchange is the effective exclusivity of the bundle of rights that constitute the asset. If the benefits of an asset can be enjoyed by others without providing the holder of the asset with a mutually acceptable *quid pro quo*, it would be folly (or perfect charity!) to pay anything for them. Another necessary condition for the existence of voluntary exchange is the transferability of at least some of the rights that inhere in the asset at least for some period of time. As indicated above, the ownership rights that inhere in a house can be transferred, in whole or in part—the part being, in this example, the right to the use of the house by another person for a stipulated period of time in exchange for a mutually acceptable rental.

However, except in a slave society, the bundle of rights that inhere in a natural person are exclusive but they are not transferable *in toto*. The individual only has the right to "rent" his own services to others for a stipulated period in exchange for a wage. Both exclusivity *and* at least the partial transferability of property rights are therefore necessary conditions for the existence of markets.

When the means to the satisfaction of human wants are scarce, choices are inescapable, for more of one desired-thing necessarily entails less of one or more other things that are also desired. To use the jargon of economics, the value of those things forgone constitutes the "opportunity cost" of that which is obtained. The essence of economic theory is this concept of opportunity cost: how can the degree of satisfaction of wants be maximized

---

[1] For a discussion of the meaning and implications of property rights, see Stein (1976).

for a given opportunity cost? Or, to put the same question the other way, how can a given degree of satisfaction be attained at minimum opportunity cost? As will be discussed later in the appendix, the market, *under some extremely stringent assumptions and conditions,* provides the ''answer.''

This ''answer,'' as it turns out, raises other questions in the minds of some, particularly questions concerning whose wants are satisfied by the market allocation of goods and services? On what basis in equity? Those dissatisfied with the purported ''answers'' to the latter kind of questions are then inclined to reject the market as the ''answer'' and seek alternative, or significantly modified, allocative systems. This brings forth questions from those who are enthusiasts for the market as an allocative device. ''If you do not accept what you call the 'gross distributive injustices perpetrated by the impersonal forces of the market', whom do *you* think should be empowered to decide who gets what? On what basis? What recourse would we have if we didn't like the distributive decisions of this person or group?''[2]

The consequences flowing from this kind of debate have radically changed the history of mankind. Despite the wars and the revolutions and the deaths and the destruction there is not now, or is there ever likely to be, a consensus, much less unanimity, concerning the ''right'' answers. Because we are so much a part of the market system (or perhaps, more accurately, our quasi-market system), it is sometimes difficult for us to keep in mind that what exists is of very recent origin among the social-political-economic structural changes that have happened in the past. The next section seeks to provide a brief historic-ideological perspective.

A.1 THE MARKET IN PERSPECTIVE

It is indisputable that Adam Smith's, *An Inquiry into the Nature and Causes of the Wealth of Nations* published in 1776 was the most important book concerned with economics ever written.[3] For not only did it set the course for what is now viewed as conventional Western market economics, it engendered, in many ways, the Marxian antithesis. These two basic and competing ideas have dramatically changed the history of the world.

Although markets had existed in feudal times (and, indeed in ancient times), they were narrowly circumscribed because of the high degree of manorial self-sufficiency, the system of land tenure, serfdom, the weakness of the king's authority relative to the lords and the princes of the church, and the consequent difficulties of transport over land or sea in the absence of national armies and navies. Rights and obligations were determined largely by tradition and custom so that choices, other than those involving

---

[2] See, for example, Milton Friedman (1962).

[3] For a succinct narrative of the life of Adam Smith and the impact of his work, see Robert Heilbroner (1972, Chap. 3).

inter-baronial conflict, were few and far between. From these so-called Dark Ages slowly emerged the medieval system that saw the shift in power from barons and church to the crown. The nation-state came into being. The declining importance of the manorial system and serfdom paralleled the increasing importance of the guilds, trade and urbanization. With increasing order and prosperity, intellectual pursuits, and, in particular, science, flourished. Many traditional rules began to be replaced by national laws. These laws greatly restricted the individual's freedom of choice but probably less than the informal rules they replaced. Guilds, for example, were empowered by the state to regulate numbers of members, training requirements, markets' qualities and prices. The attempts to ensure a "just" price meant the market was not permitted to perform its allocation of resource function as well as it otherwise might have done, although with a mixture of hypocrisy (Jews could practise "usury") and imagination, the rules concerning just prices became increasingly irrelevant. Higher taxes were imposed by the crown and monopoly licences and other crown rights were sold to raise revenues for the king. Because gold was considered the only "true" form of wealth, governments intervened to increase exports and decrease imports. This was the age of mercantilism. But as it came to full flower the seeds of the industrial revolution that had already been sown had started to sprout. These seeds were: wealth accumulation other than in the hands of the landed gentry, a labour market created by the enclosure movement that drove the peasantry from the land and forced urbanization of the serfs, and, of course, technological innovation plus a degree of domestic order that had not previously prevailed. It was Smith's role to attack what seemed in his time the old and established system and provide a rationalization, indeed what became the legitimization, for the new. His argument was as straightforward as it was convincing—particularly, of course, to the rising entrepreneurial group that was inhibited by massive state intervention that restricted the choices available to it. Basically, Smith argued that:

(1) the pursuit of self interest by individuals is a strong and immutable motive; and

(2) the energy and imagination generated by the pursuit of individual self-interest is best channelled *automatically* through the competitive forces interacting in the market ("the invisible hand") to maximize the realization of the public interest, even though the furtherance of the public interest is not intended by those involved. Order would prevail without ordering people about.

Smith, in other words, believed that government intervention which inhibited free markets, although adopted supposedly to serve "the public interest," was, in most instances, perverse in its effects. By his magic mind and pen he transformed, no doubt because the audience was most receptive, what had been thought of as the old vices of greed and covetousness into the virtue of personal ambition. If relentlessly and rationally pursued and constrained only by the competition provided by others of like drive, these would make the nation wealthy in the modern sense of achieving the highest standard of living for the residents, given its resource endowment.

Genius that he was, Smith recognized the necessity of the public provision of some services—our so-called pure public goods. He also recognized that entrepreneurs would, given the opportunity, collude to raise prices and/or reduce quality. His policy prescriptions on this front were, however, weak presumably because he did not envisage the enormous economies of scale that were possible as a result of ever extending markets and the adoption of capital intensive methods of production embodying the new technologies.

Smith certainly did not "invent" the industrial revolution and, no doubt, it would have taken place had he never written. What he did provide the rising new entrepreneurial class was a respectability *vis-à-vis* the landed gentry up to, if not beyond, the point of self-righteousness. For them, acting in accordance with narrow self-interest became a public duty. The innocent victims of the inexorable and impersonal forces interacting in the market were thought of as unfortunate. But their plight was looked upon as simply the price of progress. And had not Charles Darwin just "proven" that Mother Nature decreed that only the fittest would (and should!) survive? Such self-confidence, buttressed by growing wealth and the restriction of the franchise to the propertied, was soon manifest in the attainment of political power by the business community. The restrictions which had previously inhibited the working of the market were, in many instances, swept away and, for a period, Britain even adopted free trade.

The wealth-generating potential of the free market system espoused by Smith was certainly proven to be no delusion. What Smith had not foreseen was the enormous disparities in the distribution of that wealth and the dreadful physical and social consequences of the rapidly expanding market system.[4] While it was undoubtedly true when he wrote that the interpersonal distribution of wealth had always been, and still was, extraordinarily unequal by current western standards, Smith argued for the accumulation of wealth derived from profits that, when reinvested in the search for more profits, drew labour into ever more productive work and away from the useless service of the landed gentry living lavishly on the rents they collected without effort, imagination or risk. He probably did not imagine how rapidly industrial fortunes would be made or the misery associated with massive urbanization which was the concomitant of industrialization. Rural poverty

---

[4] This was dramatized in Benjamin Disraeli's novel, *Sybil: Or The Two Nations,* and in the works of Charles Dickens.

was one thing; urban poverty was another. The difference presumably was the greater visibility of the latter.

The callous disregard for human life and dignity for the working class in the market-oriented, capitalist-dominated nineteenth century system eventually gave rise to more and more strident protest and incited Marx to develop a theory of the capitalist exploitation of workers and the evils of private property, and, hence, free markets, that captured the minds of a few men who were later able to capture the enthusiasm of millions. Marxism-communism became a political reality.

Extreme democratic socialists, like the Marxists, abhor the personal accumulation of great wealth and the operation of competitive markets. But the democratic socialists were and are willing to press for what they perceived to be greater social justice by reforming rather than replacing the existing political order. Whether placing restrictions on the set of economic choices is compatible with maintaining the *de jure* set of political choices is a moot point.

The reason for injecting this brief sketch into a paper on government regulation is to remind the reader as forcefully as possible that the original and highly successful rationale for the capitalist market system did not attempt to persuade by an appeal to a sense of justice or equity (with the possible exception of a sense of outrage toward rental income derived from large inherited estates). Rather, the argument was that the capitalist market system created national wealth. Any untoward distributional consequences (in the unlikely event that they were not the result of personal sloth, profligacy and other moral weaknesses that had to be weeded out if humanity was to become even better) were, as we have said, thought of as the price that had to be paid for aggregate material advancement. Driven by a passion for success and a fear of failure, work effort, saving and risk taking would expand the size of the pie. Although the portions would remain unequal, competition would ensure that the largest portions were destined for those who produced and distributed at the lowest prices those goods and services that consumers wanted most. With an ever growing pie, even the smallest relative portions would grow in absolute terms (except perhaps for those without virtue!). What was completely ignored was, and remains, the notion that *perceived* interpersonal relativities are extremely important. In our view, the satisfaction that each of us derives from our own command over material things is *not* independent of what others can command, particularly if we perceive our own personal attributes, whether inherited or acquired, to be at least as admirable, if not more admirable, than those whose wealth is significantly greater. Jealousy is a powerful and persistent emotion!

The knowledge that chance (with ''chance'' taking the forms of individual inheritance: genetic, social and material) and the vagaries of market prices have a large role to play in the determination of the relative distribution of wealth is hardly an effective consolation to the losers in the game. There are many who strongly believe that a lifetime game in which the chips are distributed at birth unequally, where the successful gambler can walk away from the table with more chips won in an evening than others can earn over a lifetime of unpleasant work, is ethically unacceptable. Thus, some of them argue, once the means of physical survival are at hand, collectively we should forgo, at least to some extent, more goods and services, if that is necessary, to obtain a morally acceptable distribution of the fruits of wealth. Others believe that the rules of the game should be changed so as to ensure that wealth should accrue to people in proportion to their contributions to the size of the pie.

Another ideological dimension of the market system concerns *freedom of choice*, although it is not part of conventional welfare economics. Competitive markets can be looked upon as highly decentralized decision-making systems in which individuals and organizations can choose among alternative courses of action in the light of their objectives and the information available to them (i.e., past, present and expected future prices). Some believe that individual satisfaction is increased the greater the set of feasible choices available.[5] It is assumed that given a choice between a set of choices and a subset of that set the individual will invariably select the set. It follows that the individual obtains more satisfaction from the former than the latter. Perhaps this argument would be more persuasive if it were put the other way: an individual's satisfaction would be reduced if a feasible alternative were withdrawn even though previously it had not been selected when available. Individuals resent others who, for whatever reason, arbitrarily constrain their feasible set of choices.

The crucial issue in considering freedom of choice is, of course, the word ''feasible.'' It is often argued that, if each individual had the same feasible set of alternatives, the greater the set the better. It would be difficult to find many who would disagree with this proposition except, possibly, where moral choices were concerned. In reality, of course, this is not the situation. In particular, it is often argued that the feasible sets of the wealthy are not only greater than those of the poor but that those of the poor are less as a consequence. Greater freedom of choice for the few, it is believed, is but a reflection of the ''exploitation'' of the many. Some of the forms this exploitation may take in imperfect markets are discussed later.

Still other objections are made to the assignments of much weight to freedom of choice *per se*. Leaving aside the possibility of exploitation, there are those who *assume* that increasing individual wealth provides diminishing marginal utility. Therefore, it follows that a reduction in the set of feasible choices of the wealthy in order to increase those of the poor would raise *total*

---

[5] This assumption can in fact be traced to another assumption—the assumption of zero information costs.

satisfaction.[6] The relativities issue can also be raised. If Mr. Poor is jealous of Mr. Rich, reducing the feasibility set of Mr. Rich would afford satisfaction to Mr. Poor. Conversely, Mr. Rich may gain satisfaction just from Mr. Poor's perceived envy.

Of these several arguments pro and con freedom of choice in general, and with respect to the market system in particular, the two that seem to be most telling are the resentment of virtually all individuals against arbitrary reductions in their feasible set of alternatives, and the perceived cruelty of enormous and continuing interpersonal disparities in the range of feasible choices among individuals.

Having acknowledged that greater freedom of choice is not an unqualified "good thing," and that market "solutions" may not be effective under some circumstances—a matter we will discuss in some detail later—one substantial virtue of a reasonably free market is its *impersonality*. It is one thing to lose your job because the firm is closing as the result of losses suffered in a fire caused by lightning; it is another to be fired because your superior does not like your hairstyle. Although the adverse effects are identical, the attitude of the loser is likely to be entirely different. Being subject to arbitrary and often capricious authority is an affront to the dignity of the individual. Democratic socialists greatly emphasize the disparity in the feasible sets of Mr. R. and Mr. P, and the prevalence of exploitation as a consequence. What the adherents to that ideology seem to forget is that if market competition and private ownership were to be abolished and replaced by state ownership, at least with respect to major goods and services (e.g., steel, energy, agriculture), decisions would still have to be made and they would be made on the basis of a hierarchical allocation of authority that is constrained only by even higher authority (i.e., administratively) without the discipline of competitive market forces. It is here that the question of "legitimacy" arises. The democratic socialists assume that, because the requisite authority would be determined by majority rule, unacceptable arbitrariness would be precluded. This ignores the coercion implicit in the majority rule versus the unanimity rule. It ignores the possibility that once in authority the democratically selected incumbent of an office with authority might use it for personal advantage to such a degree that the democratic process was itself destroyed. It ignores the fact that those with authority may be able to hide what they are really doing, so they are not truly accountable to the electorate.

A.2 THE CONCEPT OF ECONOMIC EFFICIENCY

An economy is defined by economists to be efficient when it is not possible to make one or more individuals better off without making one or

---

[6] See Lerner (1944, p. 30). Lerner assumed identical marginal utility schedules for different individuals and concluded that moving towards greater equality was likely to raise total welfare.

more worse off. Pareto optimality, as this state of affairs is termed, occurs when perfect competition exists in all markets, when (but not only when) all markets are in equilibrium, and when the distribution of factor endowments is taken as given (accepted?). The principal conditions necessary for the achievement of perfectly competitive equilibrium are:

— the tastes and preferences of individuals remain constant and are independent of each other;

— technology remains constant;

— information and bargaining costs with respect to all prices and all qualities are zero (this implies, among other things, that *all* of the tastes and preferences of individuals with respect to public goods and services are revealed—there are no "free riders"—and that the magnitudes and distribution of the differences (if any) between social and private costs and benefits are known);

— there is no uncertainty;

— there are a large number of firms in each industry producing a homogeneous product; and

— there are no barriers to entry and exit in each industry.

When all these assumed conditions are met, all markets are cleared and each firm makes a normal profit with no incentive to alter the quantities or qualities of its inputs, or the method of combining them, or the level or composition of its output. Given the prevailing distribution of income, no individual can obtain greater satisfaction by altering the composition of the basket of goods and services purchased, or by saving more or less, or by working more or less.

The logic of the perfect competition model is impeccable. Given the conditions stipulated, it can be proven mathematically that Pareto optimality is achieved. Or, to put the matter the other way, if we rule out its fortuitous occurrence, Pareto optimality can only be achieved when all the conditions are met.

This simple model can and is frequently put to quasi-positivistic purposes. By relaxing the assumptions one at a time, for example, by allowing tastes and preferences to change in a certain way, the *direction* of the consequences (with no normative connotation) can be deduced. No further assumptions are needed. These uses of the model are by no means trivial. The model, used in this way, greatly assists in keeping the logic of an argument straight. But it is the normative implications of the model to which the balance of this section is primarily addressed. The reason behind this discussion of these implications is that they have provided, to a very large extent, the economic rationale for government intervention in the economy generally and for government regulation in particular. The conditions necessary for perfect competition are so crucial to government regulation that they will be considered separately in greater detail in the following section.

More or less implicit in the concept of Pareto optimality are several basic ideological precepts. These precepts, needless to say, are highly debatable. Those who reject them are, if logic prevails, almost certain to conclude that the ideal economic system, indeed the ideal political system, is substantially different than that which exists in most Western democratic nations. The more important of the precepts embodied in the concept of Pareto optimality are briefly set forth below.

(1) It is the maximization of the satisfaction of each individual within his capacity, and not of a collectivity of individuals (the "state"), that is of concern.

(2) Individuals pursue their self-interest (and/or perhaps those of third parties) without considering the interests of the second party in a transaction.

(3) The satisfaction of each individual is independent of his *perception* of the degree to which others are satisfying their own wants.

(4) Individual satisfaction is maximized only when each person can choose freely with respect to consumption, saving and work, within the feasible set of alternatives available to him, given his asset holdings and prevailing prices (over which he can exert no influence).

(5) Because the means to the satisfaction of wants are scarce, some method of rationing is inescapable. Only competitive markets serve this necessary rationing function while permitting unrestricted freedom of individual choice within the constraints imposed by personal income and wealth. As discussed earlier, markets can exist only when exclusive and transferable property rights are enforced by the state.

It is interesting to note that efficiency in the Pareto sense requires competitive markets with respect to consumption *and* saving *and* production. This in turn requires, as just mentioned, exclusive and transferable property rights in the means of production. It can be argued, therefore, that where there is state ownership of the means of production, the economy is inefficient by definition (Lange and Taylor, 1938).[7] The unwillingness to judge what others do want or should want is the hallmark of nineteenth century liberal theory although hardly a Victorian practice. In fact, as we will see, this precept is often broken by the state that places controls on the use of such things as alcohol and other mood-affecting drugs. One final observation: the importance attached to freedom of individual choice would seem to be of greater importance (as distinct from philosophic importance), the less traditional the society. In a highly traditional society, internalized cultural

---

[7] There are, of course, many gradations between "pure" capitalism and "pure" socialism: the former meaning that all property rights are held privately and the latter meaning that all property rights are held collectively. One variant might be termed "market decentralized planning." Under such a system, the state, through taxation, forces individual saving and allocates productive facilities in accordance with a central plan. Plant managers are then required to proceed under a price equals marginal cost rule and consumers are free to spend their after tax earnings as they choose. They may or may not be free to choose where they will work or how much they will work and certainly are not free to bargain as to their "wages."

values are more homogeneous and, therefore, one would expect individual wants to be more homogeneous. Individuals learn to want what they are to receive *and* both conscience and social pressures reinforce the satisfaction of those wants in the conventional manner. In less traditional societies wants are less homogeneous and the effectiveness of social reinforcement is reduced. More freedom of choice is necessary to reduce interpersonal and intergroup tensions if force is not to be perpetually invoked. To put the same point another way, the greater the diversity of individual tastes and preferences, the higher the real costs to the individual of state-enforced consumption patterns.

In the next several subsections the limitations and implications of the Pareto efficiency concept are explored that are of general application as far as government regulation is concerned. The subsequent section is concerned with each of the specific conditions enumerated above that must prevail if perfect competition is to be achieved.

A.2.1 Income/Wealth Distribution

Suppose that some hypothetical economy were Pareto optimal at some point in time and a particular distribution of income/wealth prevailed. Could the aggregate welfare of the society be increased? The answer is indeterminate unless one *presumes* to know how much satisfaction Mr. Rich would lose and how much satisfaction Mr. Poor would gain if a dollar were taken from the former and given to the latter. Such interpersonal subjective comparisons are necessarily matters of presumption, and can be neither proven nor disproven. The views of economists, *qua* economists, are not better or worse than those of anyone else on this point.

The Pareto optimality concept is silent on the merits or demerits of any particular distribution of income/wealth. What can be inferred from it, however, is that any benefits (somehow assessed) to be derived from changing the distribution of income are likely to be offset, in whole or in part, by efficiency losses resulting from the distortions introduced by the redistribution policies.[8] "Distortion" means in this context that, in the face of a tax-transfer system imposed on a Pareto optimal economy, individuals will adjust their behaviour in order to minimize their tax burden or maximize their transfer benefit. The effects on behavioural choices of the income changes *per se* brought about by the tax-transfer are *not* at issue: what is involved are the effects on behavioural choices resulting solely from changes in opportunity costs brought about by taxes and transfers. A tax imposed on earned income makes additional leisure less costly—the money income forgone is reduced; a tax on consumption expenditures makes the return on additional saving effectively higher and, therefore, reduces the relative

---

[8] An unanticipated once-and-for-all lump sum capital levy would not have significant adverse resource allocation effects. However, such a device is obviously not a practical redistributive policy instrument.

disutility of postponing some consumption expenditures. If it were feasible to impose an unexpected, once-and-for-all capital levy that had the effect of reducing the individual's subsequent income by as much as the tax collected on income, there would be no point in the individual adjusting his behaviour other than in response to the income reduction *per se*. Opportunity costs would not be altered. Every other tax, with the exception discussed below, has some effects on opportunity costs and, therefore, has some, usually unintended and/or undesired, behavioural consequences. The reduction in total welfare brought about by behavioural changes that seek to minimize the tax bite, is called the "dead-weight loss" of the tax. The individual loses satisfaction and no one benefits—except sadists and masochists!

The worst of all possible situations would be one in which a tax-transfer system were adopted that was initially effective in terms of intended effects, but later lost its effectiveness. Suppose, however, that those who were taxed gradually and successfully adjusted their behaviour in order to minimize their liabilities. (We are not speaking here of tax evasion.) Pushed to a ludicrous extreme all tax revenues might cease so that no transfers could be made. This would result in a complete dead-weight loss. The satisfaction of the well-to-do would be reduced, for the reasons given above, but there would be *no* offsetting benefit. This kind of result was obtained, to a considerable extent, when the British government imposed a tax based on the number of windows in a building. To avoid the tax, many windows were boarded and bricked up and the revenues shrank. The result was that there were virtually no revenues raised by the tax and the would-be taxpayers suffered the inconvenience to no purpose.

One of the most serious ill effects of corporate income taxes, in particular, is the fact that with an assumed rate of 50 per cent, every dollar of pre-tax net income is only "worth" fifty cents. The result is a significant reduction in management concern about minimizing costs. A dollar saved is only fifty cents earned. Productive resources are simply wasted. This kind of waste is usually designated as technical, as distinct from allocative, inefficiency—but the costs to society are the same.

Obviously, there are many different kinds of taxes and many (an infinite number!) variants of each. Generally speaking, the broader the base and the more uniform the rates, the more neutral its effects (i.e., the less the change in opportunity costs) and the less the dead-weight loss. However, where the tax is applied to something in fixed supply, no dead-weight loss will be created however narrow the base and however high the rate. An annual tax on land based on location is, for example, a tax that is immediately reflected in a reduced market value (the present value of the expected tax outlays), because no behavioural adjustments are possible that would reduce the tax, although the pace of development may be slowed.

What has been said about taxes applies, *pari passu,* with respect to transfers.

Four points are urged upon the reader.

(1) It should be noted that taxes and transfers can be readily viewed as negative and positive rights (liabilities and assets) that are contingent upon the base and rates established for the particular tax and the jurisdiction of the taxing-transferring authority.

(2) Policies adopted for a distributive purpose (at least ostensibly) usually have efficiency consequences. These efficiency consequences are likely to be negative except where they offset (intentionally or unintentionally) some other cause of inefficiency. Conversely, policy changes adopted for the enhancement of efficiency are likely to have distributional consequences. There is, therefore, frequently but not necessarily a trade-off between greater efficiency and greater equity. The ''best'' combination is necessarily a matter of personal or political judgment. Enter the adversarial process and all that that signifies, as discussed in the final section of Chapter 1 and in subsequent chapters.

(3) The concept of Pareto optimality provides a useful *standard* and framework that *aids* in assessing the efficiency costs or benefits of government policies. As we will explain later, the conditions for the full realization of Pareto optimality constitute not a blueprint for a pure and perfect economy, but rather an orderly way of approaching the answers to the question ''what determines the efficiency of an economy?''.

(4) There is an important parallel between the worst tax, as sketched above, and the worst regulation. The worst tax raises no revenue but distorts behaviour to no intended purpose. The worst regulation raises revenues from fines, but does not alter behaviour as intended.

A.2.2 Compensation and the Theory of Second Best

In the following subsections we will discuss each of the several conditions requisite for the achievement of perfect competition in a market. Assuming that there is only one imperfection and that it could be remedied by a policy change, the obvious inference is that the adoption of the policy change would improve Pareto efficiency and should be adopted if no one were to be worse off while one or more were to be made better off. It is important to recognize that unless any adverse effects on the income of one or more individuals resulting from an efficiency-improving policy change are actually offset by compensation, it is not possible to advocate them as an unqualified improvement without implicitly or explicitly making some subjective judgment about the merit of the distributional change involved. Enter once again the adversarial process discussed in the final section of Chapter 1 *and* the relevance of log-rolling and bribery and the package of policies contained in election platforms as somewhat surreptitious means of achieving a form of compensation.

Compensation of the losers in order to achieve an unqualified improvement in economic welfare, if adopted literally, could produce some rather surprising results. Suppose that, in an otherwise perfectly competitive economy there were one widely held unregulated corporation that "owned" all of the "public" utilities. Suppose further that this corporation maximized its profits and that this resulted in less output and higher prices than would prevail if competition flourished universally. These monopoly profits (profits over and above normal profits) would be capitalized in the value of the corporation's shares traded in the financial market. If a regulatory policy were implemented that resulted in prices and outputs equivalent to those that would prevail under competition, the shares would tumble in price. The compensation principle would require that the shareholders' losses be offset by grants—and these grants would be equal to the present value of the flow of monopoly profits[9] that would have existed without the regulation. If the government financed the grants by the sale of bonds, individuals would, in effect, be paying through their taxes the monopoly profits that they otherwise would have paid to the company.[10] The net gain would be restricted to the benefits accruing to the efficiency gain *per se*. One can see the difficulty a government might have in compensating the losers for the loss of something the public (other than the shareholders!) probably believes they should not have been allowed to possess in the first instance. However, not to compensate the losers could easily result in inflicting capital losses on the "innocent." Why should the individual who purchased a share in the monopoly a day before the announcement of the regulation, at a price capitalizing the monopoly profit, be singled out to pay, through the drop in the value of the share, for the correction of a situation not of his making?

Another important qualification must be brought to the reader's attention. If only one of the conditions required for pure and perfect competition, and, hence, Pareto optimality, were not met, a policy change that corrected (with compensation when appropriate) for the aberration would be salutary by definition. What is less obvious, yet much more germane from a policy point of view, are the implications of the theory of second best. It has been proven that where more than one conditon is not satisfied correcting (including offsetting) for any one of them *may* make the outcome worse rather than better from an efficiency point of view. Conceivably, two or more imperfections are removed or offset simultaneously. Because this is out of the question in practical terms, this means that the Q.E.D. arguments for particular policy changes designed to increase efficiency are not valid unless it can be proven that the imperfection being remedied has either not been countervailed and/or that some other offsets will be put in place as a package

---

[9] Here we mean the excess of the maximized profit under monopoly over that under competition.

[10] There will, of course, be different distribution effects. This is neglected in the argument.

or sequence of reforms. Clearly this attenuates any argument for reform. But more importantly, it requires the assessment of magnitudes and not simply the direction (signs) of the forces involved. "Facts" of this sort are always debatable.[11] The result is that policy pronouncements that recognize all the qualifications tend to lose their persuasive powers. Even informed men of goodwill who accept the Pareto criterion as an efficiency standard may not agree on the appropriate policy response to a particular market imperfection. (Lipsey and Lancaster, 1956).

A.2.3 Static Versus Dynamic Efficiency

Pareto optimality involves a static view of efficiency. Not only is it restricted to the situation at a point in time, but to a point in time at which each market is in equilibrium and all markets are in equilibrium *vis-à-vis* one another. This concept of static general equilibrium, a useful methodological construct, implies that relative prices and quantities of inputs and outputs have fully adjusted to any and all prior external shocks such as changes in tastes and technology. There is no incentive for anyone—consumer or producer or resource supplier—to alter their behaviour for it is already satisfaction (and profit) optimizing. As indicated above, the comparitive statics approach to the *analysis* of the impact of particular changes has proven extremely valuable. Our question, however, is different. We are concerned about the validity of the concept of Pareto optimality as a standard to guide policy in the attempt to increase economic efficiency. If we admit that all the constants are not really constant, can we say anything about the barriers to efficiency?

Almost certainly the principal limitation of the static approach lies in the field of capital investment. The static theory of perfect competition deals with an economy at rest—an economy that has fully adjusted to, among other things, the current state of technology. There is, it will be recalled, no uncertainty. Capital obtains only a "normal return" which can be thought of as simply a reflection of the rate of return required to compensate savers for waiting. With no risks there are, of course, no rewards for risk taking. There are no temporary monopoly profits attributable to innovation. Ironically, the perfectly competitive model, the epitome of capitalism, ignores innovation when the economy is in static equilibrium, by definition; yet the superior innovative capacity of the capitalist system is one of its most vaunted advantages!

There is an intertemporal version of Pareto optimality that has been developed by Arrow (1971). In essence, this approach assumes that there is,

---

[11] This is just another cause giving rise to the uncertainty faced by the policy maker. If the policy maker wants to be completely certain before making a decision, he might as well leave the policy arena.

in addition to the markets we have considered, a perfectly competitive market in which securities in risks[12] can be bought and sold. The fact is, however, that markets in risk are most imperfect and, in some investment areas, non-existent. This is largely because the transactions costs are extraordinarily high. Many risks are unique. Before anyone will assume a contingent liability, a great deal of specialized knowledge is required in order to arrive at a reasonable price. Nevertheless, the market does go some distance by pooling risks and pooling reduces the risk for each of the participants.

The point is that from society's point of view there is a *de facto* pooling of risks. Some ventures pay off; others do not. If *all* ventures were taken together, the result would be a social cost of capital even below that achieved in theory by limited private sector pooling. All of this suggests that there is too little risk investment from society's point of view precisely because the risks are real enough to the individual investor (Baumol, 1969).

Joseph Schumpeter, several decades ago, advocated a degree of market imperfection as a means of encouraging innovation. It was his argument that if competition were "too perfect," the potential innovator would not obtain an adequate rate of return to warrant the risk because, if he were unsuccessful, he would, of course, lose his investment. If he were successful, there would soon be new entrants to the industry or existing firms would expand. By so doing, they would force the price down so that only a normal rate of return would be obtained. Though certainly not rigorous, this line of argument is certainly intuitively persuasive (Schumpeter, 1942).

Like the difficulties raised by compensation and the second-best theory, recognition of the limitations implicit in the static approach to efficiency mutes the clarion call to reduce market imperfections. Here again, if one were to take the stand that "if everything cannot be perfect (no pun intended!) then nothing should be done," some feasible efficiency gains might well be forgone. On the other hand, to proceed as though the several qualifications we have discussed do not exist, or are of no importance, could lead to policy prescriptions that, if adopted, would hurt rather than help the efficiency cause. Administrative X-inefficiency—pure waste—is always undesirable. There is, of necessity, a large element of judgment (subjective values if you will) involved in analysing allocative economic efficiency and in the formulation of policy and in applying the policy to particular situations. Enter still again the adversarial process as a method of legitimizing decisions that are fraught with conflict—conflict about the facts and conflict about the theory, conflict about the underlying values and conflict among interest groups.

---

[12] Each security is a claim contingent upon the realization of a pre-specified "state of the world." The state of the world that would materialize is uncertain. See Arrow (1971, Chap. 4). See also Hirshleifer and Shapiro (1969).

In the following section we will briefly discuss the major sources of market imperfections for regulations are often rationalized as "solutions" to these imperfections.[13]

A.3 SOURCES OF MARKET IMPERFECTIONS

Although, as we have just seen, the search for greater economic efficiency is only one dimension of government policy, and the efficacy of the alternative means of achieving greater efficiency certainly is not straight-forward, nevertheless, many of the regulatory policies of government are ostensibly adopted to serve that end. Here we will briefly discuss some of the underlying causes of market imperfections and the forms they take.

Exclusive property rights are, it will be recalled, the *sine qua non* for a market in them to exist. Some of the services and facilities provided by government are sources of benefits to residents that can be thought of as non-exclusive property rights. These are the so-called "public goods," such as defence and "law and order" mentioned earlier. Such non-exclusive rights must, by definition, fall outside the scope of this section except in our discussion of externalities in subsection A.3.3.

When does a difference in degree become a difference in kind? Terms like mercantilism, capitalism and corporatism convey the image of distinct boxes with sharp edges when a many-faceted continuum extending over time is closer to the picture one wants to convey. All of this is by way of saying that the gradual evolvement of feudalism into mercantilism and then into capitalistic industrialism in the mid-nineteenth century did not mark the end of the story, of course. Successful colonialism by the European countries meant cheap raw materials and captive markets. The settling of the West served much the same purpose for the Americans. Labour was plentiful (thanks to immigration in the United States) and cheap. Dramatic capital intensive innovations fell like rain upon these economies; profits were high and taxes were low so that investment was massive. International order, thanks to the navy (and well the British could afford it for they were the biggest winners), was maintained. It is hardly surprising that growth in the developed countries was phenomenal. Or it is hardly surprising that the highly capital intensive innovations coupled with markets of unprecedented extent led to the rise of some massive industrial principalities as the bigger fish gobbled up the smaller fish by acquisition or by driving them to bankruptcy, and by reinvesting seemingly ever expanding profits. By legitimizing in the mid-1800s the limited liability corporate form of organization, the British opened up vast pools of savings for industrial investment. This can be thought of as marking the "official" end of the small

---

[13] But see quotation from Trebilcock *et al.*, reproduced in Chapter 1.

entrepreneurial era and the beginning of what one might call the "managerial era."

The recognition of the corporation as a person in the eyes of the law was of enormous significance. In effect, a new kind of property right was created, a right to a share of profits without an obligation to make good any losses beyond those covered by the original investment. Because the investor's risk was limited, his need to carry out day-to-day surveillance was reduced and effective control could be left to a few of the shareholders. Because a single corporation could hold controlling interests simultaneously in many other corporations, it was often necessary to separate, to a high degree, control and management. The result was, of course, that minority shareholders had virtually no voice in the corporation's decisions and, what is more, little concern as long as the return was not grossly out of line given the particular circumstances of the enterprise and the returns being made elsewhere. Management, for its part, was not concerned about the minority shareholders but about those in control. And even here, management's concern was limited, by and large, to meeting a target rate of return. With the target met, the controlling shareholders were willing to allow management great discretion. In some extremely widely held corporations, controlling interest shareholders and management became essentially inseparable.

The British legislative changes of 1871 that precluded charges being laid against trade unions as "conspiracies in restraint of trade" were the starting shot in the struggle that saw the gradual emergence of the turbulent labour-management era in the thirties.

With the rise of the corporate form of organization the individual entrepreneur who owned and operated his own business became increasingly rare in many industries. So-called business leaders were those who gained control of corporations, reduced competition, manipulated stock prices outrageously, and had misleading prospecti issued so that their corporations might obtain maximum leverage. The new "robber barons" were able to successfully manipulate (or if needs be, coerce) legislators and administrators alike.

In the United States, the very success of the barons, their boastful disregard for the public interest, and the joy with which some of them flaunted their affluence led to a public reaction—a reaction based on socialist principles for a few and a simple populism for many. The result was that the U.S. Congress passed the Sherman Anti-Trust Act in 1890. This was the first attempt by a government to seek to codify and thereby sanctify, if you will, Adam Smith's ideal market economy even if this meant, at least on the surface, forcing the industrial giants to divest themselves of some of their recently acquired controlling interests in competing corporations. It also should be noted that it was at about this time that Congress created the Interstate Commerce Commission to control rail rates.[14]

As is well known, the self-righteous zeal of the many was no match for the wits and wealth of the few so that reality changed much less than appearances. But the crusade had begun—a crusade for the consumer interest that has waxed and waned over the decades without a decisive victory on either side. The disappointed knights have the satisfaction, however, that without their efforts the existing situation would probably have been much worse—but this is thin gruel. Let us briefly consider some of the forces that have tended to support a high degree of industrial concentration with the attendant reduction in the prevalence of price taking rather than price making.

A.3.1 Market Structure

In many industries the optimal size of the production and/or the distribution unit is a significant fraction of the market. Indeed, in the case of the distribution facilities of a natural monopoly, it is inevitably coterminous with the market, for it is not possible to offer each user a choice among power distribution companies, gas distribution companies, telephone companies, water systems, and so on, without excessive costs. Under these circumstances, government ownership (which is regulated perforce within the government)[15] or government regulation of privately held enterprises is inescapable if users are not to be exploited. How utilities should be regulated is a question that is endlessly debated. That some form of regulation is required, if the public ownership route is not taken, is beyond question in virtually all quarters.[16]

The controversy arises primarily with respect to situations where a few firms in an industry can each be profitable but where none can disregard the effects of its own price/output decisions on the market it serves. This market structure is known as oligopolistic (competition among the few) and the firms that comprise it are called oligopolists. Industries such as steel, cement, and refined petroleum products are typically oligopolistic. All firms in each industry supply essentially homogeneous products. There are also industries, such as automobiles, major appliances, processed foods, and detergents that are also oligopolistic in structure. However, in such industries all of the several corporations that comprise it sell products that perform a similar (identical?) function but, through minor (often cosmetic) variations and through advertising, they are differentiated in the eyes of the purchaser. This is the habitat of the brand name, the trademark and the copyright—so-called

---

[14] See Case 2 in Chapter 5.

[15] One should not assume that government ownership necessarily means effective government control. Inefficiencies can abound in such enterprises—more than if they were privately held.

[16] The exception is some extremely conservative members of the Chicago school cited in Chapter 1.

intellectual property. Each corporation has created a market for its own product and therefore is a price maker, at least within limits. The width of these limits depends on the sensitivity of buyers to differential prices among roughly similar products sold by roughly similar firms. The distinction between the homogeneous product oligopolistic industries and the differentiated product oligopolistic industries is crucial. The former structure prevails because of technological factors (the plant of optimal scale is enormous) and/or the importance of tariffs or transportation costs that effectively create a protected market for each plant. The threats to competition come about through price leadership practised by the dominant firm, collusive pricing and market sharing arrangements, horizontal integration to reduce competition for the firm's product, and vertical integration to obtain secure sources of raw materials and to secure markets for the product itself.

In oligopolistic industries where product differentiation is the order of the day, the one reason is imperfect consumer information and the economies of scale in advertising (see, e.g., Comanor and Wilson, 1974). Because the buyers are not usually expert (the opposite situation holds for products such as steel), consumers tend to choose a brand they have found satisfactory in the past. New entrants are faced with extraordinarily high promotional costs if they are to induce consumers to disregard their brand loyalties that have often been built up over the decades through millions of dollars spent on advertising by the corporations. Competition among brands is intense—but it is usually competition with respect to everything but price (that is to say, quality of service, packaging and "new" gimmicks are involved). The problem from the public interest point of view is the "unnecessary" costs embedded in the products sold in their differentiated markets.The firms are usually not "unduly" profitable although what they sell is unduly expensive!

The particularly offensive practices from a competitive point of view are resale price maintenance (open or surreptitious), false or misleading advertising and "full-line forcing."[17]

It is important to note that the government, by granting patents, trademarks and copyrights, has created property rights that have, whatever their other virtues, been of great significance in creating the market structure just described.

A.3.2 Transactions Costs

In recent years, economists have paid increasing attention to what have come to be called "transaction costs." These encompass both the time and

---

[17] The retailer, in order to obtain a franchise for the sale of one brand name product that is popular, is required to carry other product lines marketed by the same corporation—sometimes exclusively.

out-of-pocket costs of bargaining and of obtaining information.[18] The former costs do not exist in perfectly competitive markets because everyone is a price taker. The latter are ubiquitous but highly variable in importance from industry to industry and from product to product. The focus of attention is upon information as an important ingredient going into the decision-making process and not upon information for its own sake.

Little will be said here about bargaining costs except to draw attention both to the enormous costs involved in bargaining in labour-management relations, and in the legislation and regulatory bodies put in place in most jurisdictions in an attempt to minimize those costs while, at the same time, making the outcome—the contract—not only binding on both parties, in a legal sense, but also binding because it was "legitimately" arrived at by legitimate parties using legitimate means to obtain the result each sought.

Brand names, as we have stated, serve to reduce the information costs of consumers. Having found a reliable brand, subsequent purchases can become virtually automatic. The result is imperfect competition in the several forms described. This is, however, but one example of the important role of information in the determination of the degree of competition. Consider the following: new, small enterprises—potentially a major source of market competition—are confronted by a formidable barrier to entry. It costs at least as much for a potential outside investor to investigate the worthiness of a request for $100,000 as it does a request for $100,000,000. The fact that the management of the new enterprise has no proven track record—a valuable source of information—compounds the problem.

The more technologically complex, the greater the cost the potential buyer faces in making an informed choice. For many goods and services decisions made in comparative ignorance are of no great concern other than to reduce competition through branding. The usual rule, *caveat emptor,* is protection enough. However, there are some goods and services that are dangerous to health and safety. The uninformed consumer (or worker) may make decisions that cannot be "chalked up to experience" for there may be no more experiences of any kind! And it is not reasonable to expect the buyer to invest heavily in the acquisition of the requisite information when this might well take years of specialized training. Governments frequently adopt regulations in order to circumvent this difficulty. These regulations include such intervention as the requirement of adequate labelling and the prohibition of certain foods and drugs except by medical prescription. But such things as regulated working conditions, automobile and boat safety and building standards are all part and parcel of the attempt by government to protect the lives and health of individuals who cannot be expected to know the risks

---

[18] Brokers' fees and commissions can be looked upon as prices paid to obtain access to potential buyers or sellers, thus economizing information costs.

involved (or who may be exposed to risks by mercenary employers or sellers).

Professional licensing is a particularly important case. The ostensible purpose of professional licensing is to protect uninformed consumers from incompetence and/or dishonest practitioners. Such licensing, which is usually carried out by the profession itself under government authority (delegated legislation), can be used, however, to restrict entry and hence competition.

Financial markets are particularly vulnerable to manipulate and/or straight dishonesty because relevant information can be withheld and biased or false information provided to investors. Conflicts of interest may not be disclosed. Governments have found it necessary to require independently audited statements by corporations, and securities markets are regulated to prevent the worst abuses—the abuses that characterized the last part of the last century.

A.3.3 Externalities

Externalities, sometimes called spill-over effects, exist when there is a difference between private costs and/or benefits and social costs and/or benefits. In essence, negative externalities exist when the individual, or more typically the firm, imposes costs on society that are not reflected in the costs taken into account by those who create them. Air and water pollution are common examples. In making its investment/output/pricing decisions the firm will consider only the money costs it must bear and ignore the costs imposed on those who breathe polluted air and the adverse impact on the downstream users of the water into which wastes have been discharged. Under these circumstances the goods and services produced by the firm will sell at prices that do not cover their full costs to society. This in turn leads to too much production of the goods and services in question. The well-being of the citizenry would be improved by government actions that, one way or another, raised the price of such goods and services.

Positive externalities have the opposite characteristic: the firm cannot capture in its selling price the full value of the goods or services it produces in terms of the social benefits provided so that, by following the profit maximization rule, too few of such goods and services are produced without government intervention. Basic scientific research perhaps provides the best example of a positive externality: because the scientist or his employer cannot capture in the selling price or in royalties what the public collectively would be willing to pay for a fundamental idea of wide application (applications of ideas are patentable but not basic scientific theories and concepts), too little basic research will be undertaken unless some outside support, such as subsidies and grants, are forthcoming from government.

Positive externalities are often attributed to:
— primary and secondary education
— public health measures
— recreation facilities resulting from public works projects (e.g., dams).

Negative externalities are often attributed to the sources of:
— noise
— congestion
— addiction
— depletion of stocks of fish and wildlife that are common property.

There is another way to approach the question that so-called externalities raise. John Dales (1968) has emphasized that there is no such thing as an "externality": the phenomenon, he believes, is better understood as the non-existence of an enforceable property right to something that is valuable (i.e., Chapter 2, Table B, Item I(A)). For example, in the past, pulp and paper companies proceeded as though their riparian rights included the use of rivers as a means of waste disposal. They demanded compensation if they were to forgo this right. Environmentalists argued, on the other hand, that the companies had no such right. Rather, they firmly believe that downstream users of the river had and still have riparian right to pure water. From the environmentalists' point of view, it should be the paper companies who should cease and desist or face damage claims.

Coase (1960) has argued that it makes no difference who *holds* the property right if the right is recognized. The reason advanced is that when established, such a right can then be bought and sold and the resulting resource allocation will be efficient. This ignores the wealth distribution question entirely and the transactions costs entailed in establishing prices for such property rights.

A.3.4 Intervention of Government

Some of the greatest barriers to perfect competition are attributable to governments themselves. Among those that immediately come to mind are: minimum wage legislation, labour-management relations legislation, real property zoning, agricultural production quotas, patents and copyrights, and licensing. The effects of each such intervention, whether intended or not, and whether admitted or not, are multidimensional although the stated purpose may not reveal the several purposes involved. Here are some examples.

Regulation	Ostensible Purpose	Some of the Side-Effects Whether Intended or Not Intended
• minimum wage	prevent "exploitation" of the worker	reduce competition for those already employed; reduce job opportunities for those unemployed

Regulation	Ostensible Purpose	Some of the Side-Effects Whether Intended or Not Intended
• labour-management relations	orderly bargaining in good faith	increase bargaining power of weak workers relative to strong employers and conversely
• real property zoning	urban planning	pork barrel to local politicians and large redistribution of wealth
• agricultural production quotas	stabilize farm incomes	raise farm incomes, and reduce efficiency in agriculture
• patents, copyrights and trademarks	reward inventor-investor to encourage innovation	restrict competition, distort allocation of innovative resources in attempts to ''invent around'' patents.

As illustrated in Chapter 5, the dominant purpose and/or effect of much of government intervention is income/wealth redistribution. In essence the basic argument for intervention is that the market works too well in the sense that resulting income/wealth distributional effects are ''unacceptable.''

A.4 WORKABLE COMPETITION

The concept of Pareto optimality and the specification of the precise conditions under which efficiency in that sense would prevail were gradually enunciated in the late nineteenth century and the first half of the twentieth century (see especially Pigou, 1920). The theory that emerged was both more and less than Smith's original theory that gave rise to it. The theory of Pareto optimal efficiency was much more precise and the logically derived conclusions much more finely spun. It served the salutory purpose of clarifying how little economists could assert dogmatically without introducing subjective judgments. On the negative side, the efficiency theory exists in a kind of vacuum. It can be easily mininterpreted as a rationalization of the capitalistic system while, at the same time, giving few clues as to how any weaknesses in that system might be corrected. At best it states, in effect, that:

(1) if all the conditions, including perfectly competitive markets, do not hold in all markets, the economy is inefficient;

(2) a policy change(s) that removed all competitive imperfections, given that all losers from the change were fully compensated, would increase efficiency—provide a bonus of additional output at no cost;

(3) this bonus would provide *the possibility* of improving overall welfare; and

(4) whether it would actually do so would depend upon how the bonus was distributed in the light of a subjective standard established by some independent authority.

This is hardly what one might describe as a persuasive call to action, as was Smith's theory. Furthermore, consideration of the necessary conditions that must prevail for even this whispered message to be valid gives one the horrible feeling that, if narrowly construed and stringently interpreted, nothing whatsoever could be proclaimed in clear conscience without putting two blind eyes to the binoculars.

What seems to make eminent good sense is to consider the Pareto optimality theory of efficiency as a framework for analysis rather than as a means of deriving universally binding Q.E.D. conclusions. The specified conditions for Pareto optimal efficiency then can be looked upon by the analyst as consisting of two kinds of assumptions. One kind consists of assumptions that cannot be tested, even in principle. When these are rejected there is nothing to be gained from analysis employing the concept. Of greater practical importance is the set of assumptions that are testable in principle. The specification of these theoretically relevant factors serves the valuable function of leading the analyst to consider whether they reasonably reflect the realities in the particular problem or are sufficiently at variance with reality that, unless modified, would lead to the derivation of meaningless or misleading conclusions.

The vital distinction between efficiency effects and distribution effects made in the theory can be looked upon in the same spirit. It is imperative that the analyst bear in mind that both are almost invariably and inextricably involved in *every* policy problem. This need not mean that the economist can contribute nothing to the resolution of a policy problem, but only that he must be constantly aware of the difference between these dimensions of it and make it perfectly clear when he is setting forth his conclusions which of these involve subjective judgments.

In other words, if economists forgo the delights of reaching conclusions that are stated as necessarily valid and content themselves with more tentative results and frankly admit that factual and subjective judgments are involved, the Pareto optimal theory of efficiency has a useful contribution to make in structuring analysis. In order to say anything of policy significance, most economists settle for second (or worse) best—to use that term loosely—as far as rigour and elegance are concerned.

Leaving aside the theory *per se,* if all of the conditions for perfect competition are unattainable in reality, what is to be gained by achieving even "workable competition," to use J.M. Clark's (1942) term, relative to what would exist in the absence of any policies that push, on a highly selective basis, towards greater market competition? As we have already stated, such estimates as have been made do *not* suggest that the strictly *economic* gains from greater efficiency would be enormous *and they ignore both the provision of compensation for the losers and the implications of the theory of second best* and the dynamics of the market process (Harberger and Bergson, 1973). In short, the empirical findings, which are highly controversial, are not a decisive vindication of the gains to be had from greater allocative efficiency. However, the losses resulting from technical inefficiencies are not reflected in these kinds of estimates *and they may well be of much greater significance.*

It is our conclusion that given the theoretical and empirical limitations of the extant theory as applied and the estimated magnitudes involved, the pursuit of net static efficiency gains is certainly not the sole and probably not the *prime* reason(s) for the almost universal advocacy of some version of workable competition by Western (non-Marxian) economists. Rather, the underlying reasons have a great deal to do with the adverse effects of severe imperfect competition on the distribution of income/wealth and of power/influence as well as with the efficient allocation of resources. To be specific, although hopelessly unrigorous, we believe that the absence of workable competition is perceived by many observers (not excluding the author) to have the following undesirable consequences.

(1) The set of choices available to individuals are often more narrowly circumscribed, with respect both to buying and selling, and with respect to price, quality and timing, than would be the case if competition were greater. There is a degree of arbitrariness and indifference towards the corporation's customers and its suppliers that is resented.

(2) The financial statements of a corporation may *not* show a persistently high rate of return on the shareholder's investment relative to other corporations, when adjusted for risk differences. This, however, does not mean that there is no cause for concern. Costs may be inordinately high through waste *and/or* management and labour may have divided the monopolistic spoils between them in their higher-than-necessary salaries, wages, fringe benefits and "perks"—some of which may carry tax advantages. This generosity is resented, as is the unusually high degree of job security and the "quiet life" that often goes with jobs in such corporations (at least up to the *most* senior levels!).

(3) By retaining monopoly profits the corporation can escape the test of the capital market. Colossal blunders can be readily hidden in a colossal industrial empire. Retained monopoly profits can be used to buy the controlling interest in other corporations that are actual or potential competitors and control can be bought in others to ensure captive markets. Innovative ideas with competitive potential can also be purchased in order to

suppress them. Not only are consumers paying more than they should for goods and services now, the excess is being deployed to ensure that the situation will continue!

(4) Most of the advertising outlays of firms under imperfect competition are resented because they provide inadequate information for the expense incurred. The public service ads of the natural monopolies (often public utilities) are thought of as an unnecessary expense ultimately borne by consumers. And the advertising carried out by corporations in oligopolistic industries is seen for what it is: unbiased information content—slight; biased information content—overwhelming; the contribution of advertising to product prices—substantial. Perhaps the waste would be less obnoxious if it were not that the credulous seem to be perpetually duped at their own expense by the incredulous.

(5) The seeming indifference of industry to sometimes irreversible adverse environmental consequences of the extraction and processing of natural resources, and of some types of production, is also resented. The same is true, of course, of products that create health and accident hazards. Industry is looked upon as indifferent to the public good and the welfare of the customer and, indeed, rapacious in grasping private benefits at public expense.

(6) Few would question the reasonableness of large rewards for successful, substantive innovation. What is resented are the rewards that bear no relationshp to the risks that were run. This resentment is intensified if the idea was generated and the most painful risks incurred by someone who did not benefit materially because he was unable to patent it or marshall the capital to exploit it. Just as unacceptable are situations where the corporate giant can engage in price wars or endless and expensive legal battles that destroy a potential competitor because of his much more limited financial backing.

(7) The political influence of large firms in imperfectly competitive markets is resented and feared by many. They can well afford the tax-deductible expenses of wining, dining and entertaining those with power or those who have influence over those who do. They can arrange to meet such people socially because they can belong to the same clubs and take their "vacations" in the right places. They can hire experts to prepare briefs, to represent them in hearings, to publicize the favourable and suppress the unfavourable, to keep them informed on what is going on behind the scenes, to arrange access to those they wish to pursuade. They can make party contributions or provide benefits in kind; they can hire the child of a powerful or influential man. Not only can corporations do all these things separately, but they can also join with other corporations of similar interest to exert collective pressure. The "public interest" enjoys no such advantages in the pursuit of policy changes.

(8) Resented too are intergenerational social inequalities that result when corporate executives, and their advisers (lawyers, accountants, PR men, and lobbyists) are so well remunerated and so secure. They live in the best neighbourhoods in expensive houses with expensive furniture, appliances, hobbies and vacations. They send their children to the best universities and/or send them to Europe to "travel." They find their children good jobs and lend them the down payment on a first home, etc., etc. Those who advocate the principle of equality of opportunity find much of this distasteful. Some of that resentment is directed towards a lack of competition that permits it in the first place and perpetuates it thereafter.

If one agrees that something akin to the feelings just described are prevalent, at least in some articulate quarters, it is hardly surprising that governments will wish to appear to be "doing something" to achieve workable competition. What is equally obvious is that intensive conflict will be involved *and* an inescapable element of subjectivity will necessarily enter the picture.

REFERENCES

Arrow, K.J. (1971) *Essays in the Theory of Risk-Bearing* (Chicago: Markam; Amsterdam and London: North Holland).

Baumol, W.J. (1969) "On the Discount Rate For Public Projects" in U.S. Congress, Joint Economic Committee, *The Analysis and Evaluation of Public Expenditure: The PPB System* (Washington, D.C.: Government Printing Office).

Clark, J.M. (1942) "Toward a Concept of Workable Competition" in American Economic Association, *Readings in the Social Control of Industry*, pp. 452-75 (Philadelphia: Blakison).

Coase, Ronald H. (1960) "The Problem of Social Cost" *Journal of Law & Economics* 3: 1-44.

Comanor, William S. and Thomas A. Wilson (1974) *Advertising and Market Power* (Cambridge, Mass.: Harvard University Press).

Dales, John (1968) *Pollution, Property and Prices* (Toronto: University of Toronto Press).

Friedman, Milton (1962) *Capitalism and Freedom* (Chicago: University of Chicago Press).

Gordon, Scott (1977) "The Demand and Supply of Government: What We Want and What We Get" Discussion Paper No. 79 (Ottawa: Economic Council of Canada).

Harberger, A.C. (May 1954) "Monopoly and Resource Allocation" *American Economic Review Proceedings* May: 77-87.

Harberger, A.C. and Abram Bergson (1973) "On Monopoly Welfare Losses" *American Economic Review* 63: 853-60.

Heilbroner, Robert (1972) *The Worldly Philosophies* (New York: Simon and Schuster).

Hirschleifer, J. and D.L. Shapiro (1969) "The Treatment of Risk and Uncertainty" in U.S. Congress, Joint Economic Committee, *The Analysis & Evaluation of Public Expenditures: The PPB System* (Washington, D.C.: Government Printing Office).

Lange, Oskar and Fred M. Taylor (1938) *On the Economic Theory of Socialism* (Minneapolis: University of Minnesota Press).

Lerner, A.P. (1944) *The Economies of Control* (New York: Macmillan).

Lipsey, R.G. and Kevin Lancaster (1956) "The General Theory of Second Best" *Review of Economic Studies* 24: 11-32.

Pigou, A.C. (1920) *The Economics of Welfare* Pt. 1 (London: Macmillan).

Schumpeter, Joseph (1942) *Capitalism, Socialism and Democracy* (New York: Harper and Row).

Stein, B.A. (June 1976) "Collective Ownership, Property Rights, and Control of the Corporation" *Journal of Economic Issues* 10:2, 298-312.

Appendix B

The Compleat Rational Actor Approach to Policy Evaluation[1]

For the present purpose, evaluation is defined as the estimation of the effects on the achievement of government goals arising from changes in government programs or policies; the purpose of evaluation is to devise strategies for the fuller realization of those goals. Evaluation involves four basic elements: (1) operationally defined goals; (2) specification of one or more statistical indicators that are taken to measure the changes in the extent to which each goal is being met; (3) specification of the full range of policy instruments that can be used to realize government goals; (4) analyses of the relationships between changes in the policy instruments and changes in the indicators of goals attainment taking into account that most instruments affect more than one goal.

B.1 THE SPECIFICATION OF OBJECTIVES

The "classic" way to approach the evaluation of a particular policy is to seek to answer the question: how well does it meet the objective or objectives relative to the alternatives? And this leads to the question: but what is the objective? Or what are the objectives? On this rock many analytic ships run aground. There are essentially five reasons why it is difficult to answer this apparently simple question.

(1) There is often more than one statement in existence with respect to a particular policy, program or organization: one or more *Acts,* the expenditure *Estimates*[2] and a number of ministerial pronouncements made in and out of Parliament. If inconsistencies exist, which statement is overriding?

---

[1] This appendix consists primarily of an integration and revision of three earlier articles and a book by the author: Hartle (Summer 1973); (Spring 1976); (Summer 1976); and (1978). It is strongly suggested that the reader refer to the alternative policy evaluation techniques, of which the "rational actor" is one, discussed in Allison (1971).

[2] The statements provided in the federal government's annual expenditure *Estimates* serve to direct attention toward the general purpose to be served by a particular expenditure and away from the minutiae of 'line by line' budgeting—travel expenses, automobile allowances, furniture, and so on. While concern with such matters is obviously legitimate, for public servants should not be able to reward themselves too generously through the provision of benefits in kind, nevertheless, there is a tendency for discussion of the most trivial matters—that everyone can understand—to drive out consideration of more basic and hence more conceptually difficult issues.

(2) Many statements of objectives are designed to persuade the largest number of voters that what is being done is in their best interest. Such statements are, as a result, couched in rhetorical language that can be interpreted in many ways.

(3) Some statements of objectives have a jurisdictional purpose. One department or agency is staking out a claim to authority vis-à-vis other departments or agencies. The objectives set forth in such statements usually provide inadequate criteria for evaluations because they are not defined operationally. That is to say, the extent to which they are being achieved can only be assessed subjectively.

(4) Some so-called objectives are, at best, intermediate steps in long causal chains between means and ultimate ends. For example, regulating the minimum number of flights/day reduces waiting time. Reduced waiting time reduces transportation costs to the individual or the shipper. This *may* increase national output (depending upon what is being transported) and hence the real per capita standard of living. It certainly will increase the level of satisfaction of air travellers flying for pleasure. However, to accept minimum waiting time as ''the'' objective precludes many alternative routes to increasing the standard of living of an individual or groups of individuals.

(5) Many existing statements of objectives assume that the particular policy or program has a single purpose and ignore the fact that, *whether intended or not,* it simultaneously affects a number of collective concerns. For example, the objectives of a minimum wage say nothing about maintaining employment. But the regulation does affect this concern. To accept the view that, because the statements of objectives do not allude to these ''side effects,'' they should not be taken into account in assessing alternatives would be to seriously reduce the relevance of the analysis.

Most statements of policy objectives are of this ''single purpose'' type. While it may be desirable to define one of the effects of a policy as its ''purpose'' in seeking to convince an interest group of the government's concern with a particular problem, such statements are of limited usefulness in assessing alternatives.

It has been emphasized above that, in principle, it is necessary to consider all of the effects of each alternative policy or program that are of concern to ministers even though each may have only one stated purpose. But the plot gets thicker. The difference between an objective and a constraint is one of perspective rather than principle. Consider two objectives: reduce the likelihood of subversion; reduce the invasion of privacy.

It is widely believed that, under some circumstances, the greater realization of one of these objectives can only be achieved at the expense of the other. There is, in other words, a trade-off between them. To the extent that this is the case, each must be looked upon as a constraint with respect to the other. For example, the two objectives could also be expressed as: reduce the likelihood of subversion subject to the constraint that the rate of increase in the number of wire-tappings is not increased; or reduce the rate of increase in the number of wire-tappings subject to the constraint that the likelihood of subversion is not increased. Seen in these terms, the failure to include all of the relevant objectives in the set is tantamount to ignoring some of the constraints that ministers will impose on their policy choices, and hence reduces the relevance of the conclusions drawn from analysis.

Obviously, the less stringently the constraints are specified, the larger the number of alternatives that are feasible. Failure to take all of the objectives (constraints) into account creates one kind of error—misleading or irrelevant evaluations. Specifying constraints too stringently (or, what is the same thing, according competing objectives inordinate weights) precludes potentially superior alternatives.

One of the most intractable problems in the evaluation of policies is that encountered in trying to reach agreement on *operational definitions* of those government goals which are conceivably quantifiable. As indicated above, the field is strewn with strategic, ideological and semantic pitfalls. But unless agreement can be reached on these government goals which can be defined operationally—that is to say, in a manner that makes it possible to assess objectively the degree to which they are being realized—analytical techniques which could make a significant contribution to the decision-making process lose their value. There is no doubt that it is impossible to define some perfectly legitimate goals operationally. The goal of increasing national pride is an example. While one would expect that the subjective evaluation of ministers will always play the dominant role in assessing the degree of goal attainment in cases such as this, there presumably are some goals that could be defined operationally and measured, at least in part, statistically. Because the goals are generally incommensurate in any case, an inability to measure all of the goals does not mean that nothing is to be gained from measuring only some of them.

Another implication of the fact that goals are usually incommensurate is the impossibility of obtaining a single measure of the extent to which a group of goals is being realized. To illustrate the point, assume that ''the economic goal'' were defined to include three subgoals: (a) increase per capita GNP; (b) reduce the unemployment rate; (c) reduce the rate of inflation. Although the changes in each of these components can be measured reasonably reliably, it is not feasible to assess the degree to which such a goal is being realized because the subcomponents are not additive except by assigning arbitrary (subjective) weights to them. This means that classification of incommensurate goals into groups that have at least one common characteristic, while no doubt useful for some purposes, has relatively little analytical significance. That is to say, evaluation and strategic planning involving incommensurate goals can only proceed at the level of individual goals because it is often not possible to say whether or not there has been an unequivocal improvement or deterioration in the degree to which they are being achieved when considered as a group.

An attempt could be made to specify for each goal one or more statistical indicators. Changes in these indicators would be taken as measures of the changes in the extent to which the goal was being realized. From an analytic point of view, the changes in these indicators that resulted from the changes in government policies and programs would constitute, in effect, their "final" outputs.

There is no doubt that the selection of the "best" achievement indicators for each goal would constitute a formidable task. For to make this determination it would be necessary to obtain some agreement about the relevant qualitative as well as quantitative dimensions of each goal *and* the most satisfactory methods of measuring them. This would be relatively simple for a few goals (particularly those related to the changes in the consumption of tangible goods and services purchased with money income); but most of them would be difficult to define with the precision required for statistical estimation. It would also be extremely difficult, in most cases, to obtain that requisite data. Attitudinal surveys would clearly have to play a major role. It might well be discovered that it was impossible to measure reliably the extent to which some goals were being realized.

Even when all of these difficulties are admitted, it is nevertheless true that: (1) at least with respect to some reasonably vague goals (e.g., education) there is already in existence much more relevant information than is usually taken into account; (2) the exercise will help to identify the major gaps in the present statistical system; (3) the attempt to determine data requirements will force a degree of rigour in defining goals that would be salutary; (4) the realization that some goals cannot be clearly defined and/or the degree of their realization cannot be measured will serve to clarify those areas where officials can be of relatively little assistance in advising ministers because they do not possess the relevant information. No attempt is made in this paper to suggest the statistical indicators that might be used for each goal. The determination of these indicators would be a major undertaking—as the extensive discussion of "social indicators" in the literature makes abundantly clear (Henderson, 1974).

Some of the foregoing difficulties in the existing statements of objectives would be less serious if all ministers and officials were single-minded in their dedication to the better assessment of present or proposed policies. But such is not the case. There is, more often than not, no desire "to get on with it" because unfavourable assessments threaten personal positions. Often the strategy is to keep redefining *the* objectives so as to describe, at least implicitly, either what is currently being done by an organization or what those responsible for it want to do to enhance its power and prestige, and hence their own. When a program's *description* is used as its *objectives* it is, by definition, perfection itself.

It is impossible to imagine a group of ministers sitting around a table for months—perhaps years—trying to agree on all of their collective objectives (constraints), for they encompass virtually all aspects of life. Moreover, the wrangling over the precise weights to be attached to each of this endless list of objectives would be interminable. There would be no time left for decision making! Furthermore, with more information available everyday, they would have to reconsider, continuously, their assignments of weights.

This pessimistic recital of the problems of the "classic" approach immediately suggests that some more pragmatic method of program and policy evaluation must be found if advisers are to be of assistance to ministers in this field. This, in turn, suggests the adoption of one great overarching criterion—the likely impact of all program and policy changes on voting behaviour. On the surface, this would appear to be the most pragmatic (indeed, some would call it pragmatic to the point of cynicism) way of proceeding.

Because a system of policy evaluation entails that all relevant public concerns be taken into account because the goals are, when policies are efficient, also constraints, it is important that the reader appreciate that the number of goals to be specified would be enormous. Tables I and II seek to capture the essence of the size of the goal definition problem by illustrating what would be involved if it were attempted. These classifications are given solely for illustrative purposes. There are an infinite number of alternatives to those provided here.

In Table I, the box on the left sets forth the fundamental assumptions that underlie the whole approach. The ultimate purpose of any policy or program is to supply more adequately the means to the satisfaction of the needs of individuals.[3] The greater the degree to which these needs are satisfied, the greater the degree of individual well-being generated, it is assumed. Government ("the state") is treated solely as a means to this end and not an end in itself as are its policies.

The centre two columns constitute the classification system as such. Twelve general sources of well-being (or "goal areas") are identified. These sources are divided into two groups: private sources and collective sources. Private sources are those over which individuals exercise some personal control and/or the benefits of which are shared among a group of individuals, in the sense that the benefits (or costs) are necessarily jointly enjoyed (or suffered), or there is some other communal aspect inherent in the provision or use of those sources. There are three goal areas in the former group and seven in the latter. Each goal area has a number of component sources (or "goals"). As explained above, it is only at the level of these goals that analysis can be carried out because, with the exception of the first goal area where the components are additive, it is not possible to assess the extent to

---

[3] It should be obvious that this assumption about the purpose of government is indeed fundamental and would not be accepted by all governments in all countries—in particular it would not be accepted by totalitarian governments.

TABLE I

BASIC ELEMENTS OF THE GOAL CLASSIFICATION SYSTEM

	Ultimate sources of the well-being of individuals and families	
'Goal areas' General classes of goals	'Goals' The particular goals that constitute the components of each 'goal area'	
PRIVATE		
1 Consumption of tangible goods and services purchased with money income		
2 Consumption of tangible goods and services received in kind		
3 Intangible personal 'assets' that are direct sources of satisfaction*		
COLLECTIVE		
4 Physical environment		
5 Intellectual environment		
6 Recreational-cultural environment		
7 Economic environment		
8 Social environment		
9 General political-legal environment		
10 Intangible shared 'assets' that are direct sources of satisfaction to Canadians		
11 International relations		
12 Federal-provincial relations		

Associated with each particular goal would be, where feasible, one or more statistical indicators. Changes in the values of these indicators over time would measure the changes in the degree to which it was being realized

The end result of improved policies and programs: the greater satisfaction of human needs (undefined). The satisfaction of these needs is assumed to generate increased individual or family well-being

* Including such diverse items as the individual's reputation with respect to honesty, charity,

Source: Hartle (1973).

which progress is being made in improving a goal area except by examining what is happening to each of its component goals because they are incommensurate.

The right-hand box indicates that, where feasible, for each goal one or more statistical indicators would be specified. The changes in the values of these indicators over time would be taken as measures of the changes in the adequacy of the particular source of well-being. For example, one of the goals included under the first goal area, ''consumption of goods and services purchased with money income,'' is labour income. The unemployment rate might be used as one of several measures of the state of this source of well-being. The unemployment rate may, of course, also be a useful indicator under goals 7 and 8, the economic and social environments.

It may be worthwhile to summarize briefly the main ideas that Table I seeks to convey. It traces four stages in the specification of goals, from the philosophically fundamental objective of social welfare based on individual well-being, through successively more detailed and concrete breakdowns of the sources of well-being, to measurable and operational indicators of the increases or decreases in these sources. Changes in these indicators then can be taken for evaluative purposes as the final outputs (as ''final'' as need be measured) of government programs and policies. For those goals for which it is not possible to be precise in this way about what underlies the general notions of social welfare and individual well-being, it follows that a comprehensive empirical evaluation of major government programs and policies is precluded.

A tentative set of goals to be included within each goal area is given in Table II. It should be noted that two types of goals are identified—positive goals and negative goals. The former are to be maintained or increased. The latter are to be reduced.[4]

There are, it will be observed, innumerable conflicts among the goals. That is to say, in many instances improving well-being from one source necessarily entails some reduction in well-being through one or more other sources. If the list of goals is complete, all of these inherent conflicts will be made explicit—for that is what decision making is all about. It is not difficult to make decisions where there are no costs!

Many generally accepted goals are not to be found in Table II. There is no reference, for example, to such an objective as the reduction of the trade deficit (dependence on foreign savings). The reason these so-called goals have been omitted is that it is assumed that their realization is sought as a means to the achievement of more fundamental goals, not for their own sake. In some instances, these subsidiary goals are now treated as ends rather than

---

[4] It perhaps should be reiterated that sets of goals, such as those described in Table II, are useless as evaluative criteria unless they are accepted by ministers. The purpose here is not to suggest that these are, in fact, the goals of ministers but rather to illustrate what is involved.

TABLE II

SOURCES OF WELL-BEING OF CANADIAN INDIVIDUALS AND FAMILIES

GOAL AREAS	GOALS	
	POSITIVE (MAINTAIN OF INCREASE)	NEGATIVE (REDUCE)
Private		
1 Consumption of tangible goods and services purchased with money income (constant value $s)	Gross money income: labour income transfer payments from all sources net investment income	Cost of 'necessities' and/or goods and services commanding social priorities such as food, shelter, health care, education, some recreational and cultural activities, some types of transportation and communication
		Taxes and compulsory contributions to governments
		'Obligations' to provide financial support to other individuals or organizations (e.g., charitable donations)
		Risk of reduced future consumption for reasons specific to the individual
2 Consumption of tangible goods and services received in kind	"Free" goods and services provided specifically to the individual by governments (e.g., primary education or garbage collection).	Conscription of services or confiscation of goods by governments
	Goods and services produced by individual for own use in leisure time	Support (non-financial) provided to other individuals or organizations (e.g., free room and board provided to an elderly relative).
	Support (non-financial) received from other individuals or organizations (e.g., free room and board provided by a religious group to an indigent)	
	Non-monetary remuneration of employees and investors (e.g. use of company car for own use)	

GOAL AREAS	GOALS	
	POSITIVE (MAINTAIN OF INCREASE)	NEGATIVE (REDUCE)
Private		
3 Intangible personal 'assets' that are direct sources of satisfaction	Knowledge (as distinct from occupational skills Health Favourable reputation derived from perception of others that the individual's behaviour is consistent with shared cultural and ethical values (e.g., the source of personal prestige) Favourable self-appraisal derived from the individual's perception that own behaviour is consistent with own cultural and ethical values (e.g., the source of self-esteem) Interpersonal relations that yield affection Perceived ability of the individual to influence the decisions of others (e.g., source of a feeling of power) Personal memberships in prestigious groups	Risk of losses through: physical and mental illness, character assassination, failure to conform to own or shared cultural or ethical values, inability to exert influence, disparities between own and shared cultural and ethical values
Collective		
4 Physical environment	The quantity and quality of common property (e.g., air and water) Unalienated property rights (e.g., crown lands, timber rights, and mineral rights)	Pollution of all kinds, including aesthetic pollution Congestion Risk of losses from natural disasters and public health hazards
5 Intellectual environment	Stock of knowledge Freedom of enquiry and expression	Cost of access to the stock of knowledge Disparities in intelligence and/or levels of educational attainment and hence perceptions of reality Risk of loss from obsolescence as result of new knowledge

TABLE II
(Continued)

GOAL AREAS	GOALS	
	POSITIVE (MAINTAIN OR INCREASE)	NEGATIVE (REDUCE)
Collective		
6 Recreational-cultural environment	Works of art, objects of historic significance, and the supply of skilled performing artists and athletes	Cost of access to cultural and recreational activities and facilities
	Facilities that make it possible for individuals to see and/or hear these objects or activities	Disparities in taste and sensitivity resulting from cultural deprivation and/or a lack of shared cultural values
	Quantity and quality of amateur sport and athletics	
	Recreational parks and facilities	
	Freedom of expression	
7 Economic environment	Information that makes markets function more effectively (e.g., full disclosure by sellers)	Barriers to the free flow of goods, services and capital
	Enforcement of contracts	Barriers to entry to occupations and businesses and other restrictive trade practices
	Freedom of choice between work and leisure, saving and consuming, alternative types of consumption	Risk of losses through changes in market conditions
	Protection of the interests of the inventor	Disparities in degree of acceptance of and/or conformity to such values as honesty diligence and prudence
8 Social environment	Social mobility (i.e., equality of opportunity)	Disparities in living standards among individuals and families resident in the same jurisdiction
	Appreciation of traditions and styles of different cultural-linguistic-religious groups	Unfavourable discrimination on the basis of sex, ethnic origin, language and religion
	Freedom of religion	

GOAL AREAS	GOALS	
	POSITIVE (MAINTAIN OF INCREASE)	NEGATIVE (REDUCE)
Collective		
9 General political-legal environment	Information on basis of which electorate can assess effectiveness of government policies and programs Rule of law under an independent judiciary Equality of treatment before law Free elections with proportionate representation Rehabilitation of convicted criminals Freedom of individuals to travel and choose their place of residence Right to privacy Freedom of speech and peaceful assembly	Disparities in living standards of the individuals living in different jurisdictions Risk of losses through war, civil insurrection, crimes against persons and property
10 Intangible shared assets that are direct sources of satisfaction to Canadians	Favourable reputation of Canada and Canadians generally among non-residents (i.e., the source of national prestige) Perception of Canadians that they generally behave in accordance with their own shared cultural and ethical values (i.e., the source of national pride) Perception of Canadians that they have the ability to exert an influence on the behaviour of non-residents (i.e., the source of a feeling of national power) Perception of Canadians that they share the same cultural and ethical values (i.e., the source of a feeling of 'belonging')	Sense of national inferiority arising from the perceptions of Canadians that the views of non-residents about them are unfavourable Sense of regional inferiority arising from the perceptions of the residents of a region that the views of them held by other Canadians are unfavourable Perception of Canadians living in different regions that the residents of other regions do not behave in accordance with 'accepted' cultural and ethical values Perception of Canadians that they do not have the ability to prevent non-residents from exerting unfavourable influences on them

TABLE II
(Continued)

GOAL AREAS	GOALS	
	POSITIVE (MAINTAIN OF INCREASE)	NEGATIVE (REDUCE)
Collective		
11 International relations	Ability of Government of Canada to influence the decisions of other national governments and their residents in order to more fully realize the goals of Canadians (as specified above)	Ability of other national governments and their residents to affect adversely the degree to which the goals of Canadians (as specified above) are realized
12 Federal-provincial relations	Ability of the Government of Canada to implement policies that will most fully realize the shared goals of Canadians Ability of provincial governments to implement policies that will most fully realize the goals shared by their residents but not by Canadians generally	Ability of provincial governments to affect adversely the degree to which the shared goals of Canadians are realized Ability of provincial governments to more fully realize the shared goals of their residents at the expense of other Canadians

Source: Hartle (1973).

means, but presumably this is because implicitly they are taken as reasonable proxy measures of the degree of attainment of something more basic that is difficult to assess.

Despite the staggering list of goals, reflection on any one of them will reveal that, in fact, many goals consist of an aggregation of many subgoals that in turn consist of sub-subgoals. There is an almost infinite regression. Consider, for example, a goal such as Number 9 in Table II—"General political legal environment"!

B.2 THE INVENTORY OF POLICY INSTRUMENTS

A classification of the inventory of policy instruments (means) available to government is given in Table III. This paper is concerned primarily with the analysis and assessment of item (9), the regulation of non-governmental activities by government. We have already defined government in Chapter 1. It remains, however, to define what we mean by "regulation." For our purpose, regulations we define as follows: rules imposed by a government acting within its constitutional and territorial jurisdiction that prescribe or proscribe certain kinds of behaviour at certain times and places by certain kinds of legal entities under certain conditions that, if effective, will neither raise significant government revenues by way of fines nor entail government expenditures for enforcement that are insignificant relative to the subsidy that would be required to yield the same effects.

The words "significant" and "insignificant" are used because some fines are so low that they may be looked upon as a fee (e.g., parking violations) while the enforcement costs of some rules are substantial (e.g., the provision of police services to enforce the Criminal Code). They are trivial relative to the amounts that would be required to pay to bribe criminals to desist or induce those who were potential law-breakers to refrain from so doing!

It is important to bear in mind what we said in the previous section. The tax-expenditure-regulation distinction is not as clear cut as it might at first appear. The differences are often a matter of degree and intent rather than in the actual effects. Indeed, we will argue later that many, if not all of the purposes for which regulations are adopted often could be realized *in principle* by taxes or subsidies (= negative tax = expenditures).

Regulations, like other policy instruments, can be considered from two points of view: the positivistic and the normative. The first is concerned with the description and the analysis of effects, whether intended or not. The second is concerned with assessing those effects against some standard. This paper purports to address the regulatory issue primarily from the former standpoint for the reasons and with the provisions stated in Section 1.1. No attempt is made to consider particular regulations in any depth. A distinction is drawn between the regulatory function and a regulatory agency. Such agencies carry out a regulatory function(s), but regulatory functions are also performed by traditional government departments that are responsible to, rather than, through a minister.

All regulations, in the final analysis, apply to persons, including corporations that are treated as persons in the eyes of the law. Rules cannot

TABLE III

CLASSIFICATION SYSTEM FOR INVENTORY OF GOVERNMENT POLICIES AND PROGRAMS

Tax System
1. Taxes (including compulsory "contributions" not included under item 5)
2. Tariffs
3. Tax concessions (subsidies made through reduction in tax otherwise payable to specific groups of individuals or businesses)

Expenditure Budget
4. Transfer payments, grants and subsidies
   Statutory
   — persons
   — businesses
   — non-profit organizations
   — provincial-municipal governments
   — other
   Non-statutory
   — persons
   — businesses
   — non-profit organizations
   — provincial-municipal governments
   — other
5. "Social insurance" plans (i.e., benefit entitlement based on contributory history)
6. Provision of goods and services
   — no user charges
   — user charges plus subsidy
   — full cost recovery

Government Financial Asset Management
7. Government borrowing and lending
8. Loan guarantees

Regulatory Activities
9. Regulation of non-government activities
10. Internal regulation-control of government activities

make inanimate or intangible "things" (other than corporations!) do something or refrain from doing something. All regulations apply to behaviour—actions or conduct. One cannot regulate for or against "being" a thing with the exception, perhaps, of "being" a corporation. Thus, when we speak about the regulation of prices, qualities, quantities of goods, services or assets, what is regulated are the prices at which persons can exchange a "thing" with another person or the kinds of things that can be transferred or the quality specifications of such things. It is the acquisition or possession or production or transfer or use of the thing that is regulated, *not* the good or service or asset as such. To be even more precise, it is not the acquisition, possession, exchange, and so on, of "things" that is at issue but rather the property rights that inhere in those "things."

Bearing all of these qualifications in mind, it is painfully obvious that regulations can be classified in a multitude of ways: the "best" way depending upon the descriptive, analytic or assessment purpose to be served. Some of the more obvious dimensions are given below.

(1) Natural persons or legal persons or both, with or without specified attributes, to whom the regulation applies (i.e., whose decisions are to be directly affected)
(2) Property rights affected:
— non-exclusive (collective)
— exclusive
— transferable
— non-transferable
(3) "Things" in which such rights inhere:
— goods (including real and personal property)
— services
— assets (including human capital; intellectual property; reputation—libel and slander; interpersonal relationships
— alienation of affection
— memberships)
(4) Kinds of rights affected by regulation:
— acquisition
— production
— possession
— transfer
— access
— rule-making procedures
(5) Means of enforcement and penalties
(6) Appeal procedures

Even if these categories and subcategories were accepted or exhaustive, and they are not, there would be an enormous number of separate "boxes" and many of them could be divided into hundreds of smaller categories (e.g., the age, sex, location and other attributes of individuals).

B.3 EVALUATION

Evaluation may be retrospective or prospective. The former seeks to determine the impact of current or abandoned expenditure programs or other policies on the degree of goal attainment in the past. The latter seeks to determine what the impact of current or proposed programs or policies is likely to be in the future. Leaving aside the question of assigning credit or blame, retrospective evaluations are undertaken as a means of improving the reliability of prospective evaluations.

Evaluation is, in turn, one of five elements of what we will call strategic planning. These elements are: (1) forecasts of the changes in the indicators of goal achievement that would occur in the absence of changes in the policy instruments; (2) the assignment by ministers of priorities to the present or emerging problems identified on the basis of this information; (3) identification of the kinds of policy instrument changes that might be used to meet these high-priority problems; (4) assessment of their relative effectiveness, taking into account any positive or negative effects on other goals (prospective evaluation); (5) selection by ministers of the changes in the policy instruments that would most effectively resolve the highest priority problems of the government.

Evaluative and strategic planning are, it can be seen, inextricably related. Evaluation proceeds from the policy instruments to their effects on goals. Strategic planning proceeds from the desired attainment of goals to the selection of the mix of policy instruments best able to achieve them using the information produced through evaluation.

These concepts can be illustrated by considering a hypothetical case: a government that has only three goals, A, B, and C, and only three alternative policy instruments, identified by the numbers 1 through 3. With each goal there is associated a statistical series. The changes in these statistical series are taken as measures of the changes in the degree to which the particular goal is realized. These statistical series are not commensurate. For example, one series might measure per capita income while another might measure the crime rate.

Let us assume that: the hypothetical government has adopted policies 1, 2, and 3 with the *intention* of furthering the degree to which goals A, B, and C, respectively, would be realized. An evaluation of these policies, in terms of the changes they have brought about in the past values of the statistical series relative to what they otherwise would have been, has yielded the results that are displayed in Table IV. Favourable effects are shown as positive signs, and conversely.

These hypothetical results would suggest that each policy had the intended favourable effect on "its" goal. But the unintended effects of the three policies on the "other" goals in some instances offset, and in other instances complemented, these intended effects. For example, all of the

TABLE IV

RETROSPECTIVE EVALUATION OF EFFECTS
OF CURRENT POLICIES ON PAST VALUES
OF GOAL ACHIEVEMENT INDICATORS

	IMPACT ON GOALS		
POLICIES	A	B	C
Intended effects			
1	+		
2		+	
3			+
Unintended effects			
1	N/A	+	+
2	−	N/A	−
3	−	+	N/A

Source: Hartle (1973).

effects of policy 1 were favourable; the two unintended effects of policy 2 were unfavourable while of the unintended effects of policy 3, one was favourable and one was unfavourable.

Three points can be made on the basis of this simple example.

(1) The distinction between intended and unintended effects, while undoubtedly significant for political and administrative purposes, is immaterial when it comes to the evaluation of policies. The effects are what they are. It is useful, however, as explained later, to distinguish between presumed effects and estimated effects.

(2) It is not possible for the analyst to determine, on the basis of the information given, whether or not policy 2 (that had one positive effect and two negative effects) made a net positive contribution to the realization of the government's goals. Even if the magnitudes of these effects were known, because the goals are incommensurate it is not possible to determine objectively if the favourable effects were ''worth'' the unfavourable effects.

(3) When all of the government's goals are included in the analysis, the costs of more fully realizing a particular goal through the use of one or more policies are the unfavourable effects they have on other goals. By definition, the mix of policies is not optimal when costless gains in goal attainment can be had by changing these policies. This is rarely the situation. In most instances a hard decision must be made in which more of something desirable can only be achieved at the expense of something else that is also desirable.

Thus far the discussion has been concerned with retrospective evaluation. But the purpose of looking backwards is to improve future decisions. The uses of prospective evaluation, and the relationship between it and strategic planning, can also be illustrated by a hypothetical example. To keep the example simple, it is assumed that: there are only four feasible policy mix alternatives (these are listed across the top of Table V); decisions are made on the basis of the expected values of the statistical indicators at a particular point in time in the future; reliable estimates of the impact of the policy options on these indicators are available and are displayed in Table V.

The hypothetical results provided in Table V indicate that if policies were left unchanged, goal A would be more fully attained (positive signs denote favourable changes), goal B less fully attained, and that there would be no change in the extent to which goal C would be realized. Whether, on

TABLE V

HYPOTHETICAL ESTIMATES OF CHANGES IN EXTENT OF GOAL ATTAINMENT UNDER ALTERNATIVE POLICY OPTIONS

GOAL ATTAINMENT INDICATORS	NO CHANGE IN CURRENT POLICIES	POLICY OPTIONS ALTERNATIVES			
		I	II	III	IV
Current values					
a $	5000				
b %	20				
c index	150				
Estimated values at some future point in time under policy options					
a $	6000	6000	6000	5000	7000
b %	10	10	20	10	0
c index	150	150	150	150	200
Estimated change from current values					
a $	+1000	+1000	+1000	0	+2000
b %	−10	−10	0	−10	−20
c index	0	0	0	0	+50
Estimated impact of alternatives relative to no change in current policies					
a $	—	0	0	−1000	+1000
b %	—	0	+10	0	−10
c index	—	0	0	0	+50

Source: Hartle (1973).

balance, the situation would improve in the absence of policy changes can only be determined if the subjective value attached to the increase is greater than that assigned to the decrease for, it will be recalled, these values are incommensurate. The comparison shown at the bottom of Table V between the policy alternatives and the "no change" option reveals that alternative I can be dismissed because nothing would be accomplished relative to current policies. The third option can also be rejected for it would not have any positive differential impact on two of the goals and would act unfavourably on the other. Alternative II is obviously preferable to the present mix of policies because it would bring about an improvement in goal B, relative to expectations under current policies, without adversely affecting achievement of the others. Alternative IV does better with respect to both goals A and C, but worse with respect to goal B. As in the case of the prospects without policy change, it is impossible to tell objectively whether or not this mix is a net gain or a net loss. Similarly it is not possible to "prove" that alternative IV is better or worse than alternative II, because this depends upon the value associated with the gains for goals A and C relative to the loss for goal B.

In the real world there are, of course, an infinite number of policy options. Consequently, the analyst can not provide ministers with the estimates of the impact of *all* feasible policy options in the spirit of Table V. The process described thus far must, in reality, work the other way if the initiative for policy change is to come from ministers rather than analysts. This reverse process that we are calling strategic planning can begin for several reasons. Let us suppose that the analyst has provided ministers with the hypothetical results given in column 1 of Table V—the estimates of the changes in the indicators of goal attainment assuming no change in policies. From this information it is apparent that a problem is emerging. If nothing is done, goal B will be less adequately realized in the future. Ministers can simply direct the analysts to search for a new policy mix that would "solve" this problem. Using the information derived from evaluations, the analyst would, ideally, discover a policy option like II that would prevent the expected problem from developing and, in this case, provide an actual improvement in goal B while, at the same time, preserving the projected gain in goal A.

Even if the forecast levels of goal attainment do not disclose emerging problems, the strategic planning process can be initiated by ministers if their preferences change or if they have reason to suspect that costless gains are to be had by changing policies. The first of these reasons perhaps needs some explanation. Suppose that the forecasts of future goal attainment showed improvements with respect to all goals, and ministers were satisfied that further improvements in one or more of the goals were not obtainable without unfavourable effects on others. If they decided that the fuller realization of one of the goals should have a higher priority, they would ask the analyst to search for a policy change that would bring about this result at the least cost in terms of other goals less adequately realized. This search would necessarily be based on evaluations of policy effectiveness as already described.

The proposed goal classification system described earlier identified twelve goal areas, and each of these goal areas included a number of component goals. It is *not* possible to assign each policy instrument to one and only one of these twelve boxes, much less to one and only one of the component boxes within each goal area. There are several reasons for this: virtually all policy instruments simultaneously affect more than one goal; to select one of these effects as the ''primary'' effect would be to prejudge both the magnitudes of the several effects and the values that ministers would assign to them—given that they are generally incommensurate. For example, suppose that a particular policy simultaneously raised the living standard of a low income group *and* increased national unity. Clearly the relative weights attached to the two effects could only be decided by ministers—and they would have to make a judgment about the relative magnitudes involved before reaching a judgment. For an official to make such a judgment without any objective evidence about the magnitudes of the effects would be doubly presumptuous.

To select the primary effect on the basis of declared intentions is not very helpful either. The gap between declared intentions and real intentions may be as great as the gap between what the effects were expected to be and what they are in realtiy. Unintended side effects may turn out to be of greater significance than intended direct effects.

All of this suggests that: (1) the same policy instrument usually must be classified under more than one goal (or goal area); (2) until the evaluation is carried out this classification can only be based on presumed effects; (3) even after reliable analyses have been completed there is little to be gained from seeking to achieve a unique classification of policy instruments in accordance with ''primary'' effects as decided by ministers because this designation will change as the priorities of ministers change.

This suggests, therefore, that the approach be adopted that the starting point for evaluation would be a matrix in which policy instruments (the rows) were cross-classified against goal areas (the columns). This initial cross-classification would be based on presumed effects until the analysis of a particular program was complete. Most policy instruments would appear under more than one goal area. Table VI illustrates the basic ideas involved.

While not made explicit in Table VI, the presumed effects are defined in terms of the probable direction of the impact of each policy instrument on the statistical indicators of goals achievement that relate to one or more of the specific goals included as elements in the goal area. To over-simplify for the moment, the evaluative process consists of estimating, on a row by row basis, the direction and magnitude of the actual effects, as distinct from the presumed effects, on these goal achievement indicators. The strategic planning process consists of trying to determine, on a column by column basis, the mix of policy instruments that will most fully realize a particular goal based on the results of these row by row evaluations. While this way of explaining the framework gets the main points across, in reality the policy instruments (rows) cannot be considered one at a time because of the interactions that exist between them. Some policy instruments are complementary while others are competitive. Similarly, strategic planning cannot proceed solely on the basis of maximizing the realization of particular goals (columns). As explained above, there are usually major conflicts among individual goals so that the more complete realization of one goal will impose a cost in terms of the less adequate realization of others. Clearly the end product of strategic planning must be the determination of these costs so that ministers can make the hard decisions that are involved.

In reality it is impossible to evaluate the joint effects of all conceivable bundles of policy instruments on the realization of all of the government's goals. It is equally impossible to devise *the* strategic plan that optimizes the degree to which all goals are realized simultaneously in the light of the preferences of ministers when conflicts among the goals are involved. The problem is to move from the definition of the task that is conceptually perfect, but hopelessly impractical, to one where material progress can be made without losing the fundamental insights provided by the framework.

The conceptual scheme outlined is neither new nor unique. It is similar to the framework developed by Tinbergen that serves as the basis for the "Netherlands" school of economic planning. Indeed, the formal structures of virtually all planning systems lead to the same basic insights. What is perhaps different in the proposal is the insistence that these structures must be made operational if they are to make a positive contribution to the decision-making process.

Three distinct tasks would have to be performed to make the conceptual framework operational. They are described briefly below.

Task 1: (a) identifying the set of particular goals that ministers seek to achieve; (b) classifying these particular goals into groups (goal areas) that have similar characteristics.

Task 2: (a) specifying for each particular goal the one or more statistical indicators that will be used to measure the degree to which it is being attained; (b) estimating the past, present and future values of each such achievement indicator assuming no change in policies.

Task 3: (a) identifying the inventory of actual and potential policy instruments that the government can use to effect the realization of its goals; (b) estimating the effects of changes in each policy instrument, and subsets of such instruments, on the projected values of the achievement indicators.

TABLE VI

CONCEPTUAL FRAMEWORK IN SCHEMATIC FORM: ESTIMATED EFFECT ON GOAL ACHIEVEMENT INDICATORS OF SPECIFIC POLICY INSTRUMENTS

SOURCES OF THE WELL-BEING OF CANADIANS

INVENTORY OF ACTUAL AND POTENTIAL POLICY INSTRUMENTS	GOAL AREA 1: the particular goals that constitute the components of the goal area			GOAL AREA 2: the particular goals that constitute the components of the goal area		GOAL AREA 3: the particular goals that constitute the components of the goal area			GOAL AREA 4: the particular goals that constitute the components of the goal area	
	1A	1B	1C	2A	2B	3A	3B	3C	4A	4B
(Associated with each particular goal would be, where feasible, one or more statistical indicators. Changes in the values of these indicators over time would measure the changes in the degree to which the goal was being realized.)										
Expenditure programs										
A	+	0	0	−	0	+	+	0	−	0
B	0	0	0	+	−	0	0	−	+	0
C	−	+	0	−	+	0	0	0	0	0
.										
.										
N	+	−	+	+	0	−	+	0	0	+
Tax system*	−	−	+	0	+	−	−	−	+	+
Government financial asset management*	0	0	+	−	+	+	−	0	−	+
Regulatory activities*	0	−	−	+	−	+	0	0	0	0

* Each of these broad classes of instrument includes an infinite number of actual and potential instruments.

Source: Hartle (1973).

B.4 IMPLICATIONS

One is immediately struck by the impossibility of creating a truly comprehensive system—for policy evaluation in the real world that encompassed all actual and potential policy instruments and all actual and potential policy objectives. There is no need here to summarize the difficulties outlined. What must be emphasized, however, is that any second best solution, even if it were attempted, would be a far cry from the ideal solution. On the other hand, the insights concerning the importance of multiple effects, the trade-offs among goals and the goals as constraints need to be constantly borne in mind. Moreover, the necessity of trying to consider alternative types of policy instruments—not only modifications of particular regulations—is also important as is the possibility of looking at *packages* of policy changes that can sometimes be used to offset the weaknesses (costs = goal realization forgone) of particular policy instruments when considered in isolation.

The most outstanding feature of the ''all goods—all instruments'' approach, aside from its infeasibility in a world rich in goals and policy instruments but poor in data, is the complete absence of interpersonal or intergroup conflict. As we emphasized in Chapter 2, the heart, if not the soul, of the political process is conflict. The rational decision model emphasizes the potential conflicts among the goals, but the conflicts in interest that lurk behind them are neatly sidestepped by imagining a Cabinet (in our case) that resolves those individual/group conflicts through assigning weights to the goals by, in effect, ''buying'' a little more of the realization of some goals at the price of sacrificing a little (or a lot) of one or the other. Assuming that the rational actor system were in place, and assuming that the optimum result were obtained, would Pareto optimality prevail? Would there be coercion (e.g., would at least one voter have to be bribed (compensated) to accept it)? The answer is almost certainly ''no'' to the first question and almost certainly ''yes'' to the second. The rational actor model basically ignores the matter of individual choice and coercion. Indeed, the whole spirit of the model is that when optimization is achieved, the *central decision-making authority* could not be made better off in some sense. Whether or not those individuals affected by the decisions would be better or worse off on balance is not addressed. Unless the ''great white father'' knew tastes, preferences and property rights of all individuals and groups (a world of zero information costs) and adopted a self-denying ordinance to only choose those policy mixes that were Pareto optimal, would coercion be precluded? In the real world where, of course, individual tastes and preferences are unknown except as they are revealed through the actual decisions of individuals, the rational actor model would necessarily involve a degree of coercion. How those coerced would react and how the great decision maker would respond is not addressed. Nor is the question of how the decision maker is selected nor the source of his (its) authority.

B.5 BENEFIT/COST AND COST EFFECTIVENESS

The compleat rational actor model is, as has been emphasized, a way of conceptualizing how an all-powerful, all-knowing, centralized decision maker would have to proceed to optimize in an uncertain, general equilibrium world, the realization of a large bundle of often conflicting objectives through the deployment of many policy instruments drawn from a potential stock of infinite size. We have seen how gigantic the task would be—at least unless there was an unbelievably large increase in the information available, individual freedom of choice were greatly circumscribed, and a high degree of coercion accepted. Nevertheless, the rational actor model does help to clarify what, in principle, is required in evaluating policy alternatives including, obviously, regulatory alternatives. Benefit/cost analysis and cost effectiveness analysis, the subject matter of this section, can be viewed as a sway-backed horse and a stripped-down buggy in comparison with Rolls Royce's best or, perhaps more aptly, a spaceship of vintage 2500 A.D. They have one thing in common, however; both provide transportation!

B.6 BENEFIT/COST ANALYSIS

Before deciding upon a major capital investment most firms attempt to estimate the expected rate of return on the alternatives available. That is to say, given that there are perhaps three alternative processes among which to choose, they will estimate the future flows of revenues and costs associated with each, then determine the rate of discount which, when applied to these flows, gives a present value of the difference between them equal to the initial capital outlay. These internal rates of return are then compared and the process with the highest rate of return is selected—assuming that this return is higher than that obtainable by investing the funds elsewhere.

Benefit/cost analysis is founded on the same basic concept. The only difference is that benefit/cost analysis seeks to take into account benefits and costs that ordinarily would not be considered by the firm. By and large, the firm is interested neither in the benefits to society for which it cannot charge a price nor the costs to society which it will not bear. The benefits and costs of a particular project which will not be reflected in its income statement (sooner or later) are ignored.

Benefit/cost analysis, on the other hand, consists of the same rate of return calculation (conceptually if not in form) where to the estimated money flows are added the imputed dollar value of these social benefits and costs of a capital investment. For example, if there were not patent laws, firms would be reluctant to undertake heavy investments in research and development. While a discovery might confer substantial benefits on society, the firm could not capture them, because other firms would soon duplicate what had been discovered. There would be under-investment in research and development.

Similarly, if there were no environmental protection laws, a firm would not be much concerned about the pollution it created. These costs would, of course, be borne by society as a whole, not by the firm. If there were effective competition, the customer of the firm would end up buying goods and services from it at prices that did not cover the full cost to society. Too many of these goods and services, relative to others where all costs were reflected in final prices, would be produced.

In other words, benefit/cost analysis seeks to include in the analysis the imputed dollar value of benefits and costs which do not have market prices, such as environmental quality, passenger travel and waiting time, changes in basic scientific knowledge, and so on.

Three things are immediately apparent. From the point of view of society as a whole, to ignore these discrepancies between social and private costs and benefits leads to a misallocation of resources. Too many of some things and too few of others are produced. In principle at least, society as a whole would be better off if production of the former were reduced and the production of the latter were expanded. Benefit/cost analysis provides a conceptual framework for examining alternatives where such intangible factors are of significance.

It is also apparent, however, that the greater the relative magnitudes of imputed benefits and costs to market value benefits and costs, and the more intangible they are, the more subjective will be the results. The analyst can obtain any result he wants by imputing benefits and/or costs which yield the required "answer." To impute the dollar value of more national unity or more national prestige may help to keep these important pay-offs in mind, but is unlikely to yield results which have great persuasive power.

There are limitations of B/C analysis which should be alluded to if not discussed in depth. It is assumed in B/C analysis that the project being considered is sufficiently small that relative market prices would not be affected if it were undertaken. This assumption is satisfactory when considering a bridge or a wharf; it is questionable, however, when applied to major projects such as the McKenzie Valley Pipeline which could, presumably, affect the foreign exchange rate, while funds borrowed from abroad flowed in and equipment and supplies were purchased abroad. Such a change, if it occurred, would affect the relative prices of goods and services throughout the economy.

As implied above, it is questionable if the technique is really appropriate when there is substantial unemployment. What is the cost of employing an unemployed man? In a financial sense it is clear that the going wage is the cost. But from the point of view of society, this labour is costless because no *output* has to be forgone. Furthermore, it is not uncommon for a government department pushing for a capital project to argue that it would generate additional employment. It is further argued that most of this additional income will be spent quickly, thus generating additional incomes for those who produce what the newly employed workers will buy; these workers will spend a large proportion of their additional incomes, and so on, *ad infinitum*—additional incomes, of ever decreasing amounts, spreading out from the initial expenditures on the capital project. This so-called multiplier, when applied to the direct benefits (labour income which would go to the currently unemployed) obviously yields a large number. The project seems to have a high rate of return.

Although one can argue whether the B/C approach is appropriate for the analysis of such problems, one thing is clear. If it makes sense to take into account the successive rounds of additional income generated by the expenditures on the project, it is also necessary to take into account the successive rounds of income which were *not* generated because of the taxes imposed or the funds borrowed to obtain money to finance these expenditures. The contribution of B/C analysis in pointing up these inconsistencies is of great importance.

Perhaps the greatest limitation of B/C analysis (it should be emphasized that this is a limitation rather than a fault) is that it usually does not take into account the distributional question: who obtains the benefits and who bears the costs? It is most unlikely that decision makers will be indifferent when considering two projects with identical expected rates of return if one would provide benefits to the rich and hit the poor with the costs while the other project would do the opposite. These distributional considerations are often of paramount importance. It is impossible to incorporate them into B/C analysis without a degree of arbitrariness which is usually unacceptable to those who ultimately have to decide, unless one calculates benefits and costs for each income group and compares the net benefits of alternative schemes rather than their overall benefit/cost ratios.

Still another problem with B/C analysis should be mentioned. There are some government programs which provide licences by regulation. It would be desirable if a benefit/cost type of analysis could be applied on a consistent basis in order to rank the requests in terms of their expected rates of return and reject those at the bottom end of the spectrum.

The difficulty is that a department usually cannot hold all applications until some magic (but arbitrary) date when all of them can be arrayed against one another: the delays would be intolerable. Decisions have to be made in sequence rather than in batches. Granting a current application may, therefore, preclude a better subsequent application, because the funds provided have been exhausted before the department is aware of the alternative.

Under these circumstances B/C analysis can be used as a kind of decision rule given to subordinates. But the cut-off point—"below this expected rate of return reject application"—can be established only on the basis of past experience with respect to the number of applications likely to be received, the dispersion of the expected rates of return on the projects for which applications will be made, and the total number of licences that would be required if any particular cut-off point were adopted. When these factors are stable, the consistent use of an approved (by ministers and senior officials) benefit/cost framework in the analysis of applications can be a valuable means of delegating authority without fear of the arbitrary exercise of power by the officers immediately responsible for "recommending" the acceptance or rejection of applicants. The word "recommending" is placed in quotes because the volume of such applications often is so great that, perforce, the minister must rely on the recommendations of his officials. He has no time to do otherwise.

The situation is generally as follows.

(1) Benefit/cost analysis is almost invariably useful as a way of conceptualizing what should be taken into account in selecting among alternative regulations where social and private costs and benefits diverge.

(2) The actual numbers generated are less valuable: the greater its influence on relative prices; the more significant unemployment prevails; the more the imputed amounts are large relative to the amounts based on market prices; and the more the imputed benefits and costs are not only arbitrary but are seen to be arbitrary.

A careful examination has not been made of the extent to which benefit/cost analysis has been used by the federal government. The author believes that it would be found that, except with respect to small, relatively homogeneous kinds of projects (e.g., selecting sites for small airports in the North), it has not been used extensively. There have been a few studies of major projects where the technique has been employed on an *ad hoc* basis, but from what can be ascertained, these analyses were rarely, if ever, the decisive factor in the ultimate decision. However, this statement is obviously debatable.

For the reasons given above, this situation is probably as it should be. That is to say, the technique almost certainly could profitably be applied much more widely than it is now, but at best the results could constitute only an additional source of intelligence to decision makers. Government by formula and arithmetic is neither here nor likely to arrive. Those who seek to keep politics out of government decisions (perish the thought!) will not find a panacea in benefit/cost analysis.[5]

Cost Effectiveness

Benefit/cost analysis requires that the numerator and denominator be in commensurate units—dollars. When the benefits cannot be so expressed, or at least not without being hopelessly, and hence unpersuasively, arbitrary,

---

[5] See *Benefit-Cost Analysis Guide (1976)* and Stokey and Zeckhauser (1978) for exposition, examples, and references.

the benefit may be expressed in real units such as automobile accidents prevented or waiting time reduced or units of pollutant eliminated.

By calculating the costs of alternative policies it is then possible to compare the cost per unit of benefit obtained with a view to selecting the most cost effective method. One can proceed either by setting a target, for example, reduce traffic deaths by 50 per cent, and then estimate the cheapest way of realizing the target or by posing the problem in another way. Given $1 million to spend per year, how should we deploy the funds to obtain the greatest reduction in the number of traffic deaths? A balanced assessment of cost effectiveness analysis is provided by Stokey and Zeckhauser (1978, pp. 153-58).

Simulation

Simulation is a valuable analytic tool that is gaining prominence particularly in dealing with problems where there is little data. In essence, the logic of a set of relationships is expressed by equations, and the values of the parameters and variables are assumed where necessary. Sometimes, using the computer, an attempt is first made to simulate the plant having more or less accomplished this task and gained some confidence in the relationships and parameters embodied in the model. Sensitivity tests can be performed to assess the effects assuming that the parameters take on different values. Some models are designed to deal with random changes in order to test the range of probable outcomes. All in all, simulation is a powerful analytic tool. The greatest limitation is, perhaps, the danger of treating the results as predictions rather than the necessary consequences of the initial assumptions *and* the difficulties of building into the models feedback, adjustment and adaptive mechanisms.

REFERENCES

Allison, Graham T. (1971) *Essence of Decision: Explaining the Cuban Missile Crisis* (Boston: Little, Brown).

Benefit-Cost Analysis Guide (March 1976) Planning Branch, Treasury Board Secretariat (Ottawa: Supply and Services Canada).

Hartle, Douglas G. (1973) "A Proposed System of Program and Policy Evaluation" *Canadian Public Administration* 16 (Summer): 243-66.

Hartle, Douglas G. (1976a) "Techniques and Processes of Administration" *Canadian Public Administration* 19 (Spring): 21-33.

Hartle, Douglas G. (1976b) "The Public Servant as Advisor: The Choice of Policy Evaluation Criteria" *Canadian Public Policy* 2 (Summer): 424-38.

Hartle, Douglas G. (1978) *The Expenditure Budget Process in the Government of Canada* (Toronto: Canadian Tax Foundation).

Henderson, D.W. (1974) *Social Indicators: A Rationale and Research Framework* (Ottawa: Economic Council of Canada).

Stokey, Edith and Richard Zeckhauser (1978) *A Primer for Policy Analysis* (New York: Norton).

Appendix C

Regulation and the Courts*

Recourse to the courts may be taken in two ways: (1) by appeals, and (2) by applying for judicial review. Each of these will be considered in turn.

(1) APPEALS

A right of appeal is acquired solely when the relevant statute grants one; there is no general right of appeal, available at common law. As such, the strength of the control exerted on appeal is determined by the legislature, in the drafting of the statute.

The Ontario Royal Commission of Inquiry into Civil Rights set out in their report an admirably comprehensive outline of the various choices available to the legislature in drafting a right of appeal. These were as follows:

(1) Whether a right of appeal would frustrate the purpose of the statute;

(2) The nature of the power conferred on the tribunal of first instance—whether it is judicial or administrative;

(3) Whether an appeal should be as of right, or conditioned upon the obtaining of leave to appeal from the tribunal of first instance or the appellate tribunal;

(4) The nature of the appeal:

    (a) The appeal may take the form of a hearing *de novo*, in which case the appellate body starts afresh as if there had been no initial decision.

    (b) The appeal may be limited to argument based upon the record of proceedings before the inferior tribunal.

    (c) The appeal may be heard partially on the record, supplemented by further material.

    (d) The appeal may take the form of an appeal by "way of stated case." In such case the tribunal of first instance prepares a statement of the point of law to be considered by the appeal court, together with a statement of the facts upon which it based its decision. The Argument is confined to the case stated and the facts as stated are accepted as correct findings of fact.

(5) The scope of appellate authority;

    Should the appeal,

    (a) relate to all matters of law or fact decided by the tribunal;

    (b) be confined to decisions on matters of law only;

---

* This Appendix was prepared by Barbara Lane, a student of the University of Toronto, Faculty of Law in the summer of 1978. Hudson N. Janisch, a Professor of Law in that Faculty has checked it for accuracy.

(c) be confined to the question of whether the matters involved fall within the powers of the tribunal to decide—the application of the principle of *ultra vires;* or

(d) relate to decisions made by the tribunal in the exercise of discretion?

(6) The powers of the appellate body;
Should it be empowered if it concludes that the initial decision was wrong,

(a) to substitute a new decision for the initial decision; or

(b) to annul the initial decision and to remit the case back for reconsideration by the initial tribunal to make a new decision?

(7) The nature and composition of the appellate body. The appeal may be made to the courts or to a special appeal tribunal;

(8) The procedure on the appeal.[1]

The potential for wide disparities of controls being exerted is thus evident. The import of certain of the choices noted above (notably (5)) will be considered under Judicial Review, below. The question of whether an appeal should be as of right or by leave may be less contentious than first appears. If the leave is required of the appellate court, and extensive argument heard in the application for leave, then a denial may serve simply to save time and expense; it is unlikely that the court would allow the appeal, if it was unwilling to grant leave in the first place. Unfortunate ramifications are, of course, the fact that the issue never gets before the courts, and so, before the public eye, in any depth.

The nature of the appeal (*de novo*, on the record, etc.) indicates the degree to which the appellate body is permitted to redecide the issue that was before the tribunal of first instance. Consistently with the separation of powers doctrine, it is not generally acceptable for a judicial court to review (or redecide) administrative, or policy decisions. The discretion afforded the tribunal is respected, and their findings of fact generally not reviewable by courts. As such, who the appellate board is may have significant impact on the nature of the appeal permitted. If the appellate board is another administrative tribunal, with qualifications to make policy determinations as the legislature wished, then they may be granted permission to review all facets of the decision of the tribunal of first instance. Courts, by comparison, are generally restricted to the findings on the record.[2]

The same considerations are present in bestowing powers on the appellate board. If it is a specially constituted tribunal, then it may be permitted to substitute a decision. Again, if it is a court, generally it is only permitted to quash the decision, and remit it to the tribunal of first instance.

All of these choices are left to the legislature, when drafting the statute. It is suggested that the more explicitly these choices are made, the more any

---

[1] Ontario Royal Commission (1968) *Royal Commission Inquiry into Civil Rights,* Report No. 1, Vol. 1, pp. 227-28 (Toronto: Queen's Printer).

[2] One exception to this is that where there is no evidence to support a conclusion made by the tribunal of first instance, then a court may review. Such a situation is considered to be an error of law, not fact.

one choice, even if insignificant in its actual effect, might serve as a signal of the degree of independence that the legislature intended to confer on a regulator.

A word should be added here, on the relationship between appeals and judicial review, to be discussed presently. The *Federal Court Act*,[3] and provisions in federal statutes since the *Federal Court Act* confer authority for appeals from most regulatory agencies on the Federal Court of Appeal. Section 29 of the *Federal Court Act* establishes that where an appeal is available under a statute, then judicial review is unavailable to the extent that the scope of both are concurrent.

(2) JUDICIAL REVIEW

There are essentially two means of direct regulation: (1) adjudication, and (2) the making of subordinate legislation, often called rules or regulations. The two mechanisms each have different controls on their use, and so will be considered separately.

(1) Judicial Review of Decisions of Regulators

The law in this area is extremely complicated; obviously, far beyond the range of this chapter. However, a rough indication of the sort of issues reviewable by the courts might assist in developing an appreciation of the relative independence of regulators.

There are essentially three grounds for obtaining review at common law: (i) where the regulator has exceeded its jurisdiction; (ii) where the regulator made an error of law which appears on the face of the record of the proceedings; or (iii) where there was a breach of the rules of natural justice committed during the course of the proceedings.[4]

These grounds have been enlarged somewhat for federal regulators, by the *Federal Court Act*.[5] These include all errors of law (whether or not they appear ''on the face of the record'') and decisions based on certain erroneous findings of fact. The significance of these grounds for review will now be considered.

(i) BREACH OF THE RULES OF NATURAL JUSTICE

Philosophically, natural justice entails the idea that certain rights are fundamental and absolute, independent of the regime or situation in which one finds oneself. Legally, natural justice requires that certain procedural safeguards be met, to ensure that justice is done. Just as basic democratic

---

[3] *Federal Court Act*, S.C. 1970-71-72, c. 1; R.S.C. 1970, 2nd Supp., c. 10.

[4] A breach of the rules of natural justice can be said to fall into the category of exceeding jurisdiction, but in the interest of clarity, they shall be separated here.

[5] See S. 28 of the *Federal Court Act*.

principles demand that the judiciary be independent of the political sphere, so do they require that if one is to be seriously affected by a decision, then one is entitled to be informed as to its nature, and given an opportunity to present one's side to the (impartial) decision maker. In the administrative sphere, complications arise because of conflicting values. This idea of natural justice may be seen to clash with the purpose of giving the issue to an administrative board for decision in the first place. That is, one of the basic characteristics of a board is that it is not a court; it is faster and more informal. Both of these characteristics incline one away from requiring full court-like procedures in the administrative setting. Yet serious consequences may frequently result to a person or body from administrative decisions. The balancing of these factors is the issue confronted by the courts, in determining whether or not to require a board to adhere to the rules of natural justice.

Again, deciding factors tend to be how judicial the function of the board is. The more it applies law or policy, the more procedural safeguards to ensure that it is fairly applied will be imposed. The more policy making that is involved, the more courts will shy away from requiring strict procedures, and leave it to the board itself to determine, as it finds such requirements necessary.

At times, the legislature will specify in the statute that certain procedures must be followed in making decisions. In these cases, failure to do so results in the loss of jurisdiction by the board.

Different standards of procedural requirements will be found needing in different statutes. A "hearing" may or may not be public. Representation by counsel may or may not be found permitted. The importance of the issues, the degree of policy-making power conferred on the decision maker, how much of a right one has to the matter involved—these are some of the considerations which go to a decision on the procedural requirements.

(ii) EXCESS OF JURISDICTION

Our system of government requires that laws be made by those who are politically responsible; this is the essence of representative self-government. As such, granting regulatory powers to non-politically responsible beings is stepping outside of the basic structure. It is acceptable so far as regulatory agencies merely carry out the will of the legislature, as outlined in the authorizing statute. Should the agencies go beyond their allotted powers, then they have exceeded their jurisdiction, and the courts can quash the action on review.

Determination of what the allotted jurisdiction is requires interpretation of the statute by the courts. The problem with this, is that the grants of power to the agencies are often framed in such vague and general terms as to be essentially meaningless. One of the common rationales given for the delegation of policy-making powers to these agencies, is that the policy is best developed as the issues are clarified through cases coming before the board for adjudication. The legislature wants to allow the board flexibility to exploit its growing expertise in the area, by not restricting it in the authorizing statute. This results in the grant of powers to regulate, often as vague as simply "in the public interest." The scope of the power conferred by such phrases is difficult to define. As such, decisions on jurisdictional questions often involve the court in imposing its own view of what the jurisdiction should be, when it decides what it maintains the statute "says." Privative clauses, purporting to restrict the amount of judicial review which can be obtained, are notoriously ineffective. The courts simply ignore them. As such, the courts can often decide themselves whether or not to review a decision, simply by construing the jurisdiction conferred on the board narrowly or broadly.

Another aspect of the concept of review for jurisdictional questions is that where there has been an abuse of discretion by the board. Discretion is conferred on the board by the legislature, yet there are certain restrictions on the way in which it may be exercised. These are basically that it must be exercised in good faith, and not taking irrelevant considerations into account, or having an improper purpose to its exercise. Failure to do so may result in a loss of jurisdiction by the board, and the quashing of the decision in question.

These grounds for review for excess of jurisdiction apply whether the function of the board is judicial or administrative. They concern the courts in their role as guardian of the system, ensuring that minimum standards are always met in regulating. The courts' function here is to maintain the integrity of democratic government, even with delegation of wide powers to non-popularly responsible beings, by ensuring that the will of the legislature is carried out. The problem, again, is when the will is that of the courts, not the legislature.

(iii) ERRORS OF LAW

The rationale for allowing review by the courts of errors of law seems to be based on an acknowledgment that the integrity of any adjudicatory process requires that no blatant error of law be tolerated. Thus, errors of law which appeared on the face of the record were held to be reviewable, and the subsequent enlargement of this ground to all errors of law (by the *Federal Court Act*) simply removed the technical requirement of finding the error somewhere stated on the record.

Review here is limited to decisions of a judicial or quasi-judicial nature.

Considered as a whole, there seems nothing offensive about permitting such review by the judiciary. The issue is necessarily legal, and so directly the sort of issue constantly confronted by the courts; as well, only judicial-type decisions are subject to it, thereby continuing the lines of accountability considered desirable, earlier. Peter W. Hogg expresses concern over it, however, on the basis that the distinctions between law, fact and policy are tenuous at best, and illusory at least. He argues against the desirability of judicial intervention, if there exists a chance that the courts can thus determine policy assigned by right to the tribunal.[6]

The tension here is, again, that between wanting to leave policy determinations to the administrative agencies, and yet wishing to maintain the integrity of the system by controls exerted by the judiciary on judicial functions of the board.

(iv) ERRORS OF FACT

This extension of the grounds of review, as found in the *Federal Court Act*, seems to invite the courts deliberately to make precisely the kind of deliberation Hogg feared them making surreptitiously under the rubric of error of law. The "erroneous findings of fact" which provoke review are: (1) those made in a "perverse or capricious manner," or (2) those made "without regard for the material before the agency."

The first seems to be a "motherhood" provision, providing protection of the sort the courts are well-equipped to handle. The second is problematical. It allows—invites!—the court to determine what conclusions the agency ought to have arrived at from the evidence. This, of course, means essentially what conclusions the court would have arrived at, had it been considering the material. This effectively grants the court the power of reviewing the entire decision of the agency.

In fact, since the proclamation of the Act in 1971, the courts have indicated an intention to interpret this section restrictively. They have suggested that the section only operates where there was no evidence to support the conclusion reached by the agency; a situation traditionally covered by error of law. Therefore, the courts seem to say that this ground for review is only a specific example of the earlier ground, of error of law. It is not yet clear whether this interpretation will stand with time, or be transformed to allow the potential review of the section to be realized.

Overall, it can be seen that the grounds for review by a court of decisions of a regulatory agency are to a great extent self-defined; a court can review generally if it defines its jurisdiction accordingly. Frequently, the degree of policy in a decision will dissuade the court from intervening, as being not appropriate for its control

The powers a court possesses, should it review and disagree with the first finding, are far more restrictive than those found on appeals. Generally,

---

[6] Peter W. Hogg (1974) "Judicial Review: How Much Do We Need?" *McGill Law Review* 20: 157-76.

a court can only either issue a writ,[7] or set aside the decision. There is no power in the court to substitute a decision.

(2) Judicial Review of Subordinate Legislation

It is clear that legislation should be made only by those who are politically responsible, and that, therefore, the grant of such powers to administrative agencies marks a departure from normal democratic theory. However, the complexity of the issues, and the perceived need for flexibility in the rule making (i.e., that it evolve out of extensive direct contact with the issues, on a day-by-day basis) has resulted in the wide granting of such powers to regulatory agencies. The courts then perform their usual role of ensuring that all such subordinate legislation is in fact authorized by the particular statute. Where wide discretionary powers have been granted to the regulator, the scope of review is, of course, correspondingly decreased. Frequently, regulations are authorized by such phrases as: "the regulator may make such regulations as he deems necessary for carrying out this Act and for its efficient administration." Such a grant of power is subjective in scope (being limited to what the regulator thinks necessary, not what is objectively necessary), and, therefore, not reviewable by the courts, who can review only by applying supposedly objective standards.

There are, however, certain presumptions that a court will make as to the intentions of the legislature, where the grant of authority is in general terms. The effect of these is to require specific authorization in the statute, before regulations attempting to effect the following:

(1) denial of access to the courts
(2) imposition of tax
(3) interference with property rights
(4) restriction of personal liberties
(5) creation of offences and penalties
(6) prescription of retroactive operation
(7) discrimination as between citizens
(8) interference with a common law right to trade.

There are no natural justice procedural protections afforded to those who are affected by the subordinate legislation, unless such requirements are specifically stated in the relevant statute. No notice need generally be given to those who might wish to make representations concerning proposed regulations before they are made. Again, once made, if they are not *ultra*

---

[7] At common law, and under S. 18 of the *Federal Court Act*, review is achieved by the court issuing a writ to the administrative decision maker. The most common writs include the writ of *certiorari*, which quashes a decision; prohibition, which can be used to prevent an order or decision being taken; *mandamus*, which compels statutory authorities to perform their public duties. Other common forms of challenging decisions were injunctions, used to restrain unauthorized interference with private rights, and declarations, which simply declare a right.

vires the authority vested by the statute, then they cannot be attacked. The desirability of the policy reflected in the regulation is not a reviewable issue.

The only procedural safeguards generally applicable to federal statutes are those contained in the *Statutory Instruments Act*.[8] This provides for political review of regulations before they are made effective, and publication to ensure that notice is given of the regulation.

It should be mentioned that not all regulations are subject to this review and publication. The Governor in Council (the Cabinet) may exempt certain regulations from either or both of these requirements, for reasons such as national security.[9] As well, the definition of what must be reviewed and published is such as excludes directives which purport to be advisory, not binding. This is so despite the fact that many such directives may in fact be viewed as binding by those who are being "advised" by them. Such directives never come to the attention of the administrators of the *Statutory Instruments Act*, and so need never come to public light.

(3) Judicial Review of Ministerial or Departmental Regulation

Statutes may confer regulatory powers on "independent" regulatory agencies (i.e., set up outside of the immediate political process, although controlled by both the political and the judicial arenas) or on governmental departments (i.e., directly within the political arena). Much of the concern with controlling the agencies stems from the fact of their status outside of immediate political control, yet their possession of essentially political functions. It would seem, therefore, that concern would be less with controlling regulators who operate within the political framework. Yet still the courts exercise their usual function of ensuring that the powers exercised are those conferred by the statute. Again, how discretion is exercised will not be reviewed, merely that its cope is that authorized.

Judicial review is a discretionary act by the courts. As such, it is likely that review will be less readily available against a body operating within the government, than for one outside of it. A court would be less willing to substitute a view of the proper jurisdiction conferred by a statute, when it is substituting for the views of those who are directly politically accountable. Review of these people belongs more in the political arena than in the judicial one. However, the potential for such review does exist, and reluctance to exercise it does not result in a lack of its use.

The position of the Governor in Council (a frequent delegate of regulatory powers under federal statutes) under the *Federal Court Act* is unclear. Review against its decisions is specifically excluded under one

---

[8] *Statutory Instruments Act*, S.C. 1970-71-72, c. 38.
[9] *Ibid.*, S. 27.

section authorizing review,[10] yet it is not mentioned in the other such section.[11] The cases thus far suggest that it is not reviewable under the Act (although there are ways around it), but there seems scope for controversy.[12]

(4) Standing to Obtain Judicial Review

Since traditionally judicial review was a discretionary act of the courts, they have been free to be more flexible with granting standing to people to bring applications for it, than has been the situation with other actions before them. As a result, statements have emerged in the cases, suggesting that even strangers to an action may bring an application for certain types of review—an unthinkable occurrence in ordinary litigation. Class actions, a highly contentious issue in Canadian courts, have been acknowledged as a possiblity in review proceedings.[13]

Generally, actions for review are brought by "persons aggrieved" by the reviewable decision or order. This may be extended to include those who are members of a class of people peculiarly affected by the offending action. The *Federal Court Act* requires (for most types of review) that the application be brought by someone who is a "party directly affected" by the decision or order.[14] How directly one must be affected is not yet clear from the scant litigation on the topic, but the general direction of the cases suggests a liberal interpretation. Therefore, it seems hopeful that standing will be granted widely for review, and the problems being battled for standing in other areas of the law avoided in this one.

---

[10] *Federal Court Act*, S. 28 (6).

[11] *Ibid.*, S. 18.

[12] See *Desjardins v. National Parole Board*, *[1976]* 2 F.C. 539 (T.D.) Generally, see David J. Mullan (1977) *The Federal Court Act: Administrative Law Jurisdiction*, pp. 18-19, Law Reform Commission of Canada (Ottawa: Supply and Services Canada).

[13] *Nat. Indian Brotherhood v. C.R.T.C. (No. 1)*, [1971] F.C. 66.

[14] *Federal Court Act*, S. 28(2).

APPENDIX D

Definitions of the "the Public Interest"*

Sooner or later any serious analyst of public policy comes up against the need for a definition of "the public interest." The concept is usually implicit (when it should be explicit) in every suggestion/recommendation about what course of action any government should undertake. Given the range of human individuality, it is hardly surprising that there are a large number of different definitions of the public interest which have been offered. Politicians or policy analysts, no doubt, will be frustrated by the conflicting perspectives such definitions provide, and by the degree of abstraction with which they are framed. Even if one definition is adopted, how can it be made operational in specific (but varying) circumstances?

While a large number of different definitions of the public interest exists, it is possible to group them in terms of a more limited number of themes or central concepts they embody. One group of definitions sees the public interest resulting from the *aggregation, weighing and balancing of a number of special interests*. It includes the following examples.

- The public interest is "determined and established" through the free competition of interest groups. "The necessary composing and compromising of their differences is the practical test of what constitutes the public interest." (Binkley and Moos, 1950, p. 7).

- The public interest "must necessarily represent a working compromise and be subject to continuous definition, as the need arises, in the process of achieving an often delicate balance among conflicting interests." (Boudreau, 1950, p. 371)

- "(Special Interests)^n = The Public Interest" (Schubert's summary of Appleby's definition, Schubert, 1960, p. 175).

- "An administrator best serves the public interest when his action creates or restores an equilibrium among all the affected group interests, or if this is not possible, when the disequilibrium following his act is minimized." (Schubert's summary of Leiserson's definition, Schubert, 1957, p. 361)

---

* This Appendix was prepared by W.T. Stanbury, Director, Regulation And Government Intervention Program, Institute for Research on Public Policy and Director, Regulation Reference, Economic Council of Canada.

213

- The public interest is the "policy resulting from the sum total of all interests in the community—possibly all of them actually private interests—which are balanced for the common good." (Marks *et al.*, 1972, p. 51)
- The definition of the public interest is "The policies government would pursue if it gave equal weight to the welfare of every member of society." (Noll, 1971, p. 15)
- "The interest of the community then is, what?—The sum of the interests of the several members who compose it." (Bentham, 1823, p. 126)

In contrast to the previous definitions, a number of writers define the public interest in terms of the *common* or *universal interests* which all (or at least almost all) members of society/nation/political unit share. The following definitions would appear to fall into this category:

- "The public interest . . . is the common interest. That which results in satisfying those wants which all members of a community share constitutes the public interest." (Held, 1970, p. 4 paraphrasing Brian Barry)
- "The 'public interest' [is] the interest that is unanimously shared with no reluctant losers . . . " (Hartle, 1979, p. 4)
- "The public interest is a standard of goodness by which political acts can be judged; action in the public interest, therefore, deserves approval because it is good. . . . To say an action is in the public interest is to judge it consistent with a political situation that is *beneficial to everyone*, if not immediately at least in the long run, and whether or not everyone realizes it. . . . The public interest is the highest ethical standard applicable to political affairs." (Cassinelli, 1962, pp. 45, 46, emphasis added)
- "What the public requires as its own good, what is specifically the *good of all without distinction*, is a sum total of general conditions under the protection of which the legitimate activities of everyone within the public may be exercised and developed comfortably." (Dabin, 1944, p. 355, emphasis added)
- "The public interest . . . may be defined as the best response to a situation in terms of all the interests and of the concepts of value which are generally accepted in our society." (Redford, 1954, p. 1108)
- The public interest consists of "those government actions that most . . . [benefit] the whole society." It is "closely related to the minimal concensus necessary for the operation of a democratic society. This consists of an implicit agreement among the preponderance of the people concerning two main areas: the basic rules of conduct and decision-making that should be followed in the society; and general principles regarding the fundamental social policies that the government ought to carry out." (Downs, 1962, pp. 2,5)
- "A decision is said to serve special interests if it furthers the ends of some part of the public at the expense of the ends of the larger public. It is said to

be in the *public interest* if it serves the ends of the whole public rather than those of some sector of the public.'' (Banfield, 1955, p. 322)

- ''Something is a public interest, if, and only if, *it is an interest of anyone who is a member of the public*; that is, if and only if it is essential for the protection, and even for the improvement, of anyone's welfare or well-being, where the means for protecting or improving this interest are out of the hands of most of the members of the public and is likely to be achieved only if the public takes a hand.'' (Benditt, 1973, p. 301, emphasis added)
- ''The common good (or public interest . . .) is best conceived as the preservation and improvement of the community itself'' i.e., ''the common human needs of men in society, needs which are more basic and essential than their temporary wants or desires.'' (Cochran, 1974, pp. 355, 353)

Not surprisingly, a number of writers have sought to define the public interest from an *idealist perspective*. Such definitions judge alternative actions or policies in relation to some absolute standard of values—in some cases independently of the preferences of individual citizens. We should note that in some formulations, the idealist approach focuses on outcomes; in others it focuses on processes.

- ''The public interest is never merely the sum of all private interests nor the sum remaining after cancelling out their various pluses and minuses. It is not wholly spearate from private interests, and it derives from citizens with many private interests; but it is something distinctive that arises within, among, apart from, and above private interests, focusing in government some of the most elevated aspiration and deepest devotion of which human beings are capable.'' (Appleby, 1952, p. 35)
- ''I suggest, that the public interest may be presumed to be what men would choose if they saw clearly, thought rationally, acted disinterestedly and benevolently.'' (Lippman, 1955, p. 42)
- ''The *public interest* is the standard that guides the administrator in executing the law. This is the verbal symbol designed to introduce unity, order, and objectivity into [public] administration. This concept is to the bureaucracy what the 'due process' clause is to the judiciary.'' (Herring, 1936, p. 23)
- ''The public interest is ultimately identified with the achievement of a society based upon or prevaded by *intelligent goodwill*.'' (Griffith, 1962, p. 19)
- ''All measures which promote, serve, and benefit the human desire for affirmative and constructive participation in the enterprise of civilization must be deemed to be in the public interest because they increase the good of all as intelligently conceived.'' (Bodenheimer, 1962, p. 213)

Several other definitions of the public interest focus on the *process by which decisions are made* rather than the specification of some ideal outcome. This group appears to include the following:

- "The public interest in a problem is limited to this: that there shall be rules, which means that the rules which prevail shall be enforced, and the unreasonable rules shall be changed according to a settled rule . . . The public is interested in law, not in the laws; in the method of the law, not in substance; in the sanctity of contract, not in particular contract; in understanding based on custom, not in this custom or that. It is concerned in these things to the end that men in their active affairs shall find a *modus vivendi*; its interest is in the workable rule which will define and predict the behaviour of men so that they can make their adjustments." (Lippman, 1925, pp. 104, 105)

- "Decisions that are the product of a process of full consideration are most likely to be decisions in the public interest . . . people accept democratic decision-making processes because these provide the maximum opportunity for diverse interests to seek to influence governmental decisions at all levels." (Schubert, 1960, pp. 205, 204)

- "The primary determination of the public interest for public servants is by the action of his political and hierarchic superiors, acting through the conventional channels, by legislation, and court decisions where applicable." In areas where the public servant has discretion he must consider the consequences to those immediately affected by the proposed action, but he most remember there are others unorganized and unrepresented and "as far as he can perceive the consequences to them, he must be their representative". (Monypenny, 1953, p. 441)

- The term "public interest" "is employed to express approval or commendation of policies adopted or proposed by government." The descriptive meaning of the term "is properly found through reasoned discourse which attempts to relate the anticipated effects of a policy to community values and to test that relation by formal principles" (i.e., universalizability). It "does not provide a divining rod or philosopher's stone for determining proper public policy." (Flathman, 1966, pp. 3, 82)

Having advanced two dozen definitions of "the public interest" it is probably useful to end on a clearly skeptical note by quoting the words of Arthur Bentley. He specifically denied there is a *public* interest since "there are always some parts of the nation to be found arrayed against other parts." In his view, "The opinion activity that reflects one group, however large it may be, always reflects the activity of that group as directed against the activity of some other group." (Bentley, 1908, pp. 220, 240)

REFERENCES

Appleby, Paul H. (1952) *Morality and Administration in Democratic Government* (Baton Rouge: Louisiana State University Press).

Banfield, Edward C. (1955) "Note on Conceptual Scheme" in Martin Myerson and Edward C. Banfield, *Politics Planning and the Public Interest*, p. 303 (Glencoe, Ill.: Free Press).

Benditt, Theodore M. (1973) "The Public Interest" *Philosophy and Public Affairs* 2 (Spring): 291-311.

Bentham, Jeremy (1960) *A Fragment on Government and an Introduction to the Principles of Morals and Legislation*, Wilfred Harrison (ed.) (Oxford:Blackwell. First published 1823).

Bentley, Arthur F. (1935) *The Process of Government* (Bloomington: Principia. First published 1908).

Binkley, Wilfred and Malcolm Moos (1950) *A Grammar of American Politics* (New York: Alfred A. Knopf). As cited in Theodore J. Lowi (1969) *The End of Liberalism*, p. 75 (New York: Norton).

Bodenheimer, Edgar (1962) "Prolegomena to a Theory of the Public Interest" in Carl Friedrich (ed.), *The Public Interest*, pp. 205-17 (New York: Atherton).

Boudreau, A.J. (1950) "Public Administration and the Public Interest" *Canadian Journal of Economics and Political Science* 16: 371-74.

Cassinelli, C.W. (1962) "The Public Interest in Political Ethics" in Carl Friedrich (ed.), *The Public Interest*, pp. 44-53 (New York: Atherton).

Cochran, Clarke E. (1974) "Political Science and 'The Public Interest'" *Journal of Politics* 36: 327-55.

Dabin, Jean (1944) "The General Theory of Law" in Kurt Wilk (tr.), *The Legal Philosophies of Lask, Radbruch, and Dabin*, pp. 227-470 (Cambridge, Mass.: Harvard University Press, 1950).

Downs, Anthony (1962) "The Public Interests: Its Meaning in a Democracy" *Social Research* 29: 1-36.

Flathman, Richard E. (1966) *The Public Interest* (New York: Wiley).

Griffith, Ernest S. (1962) "The Ethical Foundations of the Public Interest" in Carl Friedrich (ed.), *The Public Interest*, pp. 14-25 (New York: Atherton).

Hartle, Douglas G. (1979) *Public Policy Decision Making and Regulation* (Montreal: Institute for Research on Public Policy).

Held, Virginia (1970) *The Public Interest and Individual Interests* (New York: Basic Books).

Herring, E. Pendleton (1936) *Public Administration and the Public Interest* (New York: McGraw-Hill).

Lippmann, Walter (1955) *Essays in the Public Philosophy* (Boston: Little, Brown).

Lippmann, Walter (1925) *The Phantom Public* (New York: Harcourt, Brace).

Marks, F. Raymond with Kirk Leswing and Barbara A. Fortinsky (1972) *The Lawyer, the Public and Professional Responsibility* (Chicago: American Bar Foundation).

Monypenny, Phillip (1953) "A Code of Ethics for Public Administration" *George Washington Law Review* 21: 423-44.

Noll, Roger G. (1971) *Reforming Regulation* (Washington, D.C.: The Brookings Institution).

Redford, Emmette S. (1954) "The Protection of the Public Interest with Special Reference to Administrative Regulation" *American Political Science Review* 48: 1103-13.

Schubert, Glendon A., Jr. (1957) " 'The Public Interest' in Administrative Decision-Making: Theorem, Theosophy, or Theory?" *American Political Science Review* 51: 346-68.

Schubert, Glendon (1960) *The Public Interest* (Glencoe, Ill.: Free Press).